PRAYER IN PRACTICE

Pat Collins C.M.

Prayer in Practice
A BIBLICAL APPROACH

ORBIS BOOKS

Maryknoll, New York 10545

The Catholic Foreign Mission Society of America (Maryknoll) recruits and trains people for overseas missionary service. Through Orbis Books, Maryknoll aims to foster the international dialogue that is essential to mission. The books published, however, reflect the opinions of their authors and are not meant to represent the official position of the society. To obtain more information about Maryknoll and Orbis Books, please visit our website at www.maryknoll.org.

First published in 2001
in the United States by
ORBIS BOOKS
PO Box 308
Maryknoll, New York 10545-0308
www.orbisbooks.com

Origination by The Columba Press
Printed in Ireland by Colour Books Ltd, Dublin

Cataloging-in-Publication Data
available from the Library of Congress

ISBN 1-57075-353-9

Contents

More things are wrought by prayer
Than this world dreams of.
Alfred Lord Tenyson

Foreword

In 1 Thessalonians 5:18, Saint Paul gives a succinct injunction: 'Pray continually.' Anyone who takes these words to heart knows that unceasing prayer requires openness to what can only come as a gift. Prayer is, above all else, a response to God's initiative. We can only lift our mind and heart and voice to God in prayer because of the life and love that have first been given to us.

Even though prayer is first and finally a gift, it must nonetheless be nurtured, cultivated, sustained through discipline. Adherence to the tenets of religion and engaging in spiritual practices are really quite empty unless they spring from a praying heart. Prayer is the very speaking and breathing of religious and spiritual living. But living prayerfully is not a free and easy ride. It is at once a gift and a task.

When we pray unceasingly, we listen long and lovingly to the beating of the heart of God in human life, in history, in the world and in the church. Every inch and ounce of life, the whole of creation, becomes a precinct of God's constant coming. If only we would have ears to hear, and eyes to see!

A few years ago I read a little essay by Pat Collins entitled 'Is Unceasing Prayer Possible?' In this very short essay the author managed to provide one of the clearest treatments of the nature of Christian prayer that I had ever read. When I was in Dublin next, I arranged to meet with Pat Collins in the hope of learning a little more about this Irish Vincentian priest, virtually unknown to North American readers, who was able to say so much about prayer in so few pages. Our encounter was brief. Over the course of our hour-long meeting, I was struck at once by Collins' modesty as well as by the authority with which he spoke about the ways of prayer. I became convinced quickly that his simple *savoir faire* could only have been developed through years of practice, and refined through active engagement with others seeking to grow in the grace of prayerful living.

I listened attentively, knowing myself to be in the presence of someone skilled in the art of prayer, a teacher in the ways of the heart. I didn't say much, but encouraged him to keep on praying. And writing. I said quietly but firmly: 'Write! Keep writing about prayer. Write from the inside out – from the heart. Write for those who want to learn a little about prayer, for those who have heard in their deepmost parts the echo of Saint Paul's words urging us to pray all the time – but who seem to have such a hard time doing so.'

This volume is Pat Collins' response to those few encouraging words. Like his other writings, this book on the practice of prayer comes from the heart of a man who is steeped in scripture, tradition, and the liturgical life of the church. Pat Collins speaks of God and of the deep down things of the spirit in a way that enlightens the mind and touches the heart. He does not turn his back on the concerns of the world but, rather, helps us rediscover the felt presence of God amidst the nitty-gritty of everyday living. With Catholic roots long, deep, and strong, Collins' vision of God is shaped by ecumenical and interreligious sensibility, and enriched by insights from psychology and related disciplines. What's more, he demonstrates a keen sensitivity to all that is noble in the human search for meaning, purpose and value.

Prayer in Practice is contemporary Christian spiritual writing at its finest. Collins explains just what Christian prayer is, why it is so important to the religious and spiritual life, and how to engage in a disciplined life of prayer. He brings a wide range of voices and perspectives to bear on his treatment of the subject. He holds out a vision of the Christian life in which prayer is the *sine qua non*, and offers clear instruction in the ways and practices of prayer. Even though Collins is well schooled in the various methods and approaches to prayer and the spiritual life, he does not cling to any one of them. His vision of prayer is at once broad and deep; his treatment of the various methods and techniques in prayer both subtle and supple.

That there is a spiritual hunger in our postmodern culture is beyond dispute. Whether or not there are wise guides in the ways of the spirit is arguable. Many in the church and in the wider world feel that they are on a journey without a compass, on a quest with very few signposts along the way. Far too many suggest that the only really reliable guides are their own inner lights. Indeed, teachers in the ways of the heart may be few and far between; wise and reliable guides in the paths of prayer may indeed be in short supply. Pat Collins is one.

Michael Downey
Professor of Systematic Theology and Spirituality
Saint John's Seminary, Camarillo

Introduction

As a Christian I'm convinced that prayer lies at the heart of religion and spirituality. There will be no genuine revival or lasting renewal in the churches without it. Clearly, there is an urgent need for both in the Western world where we are enduring a virtual eclipse of God. It worries me, for example, that when Catholic churchmen are interviewed by the media they can appear to be ethical policemen and kill joys, rather than manna people, who feed the faithful with the spiritual bread of the numinous. The church urgently needs witnesses whose lives and words point, in a non-judgmental way, beyond the narrow confines of the secular to the sacred and the transcendental. It also needs guides who can show the pilgrims of the twenty-first century how they can come face to face with the living God by means of prayer. As one writer has sagely observed: 'Only prayer can wear away our native resistance to God.'[1]

While this book has consciously sunk its roots into the fertile soil of Christian tradition, its branches have been exposed to the rarefied atmosphere of the postmodern, secular culture in which we live on both sides of the Atlantic. The late Karl Barth once observed that the Christian of today should have the bible in one hand and the newspaper in the other. I agree entirely. Ideally, spiritual writers should aim to enculturate gospel teaching by expressing its perennial truth in the language and thought patterns of the societies in which they live.

Writing this book turned out to be an opportunity to look back over my life and to reflect upon an activity that has sustained and nourished me over the years. It quickly became apparent that, by the grace of God, I had experienced the divine presence, often in mundane, and occasionally in more memorable ways. I have also spent a good deal of time thinking and reading about different forms of prayer and giving talks about them. Like wine in a barrel, these reflections had fermented for years. Finally, I felt that they had matured to the point where they were fit for public consumption. The fact that I have confined myself to topics with which I am familiar, is at once the book's strength and greatest possible weakness. Inevitably my familiarity with the subject of prayer is limited, both in its extent and depth. That said, the book is mainly objective and didactic in orientation. It is about Christian prayer. It is not intended to be an autobiographical account of my own prayer life. In general terms I wanted the book to be biblical, Catholic, experiential and practical in its approach.

I have a strong conviction that any description of Christian prayer should be thoroughly rooted in the scriptures. I don't particularly like those studies that seem to interpret biblical truths in terms of philosophical or psychological preconceptions. It seems to me that they run the risk of cherry picking revealed texts that conform with their preconceptions. Nowadays, there is a distinct danger of watering down the teachings of scripture in order to adapt them to questionable ways of human thinking such as New Age spirituality. I have used a number of translations, mainly the *New International Version*, *Revised Standard Version*, *New Revised Standard Version*, and *The New Jerusalem Bible*. I have included relevant quotations from the Apocryphal books of the Old Testament which Catholics consider to be inspired and canonical.

I had to choose to write either in a non-denominational or in a Catholic way. As a committed ecumenist I was tempted to leave out the specifically Catholic topic of praying to Mary and the saints. But in the end I decided to include it because, from childhood onwards I have prayed to Mary. I wanted to share my experience of this kind of prayer with fellow Catholics. However, in the light of the text: 'there is one God and one mediator between God and men, the man Jesus Christ' (1 Tim 2:5), I also wanted to explain to Protestant brothers and sisters how Catholics understand this kind of prayer. Apart from that topic, and a section on the sacramental anointing of the sick, I suspect that Protestants will find they have little reason to take exception to the rest.

The book will be experiential in its approach. In modern Catholicism, as in Christianity in general, the centre of gravity is demonstrably shifting from the experience of religious authority to the authority of religious experience. Thomas Aquinas rightly observed: 'We can testify to something only in the measure that we have shared in it.'[2] When we know God by experience, Thomas added, we 'taste' God's sweetness through a Spirit-given awareness.[3] So perhaps its not surprising that Cardinal Ratzinger has written in the modern era: 'A dogmatic faith un-supported by personal experience remains empty; mere personal experience unrelated to the faith of the church remains blind.'[4] Pope John Paul II echoed this point when he observed, 'people today put more trust in witnesses than in teachers, in experience than in teaching, and in life and action than in theories.'[5] Ideally, a reciprocal relationship should exist between orthodox doc-trine and religious experience.

Prayer stands at the intersection between objective truth and subjective awareness. It is the graced means by which the one is changed into the other. Not surprisingly, therefore, I will take account of the prayer experiences of a number of Christians in-cluding my own. I do so in the belief that: 'A king's secret is pru-dent to keep, but the works of the Lord are to be declared and made known' (Tob 12:7). Ever since the end of the Second Vatican Council, the Catholic Charismatic Movement, like similar renewal movements, has become influential. It emphasises religious experience in a way that would not have been characteristic of many traditional spiritualities. Nevertheless it has received official support from Paul VI and John Paul II. They have de-scribed it as a chance for the church and the world. This senti-ment has been endorsed by the bishops' conferences in many countries including Ireland.[6] I have been involved with that movement for many years. As a result I have had first hand ex-perience of 'charismatic' ways of praying, such as loud, vocifer-ous thanksgiving and praise, either in English or in tongues. Although this book does not focus specifically on these forms of prayer, it has undoubtedly been coloured by them. I should also add that I have been deeply influenced by the teachings of Sts Vincent de Paul[7] and Ignatius of Loyola.[8]

The book will also be as practical as I can make it. I believe that when dealing with Christian issues, whether ethical or spiritual, preachers, teachers and writers should begin by describing the *nature* of a subject like prayer, while going on to recommend *motives* for engaging in it, and suggesting specific practical *means* of doing so. Throughout the book, therefore, I will propose tried and tested ways of engaging in different forms and methods of prayer. Hopefully, the guidelines will act as a helpful resource which could be consulted by those who are looking for down-to-earth help.

Those who may be familiar with my previous books will recognise that there is an element of recapitulation in this one in so far as I have recycled a number of ideas because of their relevance here. I consciously left out important topics. I have dealt with some of them elsewhere.[9] Others I have omitted, due to a lack of personal expertise, such as an exploration of liturgical prayer. I'm also aware that I have said very little about the important role of breathing exercises and posture in prayer. Anthony de Mello, among others, has made helpful suggestions in this regard, in his well-known book, *Sadhana: A Way to God*.[10]

I have also chosen to exclude a discussion of the interesting and important link that exists between psychology and prayer.[11] However I would like to briefly advert to two helpful contributions from Carl Jung, the well-known twentieth-century psychologist. He has indicated how Christians can escape from an overly rationalistic, post-Enlightenment worldview that denies that God can communicate directly with human beings. He has described the psycho-spiritual ways in which God can be revealed in an intuitive manner to the human heart, by means of such things as symbols, myths, dreams and visions which are rooted in the pre-rational, archetypal activity of the personal and collective unconscious.[12] While I would have reservations about certain aspects of Jung's psychology I would agree, in general terms, that in prayer we can have a direct, if mediated encounter with the living Lord. Other researchers have discussed the connection between Jung's sixteen personality types, as identified by the Myers-Briggs Type Indicator, and different ways of praying.[13] As a result they have made helpful suggestions about what methods might suit specific personality types.

Throughout the book I have tried to avoid sexist language,

especially when talking about God. As a result many references to the Lord, such as Godself, are awkward and abstract.[14] That is inevitable when personal pronouns such as 'him' and 'himself' are dropped. I have also used many plurals in order to avoid awkward constructions such as the repeated use of words such as his/her and himself/herself. In many instances I have substituted s/he for he and she. When quoting from others such as saints and popes I have tended to retain the non-inclusive language they used.

I am grateful to God for all the men and women who have taught me to pray and who have prayed with me and for me over the years. I owe a special dept of gratitude to my deceased parents, John and Babs, my fellow Vincentians, close friends, and members of other Christian churches, especially Cecil and Myrtle Kerr, founders of the Christian Renewal Centre in Rostrevor, County Down, in Northern Ireland. I have known and esteemed them for over a quarter of a century. This book is dedicated to these faithful servants of the Lord. I know that their commitment to the cause of reconciliation has always been rooted in prayer, energised by prayer and sustained by prayer. Finally, I owe a particular debt of gratitude to my brother Peter for his repeated generosity and practical assistance, and to Dr Michael Downey editor of *The New Dictionary of Catholic Spirituality*[15] for his encouragement. Indirectly, it has led to the writing of this book.

CHAPTER ONE

Religion and prayer

Religion has been present at all times in all cultures. It is as human an activity as language, music and dance. Objectively speaking, religion of the monotheistic kind, such as Islam, Judaism or Christianity, consists of such things as beliefs, worship, ethics, rituals and customs. Catholic Christians, for example, believe in a Trinitarian God, the Eucharist, the rosary, fasting, pilgrimages, etc. From a subjective point of view, religion is animated by religious experience. It is an intuitive, awe-inspiring awareness of the mysterious and fascinating reality of a loving God. This quasi-mystical experience of the holy leads to a joyful sense of ultimate belonging, a conviction that one is simultaneously connected to God, the universe and one's deepest self. It is *the* antidote to the anxious alienation that is so characteristic of Western societies.

The history of spirituality indicates that there is an inseparable link between formal religion, religious experience and prayer. Speaking about the relationship of religion and prayer, St Thomas Aquinas stated: 'Religion shows honour to God. Therefore anything that shows reverence to God belongs to religion. Now man shows reverence to God by means of prayer, in so far as he subjects himself to him, and by praying expresses his need of him as the author of his blessings. Hence it is evident that prayer is properly an act of religion.'[1] In the twentieth century different writers echoed this point of view. In *The Varieties of Religious Experience*, William James described prayer as: 'A conscious and voluntary relation, entered into by a soul in distress with the mysterious power upon which it feels itself to depend, and upon which its fate is contingent.'[2] He said that as such: 'Prayer ... is the very soul and essence of religion ... Whenever interior prayer is lacking, there is no religion; wherever on the other hand, this prayer rises and stirs the soul, even in the absence of forms or of doctrines, we have living religion.'[3] In his classic book entitled *Prayer*, Friedrich Heiler defined prayer as: 'A living communion of the religious man with God, conceived as personal and present in experience, a communion which reflects the forms of the social relations of humanity.'[4] Then he added: 'Religious persons and students of religion agree in testifying that prayer is the centre of religion, the soul of all piety.'[5]

Just as the lungs enable the human body to live by breathing in life-giving oxygen, so prayer enables the human soul to live by breathing in the life-giving Holy Spirit. In other words, prayer is soul-breathing. As soon as it stops, religious experience begins to expire, and one is left with lifeless beliefs, duties, worship, rituals, customs, etc. As Heiler wrote: 'Without prayer faith remains a theoretical conviction; worship is only an external and formal act; moral action is without spiritual depth; people remain at a distance from God; an abyss yawns between the finite and the Infinite.'[6] One is reminded in this regard of Jesus' observation that: 'These people honour me with their lips, but their hearts are far from me. They worship me in vain; their teachings are but rules taught by men' (Mt 15:8-9). As a result they are like 'whitewashed tombs, which look beautiful on the outside but on the inside are full of dead men's bones' (Mt 23:27).

Effects of secularisation and postmodernism

The fact that a growing number of people in secular, post-modern culture are no longer religious is quite exceptional and untypical from an historical point of view. Secularisation in Western culture first appears as the separation of a large part of the population from the churches. It also involves an increased tendency to subjectivism and relativism in the realm of ethics. Self-development and happiness replace duty and life-long commitment as priorities. Post-modernism is also a characteristic of Western societies. It maintains that, rather than being an objective fact, our knowledge of truth is partial and provisional. Nothing is absolutely certain. There is only an endless sequence of contexts and interpretations. Post-modernism is sceptical about the claims of traditional forms of knowledge. It subjects them to a methodology of suspicion, by critiquing their presuppositions in a radical way. Generally speaking, it is anti-authoritarian in outlook.[7] It does not believe in all embracing explanations of life such as Christianity. As a result, Christian beliefs and practices have become increasingly problematical and counter-cultural in Western countries. I believe that there are good reasons for believing that the consequent decline of religion is having detrimental psycho-spiritual effects.

A number of twentieth-century psychologists suggested that people cannot be truly healthy unless they have prayerful religious experiences. We will focus on the views of three of the more notable commentators, Carl Jung, Viktor Frankl and Abraham Maslow. Jung argued that the human psyche could only be fulfilled when the self – his word for the human spirit – enjoyed a conscious awareness of the divine. In *Psychology and Western Religion* he wrote: 'In thirty years I have treated many patients in the second half of life. Every one of them became ill because he or she had lost that which the living religions in every age have given their followers, (i.e. religious experience) and none of them was fully healed who did not regain his religious outlook.'[8] Viktor Frankl agreed with Jung. He felt that in modern culture a lack of prayerful religious experience left people with a vacuum, an emptiness at the centre of their lives. It caused existential frustration which he described as 'the unrewarded longing and groping of man for an ultimate meaning to his life.'[9] When people's spirits are deprived of the oxygen of meaning their psyches became disorientated and they suffer from neurotic problems. Abraham Maslow's research indicated that instead of being a sign of neurosis as Freud had maintained, prayerful religious experience seemed to be an indication of psycho-spiritual health. Not only that, such experiences served to strengthen a sense of well-being and harmony. He believed that the power of prayerful peak experiences 'could permanently affect one's attitude to life ... It is my strong suspicion that one such experience might be able to prevent suicide and perhaps many varieties of low self-destruction such as alcoholism, drug addiction, and addiction to violence.'[10]

Recent research has tended to confirm the fact that prayerful religious experience does indeed help people to enjoy greater mental health. In an article entitled 'Religious Orientation and

Psychological Well-being: The Role of the Frequency of Personal Prayer,' three researchers have examined the effects of what Gordon Allport referred to as intrinsic religion on mental health.[11] People who have intrinsic religion are those who have internalised their faith in such a way that it influences every aspect of their everyday lives. They engage in regular prayer of a personal kind and are more likely to have high self-esteem and lower levels of anxiety and depression. The authors conclude: 'The distinction between personal and public orientation toward religion may give an insight into the relationship between religiosity and psychological well-being. The present findings suggest that the relationship between religion and psychological well-being may be an aspect of the relationship between frequency of personal prayer and psychological well-being.'[12]

In the light of these related points, it seems to me that we urgently need a religious awakening both in and beyond the Christian churches. When people in our secular, post-modern culture come into a real, as opposed to a notional, awareness of God and God's love, it will counteract the insidious effects of pervasive relativism and consumerism. It also seems to me that the revival and renewal movements in the churches, with their strong emphasis on the importance of religious experience and heartfelt prayer, have already shown that they have an ability to counteract the negative effects of contemporary culture by effectively fostering religious experience. I would like, briefly, to trace the origins of some of these converging streams of revival and renewal.

Methodism and revival

The notion of revival is a Protestant one. The word refers to a work of God and not of humans, a sudden and sovereign outpouring of grace, one that rapidly brings about many conversions to Christ. It is God's answer to the prayer in Hab. 3:2: 'O Lord, I have heard of your renown, and I stand in awe, O Lord, of your work. In our own time revive it; in our own time make it known.' It would probably be true to say that, in English-speaking countries, the notion of revival can be traced back to the rise of Methodism.

John Wesley was born in Epworth in 1703. In 1720 he went to

Oxford. There he and fourteen other students formed the 'Holy Club'. A porter in the college called George Whitfield used to attend the meetings. The club members followed a strict rule of life and consequently came to be known as the 'Methodists'. When he got his degree, John was ordained as an Anglican priest. Soon afterwards he went to Georgia in the American Colonies. While he was there he had a love affair with a Miss Hopkey. J. H. Plumb, a well-known British historian, says that this experience 'seemed to destroy in him all self control and all sense of proportion.'[13] As a result of the ensuing scandal, Wesley returned to England in 1738, a disillusioned man. He set up a bookshop in London.

Around this time John Wesley met a Moravian called Peter Bohler. He recounted their conversation in his Journal on 7 February 1736. 'My brother, I must first ask you one or two questions. Have you the witness in yourself? Does the Spirit of God bear witness with your spirit that you are a child of God?' I was surprised and knew not what to answer. He observed it and asked. 'Do you know Jesus Christ?' I paused and said, 'I know he is the Saviour of the world.' 'True,' he replied, 'but do you know that he has saved you?' I answered, 'I hope he has died to save me.' He only added, 'Do you know yourself?' I said, 'I do.' But I fear they were vain words.' Then Bohler said, 'Forget your good works, your own righteousness and fly to Him – to Jesus Christ, the Saviour – to your Jesus, to your Saviour.' He said that it was only when he had experienced such a conversion that his preaching would take on a new power.

Wesley tells us in his diary that 24 May 1738 was the day of his conversion. 'In the evening I went very unwillingly to a society in Aldersgate Street, where one was reading Luther's preface to the letter to the Romans. About a quarter before nine, while he was describing the change which God works in the heart through faith in Christ, I felt my heart strangely warmed. I felt that I did trust in Christ, in Christ alone, for salvation, and an assurance was given me that He had taken away my sins, even mine, and saved me from the law of sin and death ... I then testified openly to all there what I now felt.'[14] John Wesley was 35 at this time. For the next 53 years he travelled about 240,000 miles by horse and preached thousands of sermons. He worked mainly among the poor who had been neglected by the Anglican Church. Plumb says of his outdoor meetings, 'In the exercise of religion there was no emotional restraint. Sobbing, weeping, laughter, hysteria were commonplaces of Methodist fervour – a lack of restraint that seems to us almost pathological.'[15]

At first the Methodists were a group within the Anglican Church. But eventually they split from it because of a dispute over the ordination of clergy. Years later, Wesley tells us that he went to a Methodist meeting. 'In London alone,' He says in his journal, 'I found 652 members of our society who were exceedingly clear in their experience and whose testimony I could see no reason to doubt. And every one of these, without a single exception, had declared that his deliverance from sin was instantaneous; that the change was wrought in a moment. Had half of these, or one third, or one in twenty declared that it was gradually wrought in them, I should have believed this with regard to them and thought that some were gradually sanctified and some instantaneously. But I have not found in so long a space of time, a single person speaking thus. I cannot but believe that sanctification is commonly, if not always, an instantaneous work.' The experience of sudden conversion was a typical if not essential characteristic of Protestant revivals. Incidentally, George Whitfield, the former Oxford porter, was eventually ordained and became one of the most famous and effective preachers of the day, firstly in England and later in the American Colonies.

The Great Awakening

The great revival in New England occurred among the Puritans. The most influential figure in this religious awakening was Jonathan Edwards. He was a clergyman, of Calvinist leanings, who was a brilliant philosopher and theologian, perhaps the greatest that America has ever produced. He wrote an account of what happened in his parish, entitled, 'An Account of the Revival of Religion in Northampton 1740-1742'. He says that before 1740, the people were lukewarm from a religious point of view. Then George Whitfield came to town. He had a remarkable effect. 'Mr Whitfield's sermons were suitable to the circumstances of the town; containing a just reproof on our backslidings, and a most moving and effecting manner making use of our great pro-

fessions and great mercies, as arguments with us to return to
God from whom we had departed.'[16] Within about six weeks
the New England revival was well under way.

Edward's own preaching, which followed the sudden deaths
of two young adults, also had a profound effect upon the people.
Apparently he talked a good deal about the terrible punish-
ments that awaited those who were damned. He described the
effects of the many conversions that subsequently occurred in
these eloquent words: 'The light and comfort which some of
them enjoy, give a new relish to their common blessings, and
cause all things about them to appear as it were beautiful, sweet,
and pleasant. All things abroad, the sun, moon and stars, the
clouds and sky, the heavens and earth, appear as it were with a
divine glory and sweetness about them.'[17] Apparently, the people would swing from feelings of abject guilt and virtual despair
to ecstatic feelings of elation in the realisation that they were
saved. He says: 'It was a frequent thing to see a house full of out-
cries, faintings and convulsions, and such like, both with distress, and also with admiration and joy. It was not the manner
here to hold meetings all night, as in some places, nor was it
common to continue them till very late in the night; but it was
pretty often so, that there were some so affected, and their bodies so overcome, that they could not go home, but were obliged
to stay where they were all night.'[18]

Edwards says that the revival touched people of all ages and
walks in life. By the end of 1741 it was abating a bit. Then another
preacher, called Mr Buell, came to town for a few weeks while
Edwards was away on business. His preaching seemed to rekin-
dle the first fervour of the people. When Edwards returned he
led the townspeople in making a solemn covenant to God. It was
a sort of public dedication to lead a truly Christian life. It spelt
out their ethical commitment to be honest in financial matters, to
avoid backbiting, to treat others in the way one would like to be
treated oneself, and so on.

The awakening in Northampton spread to the surrounding
towns and villages. However Edwards says that after a time, the
initial fervour died down. When the special anointing of God
was withdrawn, exaltation was succeeded by suicidal feelings.
In the event two people went mad with strange enthusiastic

delusions. The conversions ended. But Edwards says that when things settled down again the people were calmer and more joyful than they had been before the awakening.

However, Edwards was not happy about many of the more hysterical aspects of the revival in Northampton. He wondered how one could discern a true from a false work of God. Eventually he wrote two treatises on the subject. The first was entitled *The Distinguishing Marks of a Work of the Spirit of God*.[19] It was followed by a more substantial book, which has since become a theological classic, entitled *The Religious Affections*.[20] Having measured the available facts against the criteria of scripture, Edwards concluded, 'I will venture to draw this inference, viz., that the extraordinary influence that has lately appeared causing an uncommon concern and engagedness of mind about all the things of religion is undoubtedly, in general, from the Spirit of God.' In the other colonies there were smaller, less dramatic revivals, e. g. on the frontier in Kentucky and Tennessee. Other awakenings occurred at the end of the eighteenth and at the beginning of the nineteenth century. There were reports of other revivals among Protestants in places such as Wales and Northern Ireland.

Pentecostalism and Revival
During the final years of the nineteenth century there was a growing conviction, particularly among Protestant Evangelicals in America, that a new outpouring of the Holy Spirit was about to take place.[21] Many people were praying for a universal revival. There were occasional reports of healings and people speaking in tongues. There was more and more talk about a New Pentecost at conferences and in the religious press. Then in April 1906 the fire seemed to fall from heaven on to a tiny black mission on Azuza Street, in Los Angeles. It was attended by people from different denominations and races. As soon as the people were blessed they were convinced that their prayer for a great revival had been answered. As Peter Hocken, a Catholic ecumenist, remarks, 'The Inter-racial component at Azusa Street astounded all participants. This was surely an expression of divine wisdom, that such a worldwide explosion of grace should be unleashed at a gathering of the poor and dispossessed of all colours,

led by an uneducated black pastor. These origins clearly express the divine gratuitousness, and the difference between God's plans and mere human ideas.'[22]

From the beginning, Pentecostalism had a number of distinctive characteristics such as vigorous praise, melodic songs, strong expectation of the second coming, evangelistic and missionary drive, popular participation, and an active role for women. The Pentecostals believed in two interrelated blessings, being saved as a result of faith in Christ, and baptism in the Spirit which was evidenced in the ability to pray in tongues and possibly in the exercise of other gifts of the Spirit, such as prophecy and healing.

The crowds attending the meetings in Azusa Street grew larger and larger. Because they were not accepted by the established Protestant churches, they formed their own distinctive congregations. The Pentecostals were keen to spread their understanding of the Good News. Missionaries and witnesses fanned out, not only in the United States but also to many parts of the world. Everywhere they went the reports were similar, the Spirit was being poured out, the gifts were in evidence and people were being transformed.

It is significant that whereas the mainline Christian churches in Western countries, in particular, have been suffering from declining membership, Pentecostal and charismatic congregations have experienced dramatic growth. It is now estimated that there more than 400 million Pentecostals world wide,[23] many of them former Catholics. Arguably, this has been the fastest growing religious movement, not only in the twentieth century, but in the whole of Christian history. Mini-revivals, continue to revitalise what has been referred to as the 'third force' in Christianity alongside Catholicism/Orthodoxy and Protestantism. Surely the rise of Pentecostalism was the most significant religious event of the last century. It is my belief that the great revival, which was longed for over a long period of time, is already well under way and will exercise an increasing influence on the mainline churches.

Catholic Renewal
Whereas Protestants pray for revival, Catholics, with their re-

spect for tradition and the continuity of the church, tend to pray for renewal, not only of individual lives, but also of the church and through it, of entire cultures. The Second Vatican Council referred to this process of gradual transformation as *aggornimento*. A question. Should we pray for renewal or revival, or both?

I think it would be true to say that many evangelical Protestants have a firm grasp of the vital importance of revival in the Christian churches. It is an indispensable foundation stone upon which the Christian life needs to be built. However, there are good reasons for suspecting that Protestants aren't always as insightful when it comes to developing the grace of revival either in the individual, the community or the culture. That is why many of the revivals have died out. One has only to drive through rural Wales to see that many chapels which were built during earlier times of revival have since been closed and boarded up.

It would probably be equally true to say that Catholics have a deep appreciation of the importance and dynamics of renewal. In a way, the documents of Vatican II were a great blueprint for the renewal of every aspect of Christian life. However, conscientious attempts at renewal have often had disappointing results. I have long suspected that although the Council's ideas were good in themselves, we often tried to implement them by means of our own unaided efforts. But as Ps 127:1 warns: 'Unless the Lord builds the house, those who build it labour in vain.' In many instances that is what we discovered the hard way. We came to see that we had built the renewal on sand. When the storms of adversity assailed us, a good deal of the renewal collapsed. What was missing, it would seem, was the foundation stone of a graced-filled revival. A number of writers seemed to acknowledge this.

For example, during a time of religious unrest in 1967, some students from Duquesne University met for a weekend of prayer and fasting. Kevin and Dorothy Ranaghan described their state of mind: 'There was something lacking in their individual Christian lives. They couldn't quite put their finger on it, but somehow there was an emptiness, a lack of dynamism, a sapping of strength in their lives of prayer and action. It was as if their lives as Christians were too much their own creation, as if they were moving forward under their own power and of their own will. It seemed to them that the Christian life wasn't meant to be a purely human achievement.'[24] As we know, the Spirit and his gifts were poured out on that small gathering and so began the Charismatic Renewal in the Catholic Church. To be more precise, those Catholics experienced a revival that kick-started the possibility of a genuine, long-lasting renewal in the church.

I believe that what was true then is still true today. There will be no genuine renewal in the Catholic Church without the grace of revival, whether associated with the Charismatic movement or not. Toward the end of the last century, fifty different Catholic renewal movements and communities gathered in Rome, on the Vigil of Pentecost 1998. The Vatican estimated that more than half a million people attended the celebration. In its June edition, the magazine entitled *Inside the Vatican* stated in its editorial: 'What happened in May in Rome was so important we believe that future historians of the church will have to distinguish between 'before' and 'after' Pentecost 1998.' Apparently, the Pope saw the renewal movements as a hopeful sign of an impending springtime in the church.[25] Subsequently, he said: 'The abundant tears of humanity during the twentieth century open up the hope of a new spring ... I am convinced that the year 2000 will be an incomparable occasion to make the mystery of faith and the reflourishing of Christianity present in a society filled with anguish and asphyxia by secularism.'[26]

What the new movements and communities have shown is that basic evangelisation courses such as Alpha, Life in the Spirit Seminars, The Renew Program and Cursillo are vitally important. They enable people to commit their lives to Christ and to be filled with the Spirit. As the Irish bishops stated in a pastoral entitled *Life in the Spirit*, 'The outpouring of the Holy Spirit is a conversion gift through which one receives a new and significant commitment to the Lordship of Jesus and openness to the power and gifts of the Holy Spirit.' Catholic scholars Mc Donnell and Montague have pointed out that there will be no genuine renewal without this foundational, reviving grace which is both integral to the sacraments of initiation and normative for all Christians.[27] Revival and renewal are complementary. We need to pray for both.

Prayer as the key to on-going renewal

When people experience revival through an in-filling of the Spirit, they need to sustain and deepen that grace by means of frequent, heartfelt prayer. A number of writers, such as Soderblom and Heiler, have suggested that there are two main types of Christian prayer: mystical and prophetic. The biblical peoples were more interested in prophetic prayer and wisdom than they were in rational philosophy. Theirs was a personal, passionate and experiential approach to life and religion. It was epitomised by the example and teaching of Jesus and the apostles about all aspects of life, including prayer. Three of my favourite books on the subject are George Martin's *To Pray as Jesus*,[28] Arthur Wallis's *Pray in the Spirit*,[29] and at a more scholarly level, Oscar Cullmann's *Prayer in the New Testament*.[30] They indicate, in relatively brief, lucid chapters, how prophetic prayer is at once simple and profound.

Platonic mysticism

However, in the first few centuries of Christianity, eminent thinkers tried to adapt the gospel message to the Greco-Roman cultures where they lived. At the Second Vatican Council the bishops acknowledged that this had happened. 'The church learned early in its history to express the Christian message in the concepts and language of different peoples and tried to clarify the gospel to the understanding of their philosophers; it was an attempt to adapt the gospel to the understanding of all people and to the requirements of the learned, insofar as that could be done.'[31] As Platonism was the most influential philosophy at the time, religious writers such as Evagrius Ponticus (346-99), Dionysius the Pseudo-Areopagite (c. 500) and others tried to describe prayer, more or less, in Platonic terms. They saw it as an ascent of the loving will to the incomprehensible mystery of God beyond the limitations of worldly concepts and images. As the document *Some Aspects of Christian Meditation* observes, these methods of prayer 'try as far as possible to put aside everything that is worldly, sense-perceptible or conceptually limited. It is thus an attempt to ascend to, or immerse oneself in the sphere of the divine, which, as such, is neither terrestrial, sense-perceptible nor capable of conceptualisation.'[32]

In more recent years, mystical prayer of this kind has been augmented by insights and techniques which have been borrowed from Eastern forms of meditation such as breathing exercises and methods of stilling the mind. The church has given some of them conditional approval. In the document *Some Aspects of Christian Meditation* we read: 'The majority of the great religions which have sought union with God in prayer have also pointed out ways to achieve it. Just as the Catholic Church rejects nothing of what is true and holy in these religions, neither should these ways be rejected out of hand simply because they are not Christian. On the contrary, one can take from them what is useful so long as the Christian conception of prayer, its logic and requirements are never obscured.'[33] Writers such as William Johnson in his *Mystical Theology*[34] and Bernard Mc Ginn in his five volume series entitled *The Presence of God: A History of Western Christian Mysticism*, describe attempts to integrate biblical and neo-Platonic forms of religion into a synthesis that remains faithful to Catholic teaching. However, if one compares them to the books of Martin, Wallis and Cullmann, the difference in approach is immediately obvious.

Prophetic and mystical forms of prayer
It would probably be true to say that Protestants have tended to espouse the biblical understanding of prayer whereas Catholics have often championed the more contemplative approach. I believe that ultimately there is a complementarity between the two. Both of them are capable, in their differing ways, of leading people into an experiential awareness of the living God. Some scholars who favour the scriptural approach have suggested that there is little evidence of mystical experience in the bible. I believe that this is a mistaken conclusion based upon a questionable definition of mysticism. For example, Heiler says in a misleading way that mysticism is 'that form of intercourse with God in which the world and self are absolutely denied, in which human personality is dissolved, disappears and is absorbed in the infinite unity of Godhead.'[35] This Eastern notion of mysticism is too impersonal and life denying from a Christian point of view. Mysticism is more accurately described by Evelyn Underhill in her *Practical Mysticism* when she says that it is: 'The art of union with Reality.

The mystic is a person who has attained that union in greater or less degree; or who aims at and believes in such attainment.' [36]

Understood in this sense, it is clear that the Old and New Testaments contain many examples of people who were united with the reality of God. For example, the prophet Isaiah testified: 'In the year that King Uzziah died, I saw the Lord seated on a throne, high and exalted, and the train of his robe filled the temple. Above him were seraphs, each with six wings: With two wings they covered their faces, with two they covered their feet, and with two they were flying. And they were calling to one another: 'Holy, holy, holy is the Lord Almighty; the whole earth is full of his glory' (Is 6:1-3). In the New Testament we are told that Jesus had an even more profound experience when he was transfigured. 'After six days Jesus took with him Peter, James and John the brother of James, and led them up a high mountain by themselves. There he was transfigured before them. His face shone like the sun, and his clothes became as white as the light. Just then there appeared before them Moses and Elijah, talking with Jesus' (Mt 17:1-3). Later St Paul described a similar experience: 'I know a man in Christ who fourteen years ago was caught up to the third heaven. Whether it was in the body or out of the body I do not know – God knows. And I know that this man – whether in the body or apart from the body I do not know, but God knows – was caught up to paradise. He heard inexpressible things, things that man is not permitted to tell' (2 Cor 12:2-4). Surely these prophetic experiences were mystical. As John Mc Kenzie has observed: 'The only satisfactory parallel to the prophetic experience is the phenomenon of mysticism as described by writers like Teresa of Avila, John of the Cross and others. They affirm that the immediate experience of God is ineffable.'[37]

That said, while this book will focus briefly on contemplative prayer it will not deal with the neo-Platonic variety. There are a number of reasons for this. Personally, as was noted in the foreword, I prefer the biblical approach to prayer. I feel uncomfortable with the way some books deal with contemplative and mystical forms of prayer. They seem to cater for a well-educated, spiritual elite. They can also give the impression of being more influenced by philosophical presuppositions than the nuances of God's word. I prefer methods of prayer that are accessible to 'ordinary' Christians, who desire to have a deep relationship with God. I have found that the biblical approach is amenable to all, educated and uneducated alike, while enabling those who are growing in prayer to experience a deeply contemplative awareness of the love of Christ which is beyond understanding (cf. Eph 3:18). Furthermore, as a Vincentian, I admire St Vincent de Paul. As far as we know, he wasn't accustomed to having ecstatic mystical experiences like those described by Teresa of Avila or John of the Cross. His was a more practical type of Christianity where the emphasis was on the fruits of prayer. Instead of trying to enjoy union with the Mystery of God in a neo-Platonic cloud of unknowing, Vincent endeavoured to love the Lord in and through his reverential service of the poor.

Conclusion

I have suggested elsewhere that three models of spirituality are currently operating in the church.[38] Firstly there is traditional Catholic piety. It tends to be head-centred, focuses on right belief and expects obedient conformity. Secondly, there is a form of spirituality which is derived from liberation theology. It tends to be hands-centred, focuses on right action and expects to free people from spiritual and institutional oppression. Thirdly, there is a form of spirituality that emphasises the role of the Holy Spirit. It tends to be heart-centred, focuses on right experience and expects people to enjoy a conscious sense of the presence, attributes and guidance of the Lord. This third form of spirituality encourages affective prayer as the context in which adherents experience the Trinity. They would maintain that it is epitomised in the texts such as: 'Pray in the Spirit' (Jude 1:20), and 'The anointing which you received from God abides in you, and you have no need that anyone should teach you; as his anointing teaches you about everything' (1 Jn 2:27). My understanding of prayer has been influenced predominately, though not exclusively, by this third model of spirituality.

CHAPTER TWO

The prayer of Jesus

There is something mysterious and ultimately inaccessible about the inner life of Jesus. This is not surprising. After all, we are contemplating the inner life of the Son of God. However, we have reason to believe that we can gain some insight into his prayer life. Firstly, although it transcended the prayer life of the saintly men and women of Old Testament times, it had its roots in their experience of God. Secondly, the gospels not only give us information about the ways in which Jesus prayed, they also recount some of his spontaneous prayers. Thirdly, we have Jesus' teaching on prayer. Presumably, it was based on his personal experience. Fourthly, through baptism and the outpouring of the Spirit, Christ truly lives in believers and they live in him. As adopted sons and daughters of God we 'have the mind of Christ' (1 Cor 2:16). This means that our own prayer lives can enable us to have a certain affinity with the inner life of Jesus, thereby providing us with an interpretative key that can be used to unlock some of the secrets of his relationship with the Father.

Although as God, Jesus was filled with the Spirit from the first moment of his conception, we know that as a human being, he grew in age, in wisdom and grace (cf. Lk 2:40). From early childhood onwards, Joseph and Mary would have instructed him on how to pray. He first heard the psalms at home and then in the local synagogue. In one place, St Augustine referred to Mary as 'the woman of the tambourine'. It is was she, more than anyone else, who taught her Son to be 'the marvellous singer of the psalms!'[1] The varied sentiments of these scriptural prayers expressed the nascent stirrings of his own heart. Presumably, when he got a bit older, he participated in the fixed order of prayer observed by the Jewish people. He would have attended the weekly Sabbath worship, said grace before and after meals, and paused three times daily to pray, i.e. at 9 am, at 12 noon and at 3 pm (cf. Ps 55:17; Dan 6:10). He would have recited well-known Jewish prayers such as the *Shema*, *Berakah* and *Kaddish*.

The *Shema* was the Jewish confession of faith, made up of three scriptural texts, Deut 6:4-9, 11:13-21, Num 15:37-41, which, together with other appropriate prayers, formed an integral part of the evening and morning services. The name derived from the initial word of the verse 'Hear, O Israel: The Lord our God is one Lord' (Deut 6:4). The *Berakah* was a blessing, an expression of praise or thanks, which was offered to God at specific points of the synagogue liturgy, during private prayer, or on other occasions. Most blessings began with the words: 'Blessed art Thou, O Lord our God, King of the Universe.' The *Kaddish* was recited in the synagogue liturgy. The key to this prayer was the phrase 'Glorified and sanctified be God's great name throughout the world which he has created according to his will. May he establish his kingdom in your lifetime and during your days.' The congregation responded: 'May his great name be blessed forever to all eternity.' It seems pretty obvious that these lines were later to inspire the 'Our Father' to a greater or lesser extent. Besides being influenced by Jewish prayers, it is also highly likely that Jesus identified with the heroes of faith in the Old Testament, and with their prayerful encounters with the God of revelation, e.g. Ex 33:7-14.

The baptism of Jesus and his life of prayer

The baptism of Jesus is mentioned in all the gospels. As a seminal event, it seemed to have had a profound and determining influence on the way in which he prayed. Speaking of Jesus, St Paul says in 2 Cor 5:21, 'God made him who had no sin to be sin for us.' In other words, although he did not sin himself, God allowed himself to suffer some of the effects of sin.[2] I mention this because when Jesus submitted to John's baptism of repentance, he seemed to be identifying, in this qualified way, with those who had gone astray. Immediately after the event itself, Jesus spent some time in prayer (cf. Lk 21-22). As he did so, he was baptised in the Holy Spirit. The word baptism in Greek means to immerse. In other words, like a sponge plunged into water, Jesus was drenched, soaked and inundated in the heartfelt awareness of God.

We cannot be sure what Jesus was conscious of during this mystical experience. In Mk 1:11 we are told: 'a voice came from heaven: "You are my Son, whom I love; with you I am well pleased."' These words were drawn from two texts in the Old Testament. In Is 42:1 the Lord says: 'Here is my servant, whom I uphold, my chosen one in whom I delight; I will put my Spirit on him.' Again in Ps 2:7 we read: 'He said to me, "You are my Son; today I have become your Father."' There is prophetic significance in these verses.

First and foremost they suggest that as a result of the outpouring of the Spirit, Jesus became more vividly aware than ever before of the Father's infinite love for him. From that fateful day forward he was strengthened with might by the Spirit in his innermost self to the point where he was enabled to grasp the length and breadth, the height and the depth of the infinite love of God his Father that surpassed his rational understanding, so that he was filled inwardly with the very fullness of God (cf. Eph 3:16; 18-19). No wonder he could say afterwards: 'I and the Father are one' (Jn 10:30).

Child psychologists maintain that, in the days following their births, babies experience symbiotic union with their mothers. This refers to the fact that a toddler has little or no sense of 'I'ness. Because of a lack of a firm ego boundary it feels merged with its mother. Her body is an extension of the baby's body and *visa versa*. As Tennyson wrote in his poem *In Memoriam*:

The baby new to earth and sky
What time his tender palm is prest
Against the circle of the breast
Has never thought that 'This is I.'[3]

While being breast fed and cuddled satisfies its physical needs, the child is fed emotionally and spiritually by the mother's love. The mother may whisper sweet nothings, the baby may gurgle with delight, but basically there is no exchange of thoughts. The child's psycho-spiritual communication with the mother is non-verbal.

Following the outpouring of the Spirit, Jesus may have experienced a similar sense of union with God. The words of Ps 131:1-2 could be used to describe his prayerful intimacy with the Father: 'My heart is not proud, O Lord, my eyes are not haughty;

I do not concern myself with great matters or things too wonderful for me. But I have stilled and quieted my soul; like a weaned
child with its mother, like a weaned child is my soul within me.'
His deep sense of union with God, which later found expression
in such phrases as: 'You, Father are in me, and I in you' (Jn 17:21),
was fundamentally a pre-imaginative and pre-conceptual resting on the bosom of the unfathomable love of God. Pope Paul VI
observed in part three of his encyclical *On Christian Joy*: 'Jesus …
knows that he is loved by his Father. When he is baptised on the
banks of the Jordan, this love, which is present from the first moment of his incarnation, is manifested: 'You are my Son, the
Beloved; my favour rests on you' (Lk 3:22).' This certitude is inseparable from the consciousness of Jesus. It is a presence which
never leaves him all alone. It is an intimate knowledge which
fills him: '… the Father knows me and I know the Father' (Jn
10:15). It is an unceasing and total exchange: 'All I have is yours
and all you have is mine' (Jn 17:10). For Jesus it is not a question
of a passing awareness. It is the reverberation in his human consciousness of the love that he has always known as God in the
bosom of the Father: '… you loved me before the foundation of
the world' (Jn 17:24).

Child psychologists maintain that a baby's identity is formed
in the reflected light of the mother's love. If she approves, appreciates and affirms her child's unique value, the baby begins to
see itself as a person of worth and so becomes a secure and confident individual, who knows that s/he is deserving of respect
and affection. When Jesus looked at the Father looking at him he
knew that he was approving, appreciating and affirming his infinite value as the Son of God. As such he was uniquely worthy
of all the infinite love the Father could lavish upon him.
Eventually this pre-conceptual awareness of love began to articulate itself in a paradoxical way. On the one hand Jesus experienced an unimpeded sense of oneness with the Father, and on
the other he enjoyed a heightened sense of individuality separate from the Father. Jesus discovered, as never before, who he
really was. He was God's Son, the promised Messiah, and the
anointed One foretold by the prophets (cf. Lk 24:27).

As he began to know who he was in the eyes of God, Jesus
also began to have a clear sense of mission. Having heard the

Father's words on the Jordan bank, he realised that he was not being called to be the political liberator of popular messianic expectation. He recognised that his vocation was to be the suffering servant referred to in the prophecies of Isaiah. As such, Jesus felt called to show to others, especially the poor and the 'accursed' of his day (cf. Jn 7:49), the same unconditional and unrestricted love that God was showing to him. All of his words and actions were to be rooted in the love of God in order to proclaim and demonstrate it to the people. Jesus testified, in his very first sermon in his local synagogue, that: 'The Spirit of the Lord is on me, because he has anointed me to preach good news to the poor. He has sent me to proclaim freedom for the prisoners and recovery of sight for the blind, to release the oppressed, to proclaim the year of the Lord's favour' (Lk 4:18-19). It was the time of jubilee, the age of mercy when the debt of sin was being cancelled free *gratis* and for nothing.

We know that the daily activity of Jesus was closely bound up with personal prayer, and flowed from it. He often withdrew to lonely places (cf. Mk 1:35; Lk 5:16) or to the hills to pray (Lk 6:12). We are also told that he sometimes rose before dawn to converse with God. For example, Mark 1:35 recounts that: 'Very early in the morning, while it was still dark, Jesus got up, left the house and went off to a solitary place, where he prayed.' He sometimes spent the hours of darkness in prayer to God. For instance, Lk 6:12 tells us that he 'spent the night praying to God'. It is highly likely that during these times of personal prayer he reaffirmed and deepened his primordial baptismal awareness. Like a man who dives into the sea, Jesus dived into the waters of God's incomprehensible love for him and, through him, for humanity. In the light of that divine love Jesus mulled over the problems he faced and the decisions he had to make. The bigger they were the longer the time he spent in prayer.

The Jews said that the first requirement of prayer was *kawannah*. The Hebrew word referred to the way in which the mind and heart should be fixed on God.[4] It is highly likely that when Jesus prayed he was absorbed in this form of self-forgetful contemplation. In other words, he paid sustained and loving attention to the Father who loved him in such an incomprehensible manner that it couldn't be adequately expressed in words. Jesus basked in the light of that love and poured out his daily concerns in a trusting way to the Lord. As he did so he was 'led by the Spirit' (Lk 4:1), by means of the gifts of wisdom and knowledge (cf. Is 11:2) to know what to say and what to do. To paraphrase a passage of scripture, the Spirit searches all things, even the deep things of God. Jesus had not received the spirit of the world but the Spirit who is from God, that he might understand God's purposes. This is what he spoke about, not in words taught us by human wisdom but in words taught by the Spirit. He expressed spiritual truths in spiritual words (cf. 1 Cor 2:10-16). As Jesus himself was to testify: 'What the father has taught me is what I speak' (Jn 8:28). On another occasion, referring to his actions, he testified: 'The Son can only do what he sees the Father doing' (Jn 5:19). In a way, then, one could say that there was nothing original in what Jesus said and did. As a man, all his inspirations came from his Father in virtue of his prayerful union with him. But as the Son of God he could say, 'he who has seen me has seen the Father' (Jn 14:9).

On one occasion in 1656, St Vincent de Paul gave a pep talk to a young priest named Antoine Durand who had recently been appointed as the superior of a seminary. Among other things he said: 'You should also have recourse to prayer in order to beseech our Lord to provide for the needs of those entrusted to your charge. Rest assured you will gather more fruit in this way than by any other. Jesus Christ, who should be the exemplar of all your conduct, was not content with employing sermons, labours, fasts and even death itself, but he also added prayer to all that.' Then Vincent went on to observe: 'He had no need whatsoever of prayer for himself, and hence it was for us that he prayed so fervently, and also to teach us to do the same.'

Clearly, Vincent espoused what is known as Christology from above, an understanding of Christ's life which stressed his divinity more than his humanity. As a result he could make the surprising assertion that Jesus did not need to pray for himself. There are a number of obvious problems with this conclusion. Firstly, it implies that Jesus was not, in fact, like us in *all things* but sin. Secondly, Vincent implied that there was a certain degree of pretence in the prayer of Jesus. Although his petition on his own behalf in Gethsemane seemed very real, it was merely a lesson in prayer, one calculated to teach the disciples how to pray in times of distress. Jesus was going through the motions of prayer for our sake, but not for his own. This conclusion seems to contradict the teaching of Heb 5:7-9 which attests: 'During the days of Jesus' life on earth, he offered up prayers and petitions with loud cries and tears to the one who could save him from death, and he was heard because of his reverent submission.' Thirdly, it implies that the anguish of Jesus was not real, that in virtue of his divinity he was secretly enjoying the beatific vision.

If one adopts what is known as Christology from below, besides stressing the divinity of Christ, one would also stress the fact that he was truly human. As a result, one would have to conclude that as a result of emptying himself of his divine prerogatives – though not his identity as God – Jesus not only prayed for us and gave us an example of prayer, as a man he also prayed because he himself needed to do so.

Some characteristics of Jesus' prayer
It seems pretty obvious from the gospels that the apostles were very impressed by the role of prayer in Jesus' life and also by the ardent way in which he prayed. The gospels provide us with some hints about the latter point. Joachim Jeremias says that while the liturgical prayers of the time were said in Hebrew, Jesus himself prayed in Aramaic. For example, when he taught his disciples the 'Our Father' he did so in their native tongue. In doing this he 'withdrew prayer from the liturgical sphere of the sacral and put it in the centre of life, indeed in the centre of everyday life.'[5] Secondly, all four gospels attest that Jesus addressed God as Abba in all his prayers. It was a term of familiarity and endearment used by children to address their earthly fathers. In fact it is still used in much the same way in some cultures today. It means something like dear father, daddy, or papa. Instead of emphasising the transcendence and intimidating majesty of a distant and demanding God, Jesus prayed to God, like Moses of old, in an intimate and confident way. In doing so, says Jeremias, 'we are confronted with something new and unheard of which breaks through the limits of Judaism.'[6] Jesus was the One who had a natural right to address God as Abba. But by teaching outcasts and sinners to address God with

the same sense of familiarity he was showing that they too were, by God's grace, cherished members of the kingdom. It is also clear in the gospels that, as our earthly advocate, Jesus often interceded for people. For more on this point see chapter seven, below, on intercessory prayer.

Praise and thanksgiving

Jesus also offered many prayers of thanksgiving and praise. For example, in Mt 11:25-27 we read: 'At that time Jesus said, "I praise you, Father, Lord of heaven and earth, because you have hidden these things from the wise and learned, and revealed them to little children. Yes, Father, for this was your good pleasure." All things have been committed to me by my Father. No one knows the Son except the Father, and no one knows the Father except the Son and those to whom the Son chooses to reveal him.' Jesus uttered this prayer at a turning point in his life. From a human point of view his ministry was failing to bear fruit. The religious authorities of his day had rejected him. By and large the majority of his followers were disreputable figures. Nevertheless he praised and thanked God in the belief that in revealing the kingdom to the poor, God's purposes were beginning to be achieved. Again, before he raised his friend Lazarus from the dead, Jesus said: 'Father, I thank you for having heard me' (Jn 11:41). These words not only implied that God always heard his petitions but also that Jesus may have been exercising trust of the expectant kind.[7]

It is a striking fact that even during Holy Week, when he was facing torture and death, Jesus gave thanks. As we are reminded in each Eucharist, during the last supper, 'he took bread and gave you thanks and praise' and 'When supper was ended he took the cup. Again he gave you thanks and praise.' We have good reason to believe that even when he felt forsaken by his Father, Jesus thanked and praised him on the cross. We are told that he uttered the first line of Ps 22. As Gelin has pointed out, it is quite likely that he continued to pray the rest of the psalm quietly in his heart.[8] If so, he went on to say: 'in the congregation I will praise you. You who fear the Lord, praise him! ... Revere him, all you descendants of Israel! For he has not despised or disdained the suffering of the afflicted one; he has not hidden his face from him but has listened to his cry for help … they who seek the Lord will praise him! (Ps 22:22-26). As Joachim Jeremias has stated with good reason: 'We may suppose that thanksgiving dominated the life and prayer of Jesus.'[9]

Passionate prayer

There was also something passionate about the prayer of Jesus.[10] While etymologically the word 'passion' is derived from the Latin *passio*, 'to suffer', in modern English it refers to any deeply felt emotion which is evoked by a person's experience of reality.[11] There is nothing apathetic about passionate people. They are deeply affected by the events that impinge upon them. For example, when they experience the beauties and wonders of the world they are moved with joy. On the other hand, when the misfortunes of life afflict either themselves or others, they are moved with sorrow. There is clear evidence that Jesus was a man of such intense feelings. The Son of God was so in touch with his inner life that he was deeply affected by everything he experienced. Unlike other people he did not edit or censor his impressions by means of unconscious defence mechanisms. As a result he displayed an almost childlike openness and emotional vulnerability. His was the perception of an Adam or Eve before the fall, wholehearted and innocent. For example, when he rejoiced because God had revealed the mysteries of the kingdom to the poor, the text implies that he was so ecstatically happy that he leapt for joy (cf. Mt 11:25). On the other hand, we see him being almost drowned by sorrow in the garden of Gethsemane (cf. Heb 5:7-8). It would seem, then, that Jesus was a man of intense feeling. Not only did he share these emotions with his Father, he was also deeply moved by the revelation of the Father's person, word and will.

What Jesus taught about prayer

Not only was Jesus a man of fervent and frequent prayer himself, he spoke on a number of occasions about prayer. He highlighted the nature and importance of prayers of supplication. He also made strikingly unambiguous promises about God's willingness to answer such prayers while mentioning the dispositions that were necessary in order to be worthy of them. This subject is dealt with in the chapters on the prayers of petition, intercession and command. At this point we will mention some of the general points that Jesus made about praying.

Pray in secret

In Mt 6:5-6 the Lord says: 'And when you pray, do not be like the hypocrites, for they love to pray standing in the synagogues and on the street corners to be seen by men. I tell you the truth, they have received their reward in full. But when you pray, go into your room, close the door and pray to your Father, who is unseen. Then your Father, who sees what is done in secret, will reward you.' Clearly Jesus was not opposed to group prayer. After all he engaged in it himself. But he was against religious ostentation, the religious vanity that deliberately seeks to impress others. He believed that private prayer should be hidden, a matter between the person praying and God. The reference to going into one's room probably had its Old Testament roots in Is 26:20 and in 1 Kings 4:33. Interpreted in a more metaphorical way, mention of a private room probably referred to the inner tabernacle of the heart. As Jesus himself said, 'the kingdom of God is within you' (Lk 17:21).

Prayers should be short

Jesus also said: 'And when you pray, do not keep on babbling like pagans, for they think they will be heard because of their many words' (Mt 6:7). There is a striking Old Testament example of what Jesus had in mind here. 1 Kings 18:19-40 describes the religious contest between the Prophet Elijah and the four hundred prophets of Baal. They had to call on their respective Gods to ask them to consume their sacrifice with fire. We are told that the pagan prophets, 'called on the name of Baal from morning till noon. "O Baal, answer us!" they shouted. But there was no response; no one answered … At noon Elijah began to taunt them. "Shout louder!" he said, "Surely he is a god! Perhaps he is deep in thought, or busy, or travelling. Maybe he is sleeping and must be awakened." So they shouted louder' (1 Kgs 18:26-28). In marked contrast the prayer of Elijah was short and effective. 'Elijah stepped forward and said: "O Lord, God of Abraham, Isaac and Israel, let it be known today that you are God in Israel and that I am your servant and have done all these things at your command. Answer me, O Lord, answer me, so these people will know that you, O Lord, you are God ..." Then the fire of the Lord fell and burned up the sacrifice, the wood, the stones and the soil, and also licked up the water in the trench' (1 Kgs 18:36-38). What made Elijah's short prayer so effective was the fact that it was offered in a spirit of unhesitating, expectant faith. Jesus felt that the efficacy of prayer was determined more by the trust and sincerity it displayed than by its length. In any case, there was no need to be longwinded because, as Jesus observed: 'your Father knows what you need before you ask him' (Mt 6:8).

Pray always

In Lk 18:1 we read: 'Then Jesus told his disciples a parable to show them that they should always pray and not give up.' Later St Paul was to echo the same sentiment when he wrote: 'Pray constantly' (1 Thess 5:17).[12] Over the centuries there have been many interpretations, some of them mystical in nature, of what Jesus might have meant by such an injunction.[13] In biblical terms the explanation is probably more practical and down to earth. In the Old Testament the Hebrew word *tamid* can mean 'at all times' in the sense that an action is repeated on a regular basis.[14] Understood in this sense, the call to unceasing prayer could be interpreted, simply, as a call to faithfulness to regular times of prayer at morning, noon and evening. Judging by the parables about the importunate widow (Lk 18:3-8), and the friend who comes at midnight (Lk 11:5-8), the words of Jesus could also have referred to perseverance in petitionary and intercessory prayer. While Jesus taught that we should ask God to satisfy our immediate needs, we should also persist in asking the Lord to enable us to be ready for the second coming. This leads us to our next point.

Watchfulness in prayer

There are three ways of looking at Jesus' call to watchfulness in prayer. Firstly, the true disciple is always waiting for the end time. We know that Jesus seemed to think that it would come sooner rather than later. This is the subject matter of a number of parables. For example, in Mt 24:42 Jesus says: 'Keep watch, because you do not know on what day your Lord will come.' Secondly, one needs to be watchful because grace-filled moments, which are intimations of the second coming, can surprise us at any time. This kind of watchfulness consists of being aware of one's deepest desire and of paying attention to the twin bibles of creation and the scriptures in the belief that they can, at any moment, mediate the presence and the will of God to our hearts. Thirdly, there is the watchfulness of those who want to avoid temptation. Jesus spoke about this kind of alertness when he said to the apostles in the garden of Gethsemane: 'Watch and pray so that you will not fall into temptation. The spirit is willing, but the body is weak' (Mt 26:41). Following the resurrection, St Peter, one of the three apostles who witnessed the agony in the garden, could say on the basis of personal experience: 'Be self-controlled and alert. Your enemy the devil prowls around like a roaring lion looking for someone to devour. Resist him, standing firm in the faith' (1 Pet 5:8-9).

The Lord's Prayer

In New Testament times it was not uncommon for religious teachers to give their disciples a model prayer. The apostles were so impressed by the prayer life of Jesus that 'one of his disciples said to him, "Lord, teach us to pray, as John taught his disciples" (Lk 11:1).' He responded by giving them what is known as the 'Lord's Prayer,' or the 'Our Father.' There are two versions in the synoptic gospels, one in Mt 6:9-13 and the other in Lk 11:2-4. However, scripture scholars are of the opinion that the Lukan one, which is the shorter of the two, is probably the older and therefore the more authentic version. It reads:

Father, hallowed be thy name.

Thy kingdom come.

Give us each day our daily bread;

and forgive us our sins, for we ourselves forgive every

one who is indebted to us;

and lead us not into temptation.

There are many excellent commentaries[15] on this, the greatest of all prayers, notably the one in the *Catechism of the Catholic Church*.[16] What follows are brief comments on the six main components of the prayer. By way of overall elucidation it would be true to say that the object of the first two petitions is the glory of the Father, while the remaining three present our needs to the Lord.

Abba Father

Christian prayer is God-centred rather than self-centred. Consistent with the spirit of the first commandment, the very opening address of the Lord's Prayer escapes from the normal gravitational pull of self-absorption in order to focus on the Creator. The context is decidedly Trinitarian. It is offered to God the Father, through Jesus Christ in the power of the Holy Spirit. Jesus is our unique and indispensable window on God. His words and actions are like so many panes of glass in the window of his humanity. When viewed with the eyes of faith in the light of the Holy Spirit they reveal who Jesus is as the Son of God. As Jesus stated: 'I am the way, and the *truth*, and the life; no one comes to the Father but by me' (Jn 14:6).

The extent to which we grow in an intimate knowledge of who Jesus is and what he is like, is the extent that we will get to know his Father. As Jesus said: 'Anyone who has seen me has seen the Father' (Jn 14:9) and again: 'All things have been committed to me by my Father. No one knows the Son except the Father, and no one knows the Father except the Son and those to whom the Son chooses to reveal him' (Mt 11:27). St Paul tells us that as a result of receiving the Holy Spirit we not only get to know Jesus as Lord (1 Cor 12:3), through him we get to know God as our dear Father. 'For you did not receive a spirit that makes you a slave again to fear, but you received the Spirit of sonship. And by him we cry, "Abba, Father". The Spirit himself testifies with our spirit that we are God's children' (Rom 8:15-16). Again in Gal 4:6 Paul says: 'Because you are sons, God sent the Spirit of his Son into our hearts, the Spirit who calls out, "Abba, Father".'

Hallowed be thy name

For many years I thought that this petition was primarily calling on believers to praise and worship the holy name of God. Since then I have come to appreciate two important points. Firstly, rather than focusing on what we can do to bring honour to the

Lord's name, this petition primarily calls on God to demonstrate the holiness of the divine name by means of saving and liberating deeds performed among us in order to establish God's definitive reign in the world (cf. Jn 12:28). The background of this interpretation is to be found in Ezech 36:21-23, 'I had concern for my holy name, which the house of Israel profaned among the nations where they had gone … I will show the holiness of my great name, which has been profaned, among the nations, the name you have profaned among them. Then the nations will know that I am the Lord, declares the Sovereign Lord, when I show myself holy through you before their eyes.' It is true in a secondary sense that, when people see the Lord manifesting the divine holiness in the world around them, as a result of the co-operation of Spirit-filled people, they will have cause to respond in the form of heartfelt praise and worship. In the long run this petition has its eye on the manifestation of God on the last day. Understood in this sense, the words 'hallowed be thy name' could be translated as, 'Sanctify your name by bringing in your kingdom.'[17]

Thy kingdom come

When Jesus spoke about the kingdom of God and the kingdom of heaven he did so in an imaginative way. He never defined what he meant by the term. Scripture scholars maintain that he was referring to the reign of God. Writing to gentiles who were unfamiliar with Jewish religious thinking, St Paul said: 'the kingdom of God is not a matter of eating and drinking, but of righteousness, peace and joy in the Holy Spirit' (Rom 14:17). Centuries later St Gregory Nanzianzus (329-389) said, 'according to some, Thy kingdom come means, May Your Holy Spirit come upon us to purify us.' Perhaps St Luke indirectly endorsed this latter interpretation when he said: 'Which of you fathers, if your son asks for a fish, will give him a snake instead? Or if he asks for an egg, will give him a scorpion? If you then, though you are evil, know how to give good gifts to your children, how much more will your Father in heaven give the Holy Spirit to those who ask him!' (Luke 11:11-13). The implication seems to be clear. Whereas many of the things one might ask of God might not be in accord with the divine will, to ask for the outpouring of the Spirit will always help to establish the reign of God.

The petition 'thy kingdom come' can be understood in two interrelated senses which involve the 'is' and the 'not yet' of the kingdom. Firstly, God's reign is already being exercised in the here and now through the proclamation that the three great enemies of people, sin, suffering and Satan, are being overcome by the power of God. For example, on one occasion Jesus said: 'If I drive out demons by the Spirit of God, then the kingdom of God *has come* upon you' (Mt 12:28). People can participate in this kingdom of grace if they turn away from sin, believe in the gospel of God's unconditional and unrestricted mercy, and faithfully do the will of God. As Jesus warned: 'I tell you that unless your righteousness surpasses that of the Pharisees and the teachers of the law, you will certainly not enter the kingdom of heaven' (Mt 5:20).

Secondly, while God's kingdom has already come in principle, it will only be fully established in reality at the end of salvation history. As the *Catechism of the Catholic Church* points out: 'In the Lord's Prayer, 'thy kingdom come' refers primarily to the final coming of the reign of God through Christ's return.[18] So the early Christian's cry of *Maranatha*, i.e. 'come Lord Jesus' (1 Cor 16:22) was another way of saying 'thy kingdom come.' It is not really surprising, therefore, to find these words in the last chapter of the bible: 'The Spirit and the bride say, "Come!" And let him who hears say, "Come!" … He who testifies to these things says, "Yes, I am coming soon." (Rev 22:17-20). It seems to me that implicit in this petition is a prayer to see effective worldwide evangelisation. Presumably, the Lord's return will only occur when the great commission to preach the Good News to the whole of creation has been fulfilled in a way that prompts universal revival and renewal. It would seem, therefore, that when we pray 'thy kingdom come', we have both senses in mind.

Give us each day our daily bread

This petition expresses trustful dependence on the providential care of God who gives to all the living 'their food in due season' (Ps 104:27). There are a number of interrelated ways of understanding the words 'give us this day our daily bread.' At the most basic level it seems to refer to the food that sustains human life. Secondly, by extension, bread can be understood as a reference, in a more general way, to all our material needs. As Jesus said: 'So do not worry, saying, "What shall we eat?" or "What shall we drink?" or "What shall we wear?" For the pagans run after all these things, and your heavenly Father knows that you need them' (Mt 6:31-33). Thirdly, the phrase 'daily bread' refers to the word of God. When he was tempted to turn stones to bread, Jesus said to Satan: 'It is written, man shall not live by bread alone, but by every word that proceeds from the mouth of God' (Mt 4:2). Fourthly, the petition refers to the Eucharist which is food for our souls. Jesus spoke about this form of spiritual nourishment in Jn 6:32-35: 'I tell you the truth, it is not Moses who has given you the bread from heaven, but it is my Father who gives you the true bread from heaven. For the bread of God is he who comes down from heaven and gives life to the world.' 'Sir,' they said, 'from now on give us this bread.' Then Jesus declared, 'I am the bread of life. He who comes to me will never go hungry, and he who believes in me will never be thirsty.' Fifthly, the reference to bread may point forward from the Eucharist to the great banquet of heaven which will be celebrated when Christ comes again. So the petition 'Give us this day our daily bread' could be translated to read 'Give us today a foretaste of the heavenly banquet to come.'

Forgive us our sins for we ourselves forgive every one who is indebted to us

The inextricable link between God's willingness to forgive our sins, no matter how many or how bad, depends upon our willingness to forgive those who have offended us. This notion had its roots in Sir 28:2-5: 'Forgive your neighbour the wrong he has done, and then your sins will be pardoned when you pray. Does a man harbour anger against another, and yet seek for healing from the Lord? Does he have no mercy toward a man like himself, and yet pray for his own sins? If he himself, being flesh, maintains wrath, who will make expiation for his sins?' A similar point is mentioned many times by Jesus and later by the New Testament church. In Mt 6:14-15 Jesus says: 'If you forgive men when they sin against you, your heavenly Father will also forgive you. But if you do not forgive men their sins, your Father will not forgive your sins.' The same sentiment is reiterated in

Luke 6:36-38: 'Be merciful, just as your Father is merciful. Do not judge, and you will not be judged. Do not condemn, and you will not be condemned. Forgive, and you will be forgiven ... For with the measure you use, it will be measured to you.' On another occasion 'Peter came to Jesus and asked, "Lord, how many times shall I forgive my brother when he sins against me? Up to seven times?" Jesus answered, "I tell you, not seven times, but seventy-seven times"' (Mt 18:22), i.e. without number. Then he went on to tell the parable of the unforgiving servant. It ends with the words: 'Shouldn't you have had mercy on your fellow servant just as I had on you?' In anger his master turned him over to the jailers to be tortured, until he should pay back all he owed. 'This is how my heavenly Father will treat each of you unless you forgive your brother from your heart' (Mt 18:21-35). James 2:13 echoes the teaching of Jesus when he says: 'Judgement without mercy will be shown to anyone who has not been merciful. Mercy triumphs over judgement!' For more on forgiveness, see chapter six below on petitionary prayer.[19]

And lead us not into temptation

The wording of this petition is misleading because it implies that perhaps the Lord leads us into occasions of sin. It is obvious that such a view is quite absurd. As James 1:13 states: 'When tempted, no one should say, "God is tempting me". For God cannot be tempted by evil, *nor does he tempt anyone.*' This final petition could be better translated as, 'when we meet with the inevitable temptations of the evil one, do not allow us to succumb to them.' We know that having been filled with the Spirit, Jesus was led into the wilderness where he experienced three archetypal temptations. The first was the will to power represented by the kingdoms of this world. Secondly, there was the will to pleasure represented by the stones turned to bread. Finally, there was the will to charismatic irresponsibility represented by the miracle that would be performed if he threw himself from the pinnacle of the temple (cf. Mt 4:3-10). Having resisted all three temptations by wielding the inspired word of God which is the sword of the spirit (Eph 6:17), we are told that the devil left him 'until an opportune time' (Lk 4:13). He was to return on many future occasions, especially during Holy Week. Speaking of Jesus, the scriptures tell us that because 'he himself has suffered and been tempted, he is able to help those who are tempted' (Heb 2:18).

Temptation comes to all of us. St Paul assures us that: 'No temptation has seized you except what is common to man. And God is faithful; he will not let you be tempted beyond what you can bear. But when you are tempted, he will also provide a way out so that you can stand up under it' (1 Cor 10:13). I believe that this promise is true if and when a number of conditions are met. Firstly, one needs to acknowledge the existence and activity of the devil who is perverted and perverting. In the Aramaic of the Lord's Prayer in Matthew, Jesus says, 'deliver us from the evil One', i.e. Satan. As St Paul was later to comment: 'For our struggle is not against flesh and blood, but against the rulers, against the authorities, against the powers of this dark world and against the spiritual forces of evil in the heavenly realms' (Eph 6:12). As Christians we need to learn, not only to discern 'the tail of the serpent' in a realistic, non-mythological way, but how to resist him firm in faith.[20] Secondly, the person needs to have the kind of poverty of spirit and humility which are the fruit of a self-awareness that may have been the result of a disillusioning fall. Otherwise, s/he may suffer from spiritual pride. Although, the person may have the desire to resist temptation, s/he will not have the power to do so. St Peter was an example of this kind of well-intentioned presumption and spiritual immaturity. Although he promised to die with Jesus if necessary, in the event Satan sifted him like wheat. Instead of being faithful to Christ he denied him three times. Only those who truly acknowledge their desperate need of God's power can resist in the day of temptation. As St Paul discovered, God's grace is sufficient, the Lord's power is made perfect in weakness (cf. 2 Cor 12:9).

Conclusion

The heart is *the* organ of prayer in the bible. It is a good symbol. From a biological point of view it plays a vital role in the body. It is relatively small, about the size of a clenched fist. It is mostly hollow and weighs about 9 ounces. As such, it represents poverty of spirit. While the heart doesn't give life, it maintains it by circulating blood to the body and to itself. In doing so it represents absolute dependence on God. The heart is prodigious in its activity. It beats approximately seventy two times a minute as it circulates the blood through about 60,000 miles of arteries, veins and capillaries. As a result it is a metaphor for unceasing spiritual receptivity and generosity. In the Hebrew of the Old Testament and the Greek of the New, the words *leb* and *kardia* had much the same meaning. They referred to the inner person, that part of us that is open to God and capable of feeling, thought and choice. The gospels make it clear that Jesus prayed from the heart, in poverty of spirit and absolute dependence, while receiving and giving the Love of God. Not surprisingly he encouraged others to do the same.

Jesus lives in our hearts through faith (cf. Eph 3:17). St Thomas Aquinas observes: 'Every love makes the beloved to be in the lover and *visa versa.*' A little later he says, 'The beloved is contained in the lover, by being impressed on his heart and thus becoming the object of his satisfaction. On the other hand, the lover is contained in the beloved inasmuch as the lover spiritually penetrates, so to speak, into the beloved.'[21] This profound but rather abstract statement is expressed in more accessible terms by Tadhg Gaelach Ó Súilleabháin's Irish poem, *To the Heart of Jesus*. The English translation reads:

The light in my heart, O Saviour, is thy heart,
the wealth of my heart, thy heart poured out for me.
Seeing that thy heart, Love, filled with love for me
leave thy heart in keeping, hooded in mine.[22]

English poet Sir Philip Sidney expressed similar sentiments in his christological poem *True Love:*

My true love hath my heart and I have his,
By just exchange one for another given;
I hold his dear, and mine he cannot miss'
There never was a better bargain driven.
My true love hath my heart and I have his.

His heart in me keeps him and me in one,
My heart in him his thoughts and senses guides;
He loves my heart, for once it was his own,
I cherish his, because in me it bides.
My true love hath my heart and I have his.[23]

The sentiments of both poems find succinct expression in par 521 of the *Catechism of the Catholic Church*: 'Christ enables us to live in him all that he himself lived, and *he lives it in us.*' While this principle would apply to all the mysteries of Christ's life, in the context of this book it applies in a particularly relevant way to the prayer of Jesus.[24] Through the outpouring of God's Spirit in the sacraments of initiation and afterwards, we have the God given capacity, not just to imitate the prayer of Jesus, but in a very real sense to participate in it. The following chapters intend to describe some of the ways in which we can engage in this Christian conspiracy of prayer, i.e. praying through Christ, with Christ and in Christ by the breath of the Holy Spirit.

CHAPTER THREE

Prayer as self-disclosure to God

There are two main forms of prayer, one formal and vocal, the other informal and mental. In its vocal form a person reads or recites prayers, either silently or out loud. There are many of them, such as morning and night prayers, grace before and after meals, the angelus, rosary and Divine Office. This form of prayer is particularly suitable for use by groups such as a family or a community that wants to pray together on a regular basis. However it is important that mind, heart and lips work in harmony with one another. This requires three forms of attentiveness: to saying the right words, to their meaning, and to the God they address. Speaking about the rosary, which is the gospel in miniature, Pope Paul VI said that without an element of contemplative attention, 'the Rosary is a body without a soul, and its recitation is in danger of becoming a mechanical repetition of formulas that fails to take heed of the warning of Christ in Mt 6:7.'[1] Otherwise the Lord would have reason to say: 'These people come near to me with their mouth and honour me with their lips, but their hearts are far from me' (Is 29:13).

Even contemplatives, who normally engage in mental prayer, will often resort to vocal prayer. We noted in the second chapter how this was the way in Christ's life. Besides spending time in private mental prayer, he said well-known Jewish prayers at set times every day. Like Jesus, many well-known religious figures have testified how they said vocal prayers. Teresa of Avila observed: 'I must tell you that while you are repeating the Our Father or some vocal prayer, it is quite possible for the Lord to grant you perfect contemplation.'[2] Centuries later her fellow Carmelite, Thérèse of Lisieux, said in her autobiography: 'Sometimes when I am in such a state of spiritual dryness that not a single good thought occurs to me, I say very slowly the

Our Father or the Hail Mary, and these prayers suffice to take me out of myself, and wonderfully refresh me.'[3] It was reported that Jewish mystic, Simone Weil, sometimes experienced spiritual ecstasy as she slowly and devoutly recited the Lord's Prayer.

But even when prayers are recited in a sincere and thoughtful way, they can prove unsatisfactory in so far as they are not personal enough, and sometimes fail to express the nuances of what one thinks, feels and desires. As a result, vocal prayer needs to be augmented by mental prayer. It is a more informal, spontaneous type of personal prayer. However, the traditional reference to 'mental prayer' is unsatisfactory in so far as it implies that prayer is mainly an intellectual activity, whereas in reality it engages the whole personality, mind, emotions and will. This chapter and the following one will explore the nature of this kind of praying, the motives we have for engaging in it, and the practical means of doing so.

A classic definition of prayer
There are many well-known definitions of prayer. For example, the *Catechism of the Catholic Church* quotes the familiar saying of St John Damascene: 'Prayer is a matter of raising one's mind and heart to God, or the requesting of good things from God.'[4] I have long thought that it is an unsatisfactory description in so far as it emphasises what we do while neglecting to mention what it is that the Lord does. In the instruction, *Some Aspects of Christian Meditation*, there is a more satisfactory description in par. 3: 'Prayer is defined, properly speaking, as a personal, intimate and profound dialogue between man and God.' Like this definition, the best descriptions of prayer see it in relational terms as a conversation, discussion, dialogue, conference or colloquy. In prayer we do indeed raise our minds and hearts to God, but it is important to note that the Lord responds by revealing the divine mind and heart to us. In her autobiography, St Teresa of Avila offered a classic definition of prayer when she described it as 'nothing other than an intimate friendship, a frequent heart to heart conversation, with him by whom we know ourselves to be loved.'[5]

Over the years I have come to appreciate that three interrelated intimacies are involved in this form of prayer. Firstly, there is intimacy with one's deepest self. Secondly, there is intimacy with others, especially close friends. Thirdly, there is intimacy with God. Incidentally I'm using the word intimacy in its dictionary sense, meaning 'to publish, to make known that which is innermost'. Self-disclosure is involved in all the inter-linking forms of intimacy. By means of self-awareness I allow my deepest desires and feelings to be disclosed to me at a conscious level of awareness. By means of interpersonal intimacy I disclose my inner self to my trusted friends. By means of prayer I disclose my deepest experiences to God who is my second and true self, my dearest friend. In this chapter we will reflect on each of these overlapping forms of self-disclosure.

Self-awareness

There is something paradoxical about self-awareness. While it is indispensable in interpersonal friendship, and friendship with God, it is at the same time dependent upon both. Self-awareness is the point of intersection where these other enriching intimacies meet. It is not common. As Paul VI once observed, men and women today are completely extroverted, they are bewitched by the external world which is so charming, fascinating and corrupting with its delusions of false happiness.[6] On another occasion he said in similar vein that nowadays our psychology is turned outward too much. The everyday life is so absorbing that our attention is mainly directed outside, we are nearly always absent from our inner selves. We are unable to meditate or to pray. We cannot silence the hubbub inside, due to outside interests, images and passions.[7] In order to pray effectively, we need to get in touch with our deeper desires and feelings. To do this we need to have appointments with ourselves, quiet times for personal reflection. 'Each of us needs to plan to have moments of silence – exterior silence indeed, but particularly interior silence. It is a silence that can nurture and reanimate the dialogue with ourselves, that is, with our personal consciousness.'[8]

Self-awareness is a way of going beyond the narrow and arbitrary confines of the conscious ego and its roles, to get in touch with the hidden self which is pre-conscious, and the unknown-self which is unconscious. The most important way of doing this is to get in touch with one's desires and feelings. A desire is conscious awareness of an unconscious need. There are many of them, physical desires, such as a yearning for human touch; psychological desires, such as a longing for security; and spiritual desires, such as a thirst for meaning and a sense of ultimate belonging. A person can have an emotion such as anger or grief and not be aware of it. But a feeling is an emotion that has articulated itself in a conscious way. Feelings are the fingerprints of subjectivity, similar to those of other people and nevertheless unique. They put us in touch with two realities, the world of external things and our own inner world conditioned as it is by personal memories, values, beliefs and attitudes. Feelings are revelatory because they tell us what we actually perceive, believe, think and value, as opposed to what we perceive, believe, think and value at a notional level of conscious awareness. In that sense, feelings never lie. If there is anything unrealistic about our feelings it is because of the way we look at the world and ourselves. To grow in emotional self-awareness we need to acknowledge and understand our deepest desires and feelings.

Acknowledging spiritual desires
Self-awareness enables one to get in touch with what spiritual writers have called spiritual, holy, or transcendental desires that yearn for ultimate meaning. These desires, as distinct from merely physical or psychological ones, are prompted by God in our souls, in that part of us which can only be satisfied by conscious relationship with the divine. As a result it could be said that our spiritual lives are energised by holy desires. No wonder St Ignatius of Loyola said that all prayer should begin with the question, what do you want? To be out of touch with one's God-prompted desire for God is to be absent from the first and foundational way in which we experience the action of the Holy Spirit within. As Jesus once stated: 'No one can come to me unless the Father who sent me draws that person' (Jn 6:44). The Lord draws us by means of longings and desires.

The Lord prompts spiritual desires in a number of ways. Firstly, God can allow a person to suffer, e.g. as a result of predictable and un-predictable crises in life.[9] Afflictions of this kind, such as the mid-life crisis or a life-threatening illness, can attack one's ego defenses, thereby releasing the suppressed voice of the deeper self which can only be satisfied by religious experience. Secondly, the Lord can allow one to endure humiliating moral failure such as marital infidelity or alcoholism. The consequent sense of disillusionment can uncover a need for God and God's liberating power. Thirdly, desires for transcendence can be evoked by the witness of an admired person like Mother Teresa or Jean Vanier, who already enjoys a deep sense of union with the Lord.

Spiritual desires can be blocked in a number of predictable ways. Some people are inhibited by a moralistic attitude. Because they are usually motivated by an oppressive sense of duty – by what they 'ought, must, should or have to do' – they lose touch with their deeper spiritual yearnings. Unresolved feelings of a negative kind, such as grief, hurt, shame, resentment, etc., can also inhibit awareness of one's deepest desires. Finally, a self-centred preoccupation with physical or psychological satisfaction and fulfilment, by means of such things as wealth, status, power or pleasure, can deafen a person to the deeper aspirations of the Spirit within (cf. Mt 13:22-23).

Acknowledging feelings

As we have seen, a person can have an emotion such as anger or grief, and not be consciously aware of it. This is usually the case when it is buried alive in the unconscious because it was thought to be too painful or inappropriate. To recover repressed feelings a number of things are necessary. Firstly, we need to stop all activity in order to have an appointment – free from distractions – with our inner selves. Secondly, we need to relax our bodies as much as possible. There are many recognised ways of doing this. It is only as we relax physically that our feelings begin to emerge, from shadowy anonymity, to consciously declare themselves. Thirdly, we need to pay attention to our bodily sensations. The reason for this is the fact that all our emotions express themselves physically. For example, a headache, or an upset stomach could be due to repressed anger or resentment. We can dialogue with our bodies, letting images float freely into our minds. Often the unconscious mind will suggest some symbolic representation of a repressed feeling. As we savour the image, e.g. remembrance of a violent scene on TV the previous evening, we may begin to get in touch with its associated feeling such as fear or anger. Fourthly, we can recall and reflect on our dreams. So often these letters from the unconscious remain unopened and unread. In fact they are psycho-dramas which are representations of our deepest desires and feelings. Usually the main feeling in the dream is one that was evoked during the previous day or two, but went unnoticed. Frequently feelings like these will also be related to emotionally charged memories from one's earlier life. We cannot go into the subject of dream interpretation here. Suffice it to say that usually everyone and everything in a dream is a personification of some aspect of one's own personality.

Understanding desires and feelings

We come to understand our spiritual desires by means of an examen of consciousness, which enables one to discern their origin and orientation. The crucial question is this: did they come from God, from myself, or even from the evil one? Inspirations that come from God and tend towards God will normally be associated with on-going consolation, that is, positive feelings such as peace, joy, hope, etc. Sooner or later, those that are not from God will be associated with desolation, that is, negative feelings such as agitation, sadness, morbidity, and aridity. St Ignatius wrote: 'Desolation is the contrary to consolation. Contrary to peace there is conflict; contrary to joy, sadness; contrary to hope in higher things, hope in base things; contrary to heavenly love, earthly love; contrary to tears, dryness; contrary to elevation of mind, wandering of mind to contemptible things.'[10]

Noted psychologist Albert Ellis has indicated how we can understand our feelings. He says that they are not directly evoked by people and events, but rather by the way we *perceive* them. Our perceptions are coloured by a unique cocktail of our values, beliefs and past experiences. For example, a man hates being licked by a cat. He feels disgust, aversion and fear. He himself had no animals at home as a child. As a result he has grown up with the questionable belief that cats are dirty and liable to attack for no good reason. So when we want to understand a feeling we can ask ourselves three important questions:

What perception or belief evoked my feeling? What in my earlier life conditioned the way I perceive and believe? Is my way of perceiving and believing realistic?

Friendship love

From the 1960s onward the developmental psychology of Erik Erikson has exercised increasing influence. It maintains that the life of men and women involves a succession of stages, each one of which is characterised by a specific developmental task. For example, while one attains a sense of identity in adolescence, the basic challenge of early adulthood is to develop a capacity for committed intimacy with other persons. It involves an ability to go beyond one's public persona, which is made up of roles and masks, in order to increasingly reveal one's true self to a trusted confidant or friend. This will only be possible to the extent that we are in touch with our own inner lives. Erikson maintains that while our sense of identity is actualised and consolidated through self-disclosure, when it is avoided we feel lonely, dispirited and unfulfilled.

Robert J. Sternberg has suggested that there are three main components involved in adult relationships, intimacy, romantic passion and commitment.[11] He says that the intimacy in loving relationships refers to close, connected and bonded feelings. Passion refers to the drives that lead to romance, physical attraction and sexual consummation. Loving commitment consists of a decision that one loves someone and is committed to maintaining that love. Sternberg maintains there are two main forms of adult intimacy, consummate and companionate. Consummate love is experienced by couples who are romantically attracted to one another and who share deeply within the context of a committed erotic relationship, ideally marriage. Companionate love is experienced by people who love one another in a non-romantic way, but who communicate deeply within the context of a committed friendship.

Despite its importance, researchers have indicated that only a minority of men enjoy such consummate or companionate love. In his well-known *Seasons of a Man's Life*, Daniel Levinson wrote: 'As a tentative generalisation we would say that close friendship with a man or woman is rarely experienced by

American men ... The distinction between friend and acquaintance is often blurred.' Writing in *Male Intimacy*, Michael Gill said that research had confirmed Levinson's impression: 'To say that men have no intimate relationships seems on the surface too harsh, and it raises quick objections from most men. But the data indicate that it is not far from the truth. Even the most intimate of male friendships rarely approach the depth of disclosure a woman commonly has with other women. We know that very few men reveal anything of their private and personal selves even to their spouses; fewer still make these intimate disclosures to other men. One man in ten has a friend with whom he discusses work, money, marriage; only one in more than twenty has a friendship where he discloses his feelings about himself or his sexual feelings.'[12]

This lack of interpersonal intimacy in the lives of men has many causes. Chodorow and Stoller have suggested that in early childhood boys develop their sense of male identity by suppressing their empathy for their female mothers. On the other hand girls develop their sense of female identity by doing the opposite. As a result, in adult life males find it harder either to tune in to their feelings, or to express them to other people, especially to other men. A sense of emotional closeness, i.e. feelings of affinity, affection, warmth, etc., is often substituted for intimacy, i.e. honest disclosure of feelings and experiences. Men are also competitive and hampered in relationships by macho stereotypes that imply that all sense of vulnerability has to be hidden.

Research indicates that a greater percentage of women form intimate friendships. For example, Lillian Rubin studied friendships in the lives of single men and women. 'The results of the research are unequivocal,' she says, 'women have more friendships than men, and the difference in the content and quality of their friendships is marked and unmistakable ... Women's friendships with each other rest on shared intimacies, self-revelation, nurturance, and emotional support.'[13] She goes on to say that three fourths of the single women surveyed had no problem in identifying a best friend.

Same-sex and heterosexual friendships have many good effects. We will look at one of them, in particular, because it is the result of honest self-disclosure. In adult life most of us are aware of inner hurts. We lack integration. As a result, we are debilitated by neurotic fears and compulsions. Psychologists argue that many of our adult problems can be traced back to childhood experiences. Some of these experts maintain that healing can only come through psychotherapy or psychoanalysis. However, both are expensive and time-consuming. Other experts, e.g. Erikson and Rogers, believe that emotional and spiritual healing, of a retrospective kind, can be the result of intimate relationships. When we are aware of the love of friends, we begin to have the freedom to take off our masks. We sense a growing urge to give our friend the greatest gift we have, the gift of our true selves. As this desire strengthens, it begins to override our fear of rejection which echoes back to childhood. We begin to lower our defences and to courageously tell our friend about the more vulnerable side of our nature. As we sense the understanding, acceptance and love of our friend a wonderful healing begins to take place. In the light of this friendship love we begin to understand, accept, and love ourselves as we are, and not as we have pretended to be. It is worth noting, in this context, that in many ways the effectiveness of the twelve steps of Alcoholics Anonymous revolves around step five which states, 'We admitted to God, to ourselves, *and to another human being* the exact nature of our wrongs.' The extent to which we experience the empathic understanding of friends or confidants is the extent to which, by God's grace, we experience healing. Alienation gives way to harmony, disturbance to peace.

Prayer as friendship with God

Self-awareness enables us to get in touch with our own experience. Friendship schools us in the arts of self-disclosure. Not only are these two forms of intimacy a prerequisite for prayerful intimacy with God, they find their fulfilment in this way. Indeed, one could say that we are no closer to God than we are to our true self and our closest neighbours. As St Aelred of Rievaulx wrote: 'God is friendship ... I would not hesitate to attribute to friendship anything associated with charity, as for instance, he who abides in friendship abides in God and God abides in him.'[14] As we relate to others, so we will pray. If our human relationships are formal, it is almost inevitable that our prayerful relationship with God will be much the same. But if some of our human relationships are intimate our prayerful relationship with God will tend to be more personal.

A foundational experience of love
St Teresa says that prayerful self-disclosure is made possible by the fact that 'we know ourselves to be loved' by God. This awareness is an essential prerequisite for prayerful friendship with God. Trust is a key characteristic of any intimate relationship. Our trust in God is evoked by a heartfelt experience of divine love. It is usually the result of a religious awakening, a graced moment, or moments, when we become consciously aware of the love of God and thereby appropriate the graces first received in the sacraments of initiation. This is the indispensable foundation stone upon which the edifice of prayer has to be built. To do otherwise would be to build on sand. The sad fact is that although they have been sacramentalised, many people have not been effectively evangelised. As a result they haven't the power to grasp the true nature of the unrestricted and uncond-itional love of God. While they might have a notional appreciation of God and God's loving mercy, these life-giving truths often fail to fall from head to heart. Not surprisingly, therefore, God may seem remote, impersonal, demanding and forbidding. In other words, the Lord would not be the kind of deity that such people would want to trust or to confide in.

The in-filling of the Spirit, which is sometimes referred to as 'baptism in the Spirit', is a religious experience that inaugurates a decisively new awareness of the loving presence and activity of God in one's life. As a result, the person has an experiential understanding of the unconditional acceptance and love of God. There is a Jewish hymn which was associated with the feast of Pentecost for hundreds of years. It was written in Aramaic by a rabbi named Meir who was martyred, together with his wife and son, during the first Crusade in 1096. It describes the love of God in the following eloquent words: 'Could we with ink the ocean fill, were every blade of grass a quill, were the whole world of parchment made, and every man a scribe by trade, to write the love of God above, would drain the ocean dry; nor would the scroll contain the whole, though stretched from sky to sky.'[15] It is this awareness that needs to inform the heart-to-heart conversation between the praying person and the Lord. As Bill Barry has rightly observed: 'If I do not know in my bones that God loves me with an everlasting love, I will not dare to open myself to his gaze and to ask to see myself as he sees me.'[16]

A few years ago I had a memorable experience of God's grace. I had been telling the Lord for months that I wanted to experience God's love more deeply than ever before. I repeatedly asked God for this gift. But nothing seemed to happen. Then I went on an eight-day directed retreat. When I arrived at the retreat centre I was told that we were beginning with Mass. When the gospel was read, the priest said he wasn't going to give a homily. Rather, he wanted us to engage in a prayer exercise. He asked us to close our eyes and to allow a scene from the passion of Christ to spontaneously come to mind. When I closed mine, I immediately imagined Simon of Cyrene reluctantly helping Jesus to carry his cross to Calvary. A few moments later I imagined myself taking his place. Then the priest said, 'Have you got an image from the passion in your mind? I want you to imagine that Jesus looks at you and says, "I'm glad that you are with me, accompanying me in my sufferings".' In my heart I heard Jesus say those words to me. I was strangely moved and my eyes became moist. I must admit that I weep easily at funerals, watching TV or listening to great music, but never when I pray. So I was surprised that I was on the verge of tears on this occasion. I thought to myself, what did the priest say? 'Imagine that Jesus looks at you and says, "Pat I'm glad that you are with me, accompanying me in my sufferings".'

At that moment copious tears poured from my eyes. Without thinking, I was vividly aware of a number of things. The truth was, although I sometimes felt as a teenager that I was being called to be a priest, I wasn't enthusiastic about the idea. I didn't find the prospect of being poor, celibate and obedient very attractive. But when I was 18 I had a religious experience overlooking Kinsale harbour in county Cork. I felt that just as Simon had been press-ganged by the soldiers when he was on his way to do his worldly thing in Jerusalem, so God was hijacking me when I had intended studying medicine in the Royal College of Surgeons in Dublin. As a result, I joined the seminary three days later.

I must admit that sometimes I half hoped that I would get sick or would be asked to leave. In the event most of the other students left, but after eight years I was ordained. Although I had tried to give my best to the priesthood, I often felt guilty because I had a divided heart. Part of me wanted to serve God, while the other part still wanted to do my own worldly thing. I often recalled the words of Jesus in Rev 3:15: 'I know your deeds, that you are neither cold nor hot. I wish you were either one or the other! So, because you are lukewarm – neither hot nor cold – I am about to spit you out of my mouth.' So I wondered how could the Lord love me, or act powerfully through me? But when Jesus looked at me and said, 'I'm glad that you are accompanying me in my passion', I knew that he knew all about my divided heart, and that, despite this knowledge, he loved and accepted me the way I was. I felt that he was overlooking all my faults and honouring my good intentions while saying 'Well done good and faithful servant, my favour rests upon you.' This knowledge of the Divine Mercy so filled me with joy that the tears poured down my cheeks on to the light grey shirt I was wearing. In the words of 1 Jn 4:16, I knew and believed in the love that God had for me in Christ. In the depths of my heart I received the grace to accept that I was accepted by God and that God lived in me. In fact, every time I recalled the Lord's words over the next eight days, tears of joy flowed again. I knew from first hand experience what St Peter meant when he said: 'Though you do not see him you believe in him and rejoice with unutterable and exalted joy' (1 Pt 1:8).

Self-disclosure to God

What makes friendship different from other relationships is the degree of self-disclosure involved. In his classic book, *Christian Friendship,* St Aelred of Rievaulx wrote, 'A friend shares all the innermost secrets of your heart … to him you confide everything as if he were your other self.' When Jesus referred to the apostles as his friends, he went on to add that they would know he was their true friend because he had made known to them all that he had heard from his Father (cf. Jn 15:15). Because we know that Jesus loves and accepts us as we are, we disclose all our innermost secrets to him. Why share such things with the

Lord? Doesn't he know them all anyway? Yes. But the Lord wants us to reveal our real selves, not because God needs it, but because God knows that we do. There are a number of reasons for this. Firstly, when you love someone, you experience joy in being generous to him or to her. But the greatest gift one can give to a friend or, for that matter, to the Lord, is the gift of one's true self. Secondly, a person never feels truly loved and accepted by a friend, or by the Lord, unless s/he knows that s/he is loved as s/he is and not as s/he pretends to be. Thirdly, this kind of honesty opens up the heart and prepares it to receive either the self-revelation of a friend or of the Lord. Experience teaches that the extent to which we control our dialogue with the Lord, by failing to reveal all of our true feelings and desires, is the extent to which we will be unreceptive to God's self-revelation and in-spirations.

It is relatively easy to come to God in the Sunday best of our good, positive feelings such as gratitude, love, appreciation, sweetness, etc. The trouble arises when we have to come to the Lord in the ragged and unimpressive clothes of our negative feelings. These would include our feelings about ourselves, such as shame; about others, such as envy or jealousy; and about events we have experienced or heard about, such as sadness, horror, etc. Over the years I have come to see that it is particularly important to acknowledge, understand and express negative feelings about God such as anger and fear. They are often associ-ated with negative images of God. Just as it is hard to cope with such negative feelings in human relationships, so it is just as hard to cope with them in our relationship with the Lord.

Disclosing anger
Deep down we all have a sense of justice. At an unconscious level it gives rise to what has been referred to as the 'just world hypothesis'. It assumes that the world is governed by the provi-dence of God and that we get what our behaviour deserves. In other words if we try to live good, honest, decent lives, we are entitled to good luck and good fortune, and *vice versa*. As Job discovered, however, things don't always work out the way we would expect. The fact is that bad things happen to good people. When they do, we feel hurt, loss and anger. We are angry with

life but deep down we may be angry with God for not protecting us from misfortune. There are two unhealthy ways of handling this kind of anger which can inhibit our prayerful relationship with God.

Many of us were brought up in homes where anger was not acceptable. It may have been that our parents gave us the impression that anger itself was wrong, or perhaps they were bad tempered and we were afraid to express our own legitimate anger lest it evoke their irrational ire. As a result we learned to suppress it in order to retain the love and acceptance of our parents and carers. Such anger doesn't go away. It gets buried alive in the unconscious where it tends to turn against us in two harmful ways. Firstly, it is transformed into feelings of guilty insecurity. Secondly, it can turn into either mild or severe depression. So when, in spite of our many prayers, a relative dies prematurely because of a painful form of cancer, we can feel hurt and angry with the medical profession and also with God for not having saved the person. But if that anger is neither acknowledged nor expressed it will have the effect of distancing the praying person from God. Although s/he may continue to go through the motions of prayer, his or her heart won't be in it. Their relationship with God will become formal rather than personal.

Some people have no problem in acknowledging their hurt and anger. But instead of expressing it in a constructive way, it causes them to turn their backs on people and on God. I can recall the case of a woman whose husband died following a long fight with motor neurone disease. She was so angry with God that she decided to protest against the Lord's failure to answer her prayers and those of her children. She went on strike. She literally stopped praying or going to church for many years. During that time she had a brief affair with a married man. When I asked her why she had come back to church she said, 'I have mellowed over the years. I have come to terms with my husband's death. I have decided to give the Lord a second chance.'

There is a *via media* between repressive and aggressive anger. When people acknowledge their hurt and anger to themselves they can and should honestly express it to the Lord. Instead of inhibiting relationship it becomes part of it. Usually when a

person expresses such anger, fury or rage in prayer, deeper, repressed feelings of desire surface in the heart. So it is important
not to ignore negative feelings in a dutiful way that is prompted
by scriptural injunctions such as, '*always* and for *everything* give
thanks to the Lord' (1 Thess 5:18). The healthy way of coping is
firstly, to acknowledge and express one's negative feelings, and
secondly, to express one's desire for a renewed relationship with
God in a spirit of honesty and anticipatory thanksgiving. As
Paul says: 'In everything, by prayer and petition, with thanksgiving, present your requests to God' (Phil 4:6).

Disclosing fear
When people have a genuine religious experience their initial
emotional *response* is usually followed by an emotional *reaction*.
The initial emotional response is spontaneous, rooted in the
deeper spiritual self and is positive in nature. For example, as
people become aware of the presence and attributes of God, they
commonly feel a sense of reassurance and joy. The secondary
emotional reaction, which takes the form of a backlash, is rooted
in the controlling ego and more often than not it is negative in
nature. For example, people commonly experience what spiritual
directors refer to as resistance. It is a form of fear that is prompted
by the prospect of deepening relationship with God. It can have
three possible causes.

Firstly, at the conscious level of professed theology, many
people maintain that God is loving and trustworthy. But at the
unconscious level of operative theology they may have many
negative images of God lurking in recesses of their minds. They
are usually formed in childhood and associated with negative
feelings. Over the years these emotions can unconsciously inhibit prayer relationship with God. For example, some people
have the impression that if they get close to God they will suffer
misfortunes and possibly die young like some of the saints.
When they do have a genuine experience of the living God, one
that challenges their false images, resistance sets in. The unconscious seems to react in fear, as if it were saying, 'This is too good
to be true!' and so they revert to their familiar but intimidating
images of God.

I experienced ambivalent feelings of this kind following the awareness of God's love during the retreat mentioned above. Each day I went to see my director for a chat. On the fourth day he encouraged me to meditate on the parable of the king who invited people to his feast (cf. Lk 14:16-24). I'm sure that he hoped that I would see the banquet as a symbol of the many graces the Lord had prepared for me. However, when I reflected on the passage it filled me with anger. I disliked the king intensely. To me he seemed to be demanding, insensitive, self-centred, unreasonable and vindictive. I felt I could have nothing to do with him. As a result, I was filled with turmoil and all my joy disappeared.

When I went to see my director the following day he asked, 'Well, how did your prayer go?' I told him what had happened. After about half an hour he said, 'What is it exactly that you dislike about the king?' Spontaneously I blurted out, 'He is impossible to please!' After a long pause, the director said, 'Have you ever felt that way about anyone in your own life?' Immediately I retorted: 'Yes, my late mother. I felt she was impossible to please. As soon as I'd try to live up to her expectations in one area of my life she would move the goalposts and expect something else. I'm afraid that God is much the same.' Then the director said, 'You seem to have met with two Gods on this retreat. Firstly, there was the accepting God who was revealed to you during the first days of the retreat. The awareness of that God filled you with joy. Then there was the God you met yesterday, the One who is impossible to please. The thought of that God fills you with anger and inner turmoil. Which do you think is the living God of revelation?' Immediately I answered, 'The God of mercy, and consolation.' Since then I have come to see that a revelation of the God of Divine Mercy not only brings false images into the light, it often replaces them. As a result the Good News of God's love makes the innermost self grow increasingly strong in the Spirit (Eph 3:16).

Secondly, resistance to growing relationship with God can be rooted in the fact that religious experience tends to challenge our sense of self in two interrelated ways. If people have suffered from low self-esteem their awareness of God's love may challenge their negative self-image. In the light of God's love they may sense that they have greater worth and dignity than they ever suspected. Furthermore, those who suffer from a lack of self-acceptance often live from their egos and try to control their experience of a threatening world, by means of rational thought and will power. In the light of God's love they may sense that they could live more freely and spontaneously from their deeper spiritual selves. While these two prospects might appear to have attractive and welcome effects, ironically they can evoke a sense of apprehension. Living in a freer, more trusting way from the spiritual self seems too challenging. Better to stick to familiar perceptions, attitudes and feelings than to embrace unfamiliar ones.

Thirdly, resistance to growing relationship with God can be rooted in peoples' fear of the possible ethical and practical implications. Perhaps the Lord would ask them to change their lifestyle in some demanding way. A business man might have to modify some of his financial practices, a nun might be sent on the foreign missions, a married woman might have to forego her current preoccupation with fashion, a young adult might have to question his or her worldview and replace a materialistic perspective with a more spiritual one. As a result they back away from more intimate relationship with God in the belief that if they keep the Lord at arm's length, so to speak, they will avoid the scary prospect of demanding change and sacrifice. After all, the devil you know is better than the devil you don't know!

Conclusion

Religious people are those who experience a triple sense of intimacy that leads to a joyful sense of belonging. Firstly, there is self-intimacy, whereby I am receptive to my neglected self as it discloses itself to consciousness. Secondly, there is interpersonal intimacy, whereby I disclose to a few trusted friends the truth, the whole truth and nothing but the truth about myself. Finally, these two intimacies reach their fulfilment when I disclose my true self to the God who sees and loves in me what the Father sees and loves in Jesus.[17] Prayer is a matter of being honest *to* God. As Luther is reputed to have said, 'Prayer is not telling lies to God.' Whereas individualistic and rationalistic culture tends to undermine a sense of ultimate belonging, prayer as self-disclosure strengthens it. Any holistic understanding of prayer needs to keep these interrelated forms of intimacy in harmony. Although self-disclosure is a necessary pre-condition of prayerful relationship with God, it is not its essence. Prayer, as heart-to-heart conversation, reaches its high point when the Lord reveals the God-Self to those who are attentive and receptive. It is this important subject that we explore in the next chapter.

CHAPTER FOUR

Prayer as self-forgetful
attention to God

Besides being lovers, married couple George and Helen are best friends. They are committed to mutual self-disclosure. Nevertheless, there is something lacking in their intimacy. Despite the fact that they talk a lot about their thoughts, feelings, and desires they don't feel as close to one another as they would like. Eventually they agree to go to see Maureen, a local marriage counsellor. Having asked them many questions about their way of communicating, Maureen helps them to see that, because both of them came from fairly dysfunctional families, they are insecure and emotionally needy. While they speak fairly openly and honestly about their inner lives they are not good at listening to one another in an empathic way. They seek to be understood more than they seek to understand. Consequently, both George and Helen fail to meet one another's needs. They feel strangely alone in spite of the fact that they talk a lot. Maureen suggests practical ways in which they could put their respective thoughts, feelings and memories on hold, in order to listen in a self-forgetful way to one another.

The problem that has been troubling George and Helen's relationship can also undermine one's desire to have an intimate relationship with God. While many of us are quite good at disclosing our innermost selves to the Lord, we are not as good at paying self-forgetful attention to the self-disclosure of the Lord's presence, word and will. In this chapter we will look at some of the ways in which we can attend to the presence and word of God. In the next chapter we will explore ways in which we can seek and discover God's will in a prayerful way.

Desire for a revelation of God
Just as friends desire to get know one another better, so in

prayer, we need to have a single-minded desire to know the Lord. It is important to become consciously aware of such a desire and it needs to be disclosed to God. St Ignatius of Loyola thought that this was a point of fundamental religious importance. He maintained that at the beginning of any retreat and prayer time, the person's first question should be, what grace do I most want? Having identified what that longing might be, it is reassuring to know that the Lord promises to reveal the God-self to those who desire to know it. In Deut 4:29 we read: 'If from there you seek the Lord your God, you will find him if you look for him with all your heart and with all your soul.'Again in Jer 33:3 the Lord promises: 'Call to me and I will answer you and tell you great and unsearchable things you do not know.' In the New Testament the Lord adds: 'This is the covenant I will make with the house of Israel after that time. I will put my laws in their minds and write them on their hearts ... No longer will a man teach his neighbour, or a man his brother, saying, "Know the Lord," because they will all know me, from the least of them to the greatest' (Heb 8:10-11).

The Holy Spirit has a central, if sometimes hidden, role to play in revealing the presence, word and will of the Lord. In Jn 15:26 Jesus assured believers that: 'The Helper will come – the Spirit who reveals the truth about God and who comes from the Father. I will send him to you from the Father, and he will speak about me.' In Jn 14:26 Jesus promised: 'The Helper, the Holy Spirit, whom the Father will send in my name, will teach you everything and make you remember all that I have told you.' St Paul makes it clear that by means of the Spirit-given gifts of wisdom and knowledge, we can come into an experiential knowledge of God in and through Jesus Christ. In Rom 11:34, Paul asks: 'Who has known the mind of the Lord or who has been his counsellor?' Many Christians quote this verse to support the contention that God is unknowable. This is not a sustainable thesis. In one of the most profound passages in the New Testament, Paul says: 'As it is written: "No eye has seen, no ear has heard, no mind has conceived what God has prepared for those who love him" – *but God has revealed it to us by his Spirit*. The Spirit searches all things, even the deep things of God ... we have not received the spirit of the world but the Spirit who is from God,

... For who has known the mind of the Lord that he may instruct him? *But we have the mind of Christ'* (1 Cor 2:9-16).

Mediated immediacy

When we are with our human friends we can see, hear, and touch them. But our relationship with God is different. The Lord is pure Spirit and cannot be directly perceived by the human senses. So how can the Lord reveal the God-self to us? Clearly, a principle of mediation is needed. We can only encounter God indirectly through created things. St Thomas Aquinas, the greatest theologian of the medieval era, stated in his *Summa Theologica*: 'Our natural knowledge begins from sense. Hence our natural knowledge can go as far as it can be led by sensible things. But our mind cannot be led by sense so far as to see the essence of God; because the sensible effects of God do not equal the power of God as their cause. Hence from the knowledge of sensible things the whole power of God cannot be known; nor therefore can his essence be seen.'[1] Later on he added: 'The nature of man requires that he be led to the invisible by visible things. Therefore, the invisible things of God must be made manifest to man by the things that are visible.'[2]

The natural world can mediate a sense of God's presence. As St Paul observes in Rom 1:20: 'Since the creation of the world God's invisible qualities – his eternal power and divine nature – have been clearly seen, being understood from what has been made.' Speaking of the ability of people to mediate God's presence, Karl Rahner, possibly the greatest Catholic theologian of the twentieth century, wrote: 'The human person's first personal partner ... cannot be God, because a mediation is always needed ... the human person ... can be the mediator.'[3] God's presence and attributes are more clearly mediated by the sacraments and sacred scripture that by any other created reality. This is particularly true in so far as they put the praying believer in touch with Christ. St Thomas wrote: 'Such is the weakness of the human mind that it needs a guide ... to divine things by means of certain sensible objects known to us. Chief among these is the humanity of Christ ... Accordingly, things relating to the humanity of Christ are the chief incentive to devotion.'[4] Although she was a great mystic, St Teresa of Avila had a strong appreciation of this point. She was, rightly, wary of any method of prayer, such as using mantras, that tried to side-step the humanity of Christ. She wrote: 'I clearly see … that God desires that the graces of prayer must come to us from the hands of Christ, through his most sacred humanity, in which God takes delight. Many, many times I have perceived this as a result of experience. The Lord has told it to me. I have definitely seen that we must enter by this gate if we wish His Sovereign Majesty to reveal to us great and hidden mysteries. A person *should desire no other path* (my italics) even if he or she is at the summit of contemplation; on this road he or she walks safely. All blessings come to us through the Lord.'[5]

Perhaps the nearest we get to a direct encounter with the Lord is when Christ's presence is experientially encountered within the self. But even there mediation is involved, because we can only know the self to the extent that its potential has been activated by means of relationship with other people, the world around us, and through both with the Lord. God uses this kind of relationship to mediate the divine presence to the self. This ability to move from created things to an awareness of their Creator is known as the principle of mediated immediacy. It is a matter of having intimations of divinity rather than a direct awareness of God (cf. 1 Cor 13:12).

Self-forgetful attention

There is an archetypal passage in Ex 33:11 which tells us that having poured out his heart to God, Moses paid undivided attention to the Lord. It goes on to say that: 'The Lord would speak to Moses face to face, as a man speaks with his friend.' Our desire to know God will be satisfied to the extent that we too are able to pay self-forgetful attention to the twin bibles of the created world and the holy scriptures, both of which can mediate the presence, word and will of the Lord. The etymology of the word 'attention' is interesting. It means 'to stretch' or to 'incline' the mind, in order to understand the realities we perceive. This kind of attention has a number of discernible characteristics.

Qualities of self-forgetful attention

Firstly, it is contemplative in nature. It is an ability to attend to

things in a sustained and interested way. It is sometimes referred to as passive attention because, on the one hand, it is energised by a dynamic desire to know reality, while on the other, it
is characterised by a quiet openness and receptivity. Secondly,
this kind of attention surrenders wilful control over experience.
It is willing to let reality be its unique self without projecting
one's own thoughts and interpretations upon it.[6] It is interesting
to note that in Greek the word for 'attention' is virtually the
same as the word for 'conversion'. In other words, self-forgetful
attention to reality can involve an invitation to change, to let go
of pre-conceived ideas and impressions in order to encounter
the surprise of the unfamiliar and the new. Thirdly, self-forgetful attention to people is empathic. The word is derived from the
Greek, and literally means 'feeling into.' It is the ability to sense
in an understanding way what another person is experiencing,
and to convey that understanding to him or her. Fourthly, self-
forgetful attention is intuitive. It is a form of knowing that seems
to operate beyond the limitations of merely rational, analytical
processes. By means of intuition, one can go beyond appearances to 'see within' to the inner reality of people and things.

Impediments to self-forgetful attention
There are many blocks to self-forgetful attention of this kind. To
begin with, there is the problem of self-absorption, a tendency to
be overly preoccupied with one's own needs, experiences,
thoughts, feelings and desires. Besides being a result of a willful
selfishness, it is often due to the effects of unacknowledged and
unresolved psychological pain which is rooted in the hurts and
deprivations of the past. They can give rise to distracting feelings such as mistrust, fear, shame, etc. When people with emotional problems try to pay attention to nature, to another person
or to a scripture text, their desire to concentrate on them can be
subverted by unconscious attitudes and feelings of a negative
kind. As they try to focus on realities such as the thoughts, feelings and memories of another person, their attention tends to
boomerang back to themselves. Instead of entering into an
awareness of objective reality, such as the other person's story, it
tends to remind them of their own. And so in interpersonal relationships, for example, they are inclined to say: 'I know exactly

what you are going through. I went through something very similar some time ago.' Instead of paying self-forgetful attention to the person who is sharing, they get him or her to listen to them.

Genuine attention can also be inhibited by adopting an evaluative attitude to life. Instead of accepting experiences in a non-critical, non-judgmental way, perfectionists are inclined to assess them in terms of ideals. For example, when they read the scriptures they tend to interpret them in a moralistic way. For instance, they can focus on the words spoken by Jesus at the very start of his public ministry: 'The time has come,' he said, 'The kingdom of God is near. Repent and believe the good news!' (Mk 1:15). Notice that Jesus begins with a glorious and fundamental proclamation, 'The kingdom of God is near.' Implicit in this declaration is the Good News of the outpouring of God's unconditional mercy and love. Instead of taking those liberating words to heart, a moralistic person concentrates on the ethical injunction, 'Repent'. Rather than focusing on what God is freely offering, such a person becomes morbidly introspective. Ironically, the repentance s/he highlights has to be the fruit of a heart that has firstly been evangelised by the gospel message.

Prejudice of any kind is another impediment to self-forgetful attention. Instead of savouring reality as it is, prejudiced people can unwittingly interpret and censor experiences in terms of preconceived ideas and stereotypes, whether racial, sexual, or religious. In chapter three we noted how unresolved anger and fear can also inhibit self-forgetful attention. These emotions can cause mistrust and resistance, especially when they are consciously or unconsciously focused on God. For example, some people fear that if they get close to the Lord in prayer, they might have to reassess their priorities, make big sacrifices, etc. As a number of writers have pointed out, negative feelings of this kind are often connected to negative, forbidding images of God which were formed earlier in life.[7]

Effects of self-forgetful attention
When we pay self-forgetful attention to created things, we can experience two levels of awareness. There is a consciousness of the immediate object of attention such as a majestic waterfall or

a liturgical event. At the same time these created things can mediate an awareness of the presence of the Beyond in the midst of everyday life. It could be referred to as the halo effect, or a sense of the numinous. It is a spiritual experience that hints at the mysterious presence of the divine in such a way that one would be inclined, in a metaphorical sense, to bow one's head in reverence. The two forms of presence can be discerned by means of our emotional responses which have two interrelated dimensions. To begin with, there is the feeling reaction which is evoked by the immediate object of attention, e.g. the waterfall or liturgical event, and there are other feelings which are evoked not so much by the waterfall or the liturgical event itself, as by a sense of an invisible Presence which they mediate.

No wonder, then, that the *Catholic Encyclopedia* comments, 'Attention is the very essence of prayer; as soon as attention ceases, prayer ceases.' The Jewish philosopher and mystic, Simone Weil, endorsed this point of view when she wrote, 'Prayer consists of attention. It is the orientation of all the attention of which the soul is capable toward God. The quality of attention counts for much of the quality of the prayer. Warmth of heart cannot make up for it. It is the highest part of the attention only which makes contact with God, i.e. when prayer is intense and pure enough for such contact to be established.'[8]

Attending to the word of God and the God of the word
At this point we will look at the way in which people who desire to know God pay attention to the word of God. One ecclesial document observes: 'The church recommends the reading of the word of God as a source of Christian prayer, and at the same time exhorts all to discover the deep meaning of sacred scripture through prayer', so that a dialogue takes place between God and man. For, 'we speak to him when we pray; we listen to him when we read the divine sayings.'[9] First, a few comments about the biblical notion of God's word.

In Western culture reality is primary, language is secondary and is used to reflect it. But in the bible it is the other way around. God's word comes first. It is dynamic. It creates reality because it contains within itself the power of its own fulfilment. As Is 55:11 says: 'my word that goes out from my mouth: It will not return to me empty, but will accomplish what I desire and achieve the purpose for which I sent it.' In the Old Testament the term for word is *Dabar*. It means 'to drive, to get behind, to push.' It can be used as a noun or as a verb. As a noun it is objective. It refers to the word of God which is true in itself. As a verb the word has a subjective aspect. It refers to the spoken word of God which is true for a particular individual in a particular situation. When people pay prayerful attention to the scriptures they do so in the hope that God's word would leap alive off the page into their hearts as an inspired and inspiring word of revelation.

Abraham and Mary are the two outstanding exemplars of this kind of self-forgetful attention. Their attitude is encapsulated in Is 50:4-5 where it says: 'The Sovereign Lord ... wakens me morning by morning, wakens my ear to listen like one being taught. The Sovereign Lord has opened my ears, and I have not been rebellious; I have not drawn back.' They were blessed because they believed that the word spoken to them by the Lord would be fulfilled. In the Old Testament, Abraham was told that although he and his wife Sarah were senior citizens they would have a child who would become the father of a great nation. Eventually Isaac was born. His name means 'laughter'. It was God who had the last laugh. Speaking of Abraham, St Paul says in Rom 4:20-21: 'He did not waver through unbelief regarding the promise of God, but was strengthened in his faith and gave glory to God, being fully persuaded that God had power to do what he had promised.' In the New Testament, the angel Gabriel promised Mary, a virgin, that she would become the mother of Jesus by the overshadowing of the Holy Spirit. She responded: 'Here am I the servant of the Lord: let it be with me according to your word' (Lk 1:38). Sometime later, when she visited her cousin Elizabeth, the latter was inspired to declare: 'Blessed are you among women ... and blessed is she who believed that the promise of God would be fulfilled' (Lk 1:45).

Lectio Divina
The best known means of paying attention to God's word in the scriptures is the Benedictine Method. It is known as the *Lectio Divina,* or sacred reading. It is a personal or communal reading

of a scripture passage of any length, received as the word of
God, which through the impulse of the Holy Spirit leads to meditation, prayer and contemplation.[10] A twelfth-century writer
described its purpose in these words: '*Reading* you should seek;
meditating you will find; *praying* you shall call; and *contemplating*
the door will be opened to you.' Before engaging in the *Lectio
Divina*, we ask the Lord to bless our prayer time. There is a succinct verse in the *Divine Office* which is particularly apt. 'In the
scriptures by the Spirit, may we see the Saviour's face, hear his
word and heed his calling, know his will and grow in grace.
Amen.' A shorter prayer says: 'I open the scriptures to meet you
again. Reveal yourself to me.'

Reading

One goes on to select a passage to read. It might come from the
liturgy of the day, or the following Sunday, or one could choose
a passage that would speak to one's needs at that particular
time, such as how to cope with bereavement, anger, temptation,
etc. Admittedly, one needs to have a fairly good knowledge of
the bible in order to choose such an apt passage. Others buy
booklets which contain thematic scripture meditations. The
bible societies in different English-speaking countries produce
useful materials of this kind. Ideally, the passage chosen should
not be too long. Then one goes on to read the verses slowly and
attentively. I have found that it is good to read the passage two
or three times. St Anselm wrote in the eleventh century, 'The
scriptures are not to be read in a noisy situation, but where
things are quiet, not superficially and in a rush, but a little at a
time.' By way of example, we will suppose that the person
chooses to meditate on two short descriptions of the same incident in Mk 6:31-34 and Mt 9:36:

> Then, because so many people were coming and going
> that they did not even have a chance to eat, he said to
> them, 'Come with me by yourselves to a quiet place and
> get some rest.' So they went away by themselves in a boat
> to a solitary place. But many who saw them leaving
> recognised them and ran on foot from all the towns and
> got there ahead of them. When Jesus landed and saw a
> large crowd … he had compassion on them, because they

were harassed and helpless, like sheep without a shepherd ... So he began teaching them many things ... Then he said to his disciples, 'The harvest is plentiful but the workers are few. Ask the Lord of the harvest, therefore, to send out workers into his harvest field.'

Meditating

We can usefully begin this section with a succinct definition from the *Catechism of the Catholic Church*. 'Meditation is a prayerful quest, engaging thought, imagination, emotion and desire. Its goal is to make our own in faith the subject considered, by confronting it with the reality of our own life.'[11] In Prov 4:20-5:1 we are told how to internalise a scripture text: 'My son, pay attention to what I say; listen closely to my words. Do not let them out of your sight, keep them within your heart; for they are life to those who find them ... Above all else, guard your heart, for it is the wellspring of life ... My child, pay attention to my wisdom, listen well to my words of insight.' I often read a bible commentary as part of my meditative exploration of the passage. It can throw light on the context and the true meaning of the verses. During the meditative stage, one ponders the import of the text, thinks about obscure or difficult points, and tries to see how these truths relate to one's own life and the life of the world about us. For example, one might consider how, regardless of their education and material prosperity, many people in modern society also seem to be harassed and dejected like the people in the gospel story. Indeed one might reluctantly have to admit that, because of personal unhappiness, emotional problems, addictions or obsessions, one could personally identify with the needy crowd.

There are two ways of meditating. If you are reflecting on a doctrinal point, for example, from the letters of St Paul, it can be helpful to repeat a chosen word or sentence, over and over again, while letting its meaning sink into the heart. It is rather like sucking a candy. You let it dissolve in order to savour its taste and flavour. If you are reflecting on a scriptural incident, such as the one mentioned above, it can be helpful, as Ignatius of Loyola suggested, to imagine it as if you were making a mental video. *See* the scene and the people who are mentioned. You may choose to see yourself as one of the characters involved. *Hear* what is said. You may want to add to the dialogue that is recorded in the text. *Notice* what the characters do. Finally, try to *sense* what the people feel. I have found that if the story is about Jesus I can try to empathise with him empathising with the people of his time. I attempt to get inside his skin, so to speak, in order to sense in an understanding way what he felt. Empathy has five characteristics.

1. By means of empathy one person becomes aware of the inner life of another. It involves moment by moment sensitivity to the changing feelings which animate other people.

2. Empathy seeks to understand other people's lives, by becoming aware of the unique perceptions, attitudes, values, and beliefs that evoked their feelings, coloured as they are by their past experiences and memories.

3. Empathy studiously avoids judging, condemning or even assessing other people's experiences in the light of abstract ideals or norms of perfection.

4. Empathic men and women mirror back their awareness of other people's feelings. It means checking frequently with them to establish whether their sense of their experience is accurate or not.

5. Empathic people don't share the feelings of others, but they are not only aware of them, they spontaneously respond to them at the emotional level.

Read and meditate on the encounter between Jesus and the crowd in the wilderness. As you read, refer to the characteristics of empathy just mentioned. Notice how Jesus illustrates each one of them in his reaction to the needy people.

1. What feelings does he sense in the crowd? The text intimates that they felt sad, dejected, abandoned, and needy. How did Jesus feel? The text suggests that when he sensed what the people were feeling he was moved with compassion. The Greek word used in the verse is a strong one. It implies that he was moved to the pit of his stomach by the sufferings of the crowd.

2. Does he understand why they felt the way they did? Clearly he did. He knew from personal experience what they

had to endure. Taxes were heavy. Famines were frequent. Emigration was high. Roman rule was cruel. Physical and mental diseases were many and incurable. But the principal suffering of the poor was shame and disgrace. The sinners of the time included most of the rural poor, e.g. those who engaged in unclean professions such as prostitutes, tax collectors, robbers, herdsmen, usurers, gamblers, those who did not pay their tithes or neglected the Sabbath day rest and ritual cleanliness, and also those who through no fault of their own didn't know the law. There was no way out for them. As a result they suffered from chronic guilt feelings which led them to fear divine punishment. In Jn 7:49, the Pharisees refer to the poor as 'the accursed', i.e. those who have no hope of salvation.

3. How does Jesus show his acceptance of the people? Unlike false shepherds 'who only take care of themselves' (Ezech 34:2), he did not get angry or impatient with the crowd even though they had frustrated his plans to take a much needed rest with the apostles. Despite his tiredness there is no hint of complaint.

4. Does he reflect back his understanding of what the crowd has had to endure? He does. His feeling reactions were evident in his body language and in the sympathetic way he spoke.

5. How does Jesus respond to the people's heartfelt needs? Although they were materially poor, he saw that they suffered from a deeper poverty of a spiritual and emotional kind. They were victims of a famine of the knowledge of God, of the assurance that they were accepted by God and that they had a future and a hope. Jesus met this need by firstly proclaiming the good news of God's unconditional and unrestricted love to them. Later on, the text says that he also demonstrated the truth of the gospel message by satisfying their bodily hunger by means of the miraculous multiplication of the loaves and fish.

In a medieval document named *Scala Claustralium*, Guigo the Carthusian described the outcome of a reflective process of this kind. 'When meditation busily applies itself in this way, it does not remain on the outside, it goes to the heart of the matter. When the soul is set alight by this spark it appreciates how sweet it would be to know by experience, yet it can find no means of its own to have what it longs for. So the soul, seeing that by itself it cannot attain to that sweetness of knowing and feeling which it longs for, humbles itself, and resorts to prayer.'[12]

Praying

As a person begins to react at a personal level to the text, meditation gives way to prayer. Rational thinking gives way to the disclosure of the feelings and desires that have been evoked by one's reading and reflection. S/he may be moved to offer prayers of contrition, petition, intercession, thanksgiving, praise and adoration. As we have dealt with the subject of prayer as honest self-disclosure in the preceding chapter, there is no need to reiterate the points mentioned there. Suffice it to say that as St Benedict counselled, 'let the prayer be brief and pure.'As we pray, the Lord may be revealed to our hearts. This kind of religious experience brings us to the threshold of contemplative awareness. Up to this point we have been active, desiring, and attending by means of reading, meditation and prayer. But at this stage we make fewer efforts in order to let the Lord take the initiative. St Vincent de Paul used a number of homely images to describe this transition. In one of them he says that one uses a flint to kindle tinder in order to light a candle. Once the wick is burning there is no need to keep on striking the flint to create sparks. Meditation is the flint, it is used until the candle of prayer is lighting. Then it is no longer needed unless the candle splutters out. Referring to another contemporary image he said that the soul was like a sailboat equipped with oars. The oars were not used unless the wind failed, and then progress wasn't as rapid or pleasant as when the ship was moving along under a good breeze. Similarly, we need to reflect when special assistance from the Holy Spirit is not forthcoming, but when the heavenly breeze blows upon the heart, we must yield ourselves to its influence. When inspiration comes, meditation gives way to heartfelt prayer.

Contemplating

In the *Catechism of the Catholic Church* we read: 'Contemplative prayer is the simple expression of the mystery of prayer. It is a gaze of faith fixed on Jesus, an attentiveness to the Word of God, a silent love. It achieves real union with the prayer of Christ to the extent that it makes us share in his mystery.'[13] As a person reads, meditates and prays, there can be moments when these activities give way to a graced sense of God's presence. Speaking about this kind of religious experience, St Vincent de Paul wrote, 'It is not the result of human teaching. It is not attainable by human effort, and it is not bestowed on everyone … In this state of quiet, the soul finds itself suddenly filled with spiritual illuminations and holy affections (i.e. feelings and desires).'[14] I suspect that such experiences are not only religious but at least mildly mystical in nature. The phrase 'religious experience' refers not so much to talk or thought *about* transcendental reality, as conscious, mediated awareness *of* that reality. A religious experience therefore is an experience in which one has intimations of the immediate presence of 'the divine'. Because the word mysticism can mean so many different things, it is difficult to define. Etymologically, it refers to a person who has been initiated into a 'mystery'. A mystic, therefore, is a person who has a certain experiential sense of what eye has not seen nor ear heard (cf. 1 Cor 2:9) and whose religion and life are centred, not merely on an accepted belief, but on that which he or she regards as first-hand spiritual knowledge. Understood in that way, all genuinely religious experiences are at least mildly mystical in nature.

Attention to the God of active imagination

The bible makes it clear that God can be revealed in and through our imaginations by means of such things as dreams, visions and creative visualisation. In Greco-Roman thought, human beings were thought to be made up of body and mind. As a result the notion of the human spirit was often mistakenly understood in terms of the psyche. The bible, on the other hand, sees the human person as an inseparable unity of body, psyche and spirit. St Paul adverts to this when he prays, 'may God … keep your whole being, spirit, mind and body free from fault' (1 Thess 5:22).

The role of the body is pretty clear, but what is the difference between the psyche and the spirit? The psyche includes thought, memory, emotion, and will. The spirit refers to the God-created blank within us that can only be fulfilled by means of heartfelt relationship with the transcendent God. It consciously or unconsciously thirsts for such relationship, and is only fulfilled when it is satisfied. As a result our imaginations can experience dreams, visions and images that either originate in the mind, i.e. the psyche, or in the spirit. The latter are prompted by God's Spirit active in our spirits. The Holy One uses emotionally charged psychic symbols to express a spiritual revelation.

In his book *Sadhana* Antony de Mello suggests many ways of paying attention to the things of God. There are two imaginative exercises that I like to combine. I begin by recalling the words, 'God is Love' (Jn 15:9) and 'As the Father has loved me, so I have loved you; abide in my love' (Jn 15:9). Then I imagine that Jesus is kneeling before me with a towel around his waist. I notice as, St Teresa of Avila used to recommend, that he is looking at me with eyes filled with love and humility. He is not there to tell me what he wants. Rather he wants to know what my God-prompted desire might be. So I tell him that I want to experience his love in a deeper way than ever before, so that I might return it to him in and through my love for the people I meet. Sometimes I imagine that I can hear the Lord saying: 'I love and accept you as you are. You don't have to become better, or give up your faults and failings. Obviously I would want you to do so. But that is not a condition for receiving my love and acceptance. That you have already, before you change, even if you decide never to change at all. Do you believe me? Do you believe that I love and accept you as you are, right now, and not as you could be, or should be, or may be some day? Ponder what I'm saying to you and tell me what you really feel.'[15]

Visionary experiences of God are more spontaneous than the imaginative kind we have just described. Prompted by the Spirit, and expressed in images that emanate from the unconscious, these religious day-dreams can reveal something of God and God's love. For example, some time ago I was on retreat. One evening I spent time before the Blessed Sacrament in the chapel. At the beginning I told Jesus that I desired to know his love more deeply than ever before, in order to love him more effectively in and through other people. As I focused in faith upon the real presence, a fairly vivid image came to mind. I could see a youthful looking Jesus standing in front of the altar. He was clean shaven and wore a creamy white garment of great simplicity. I could see that red light streamed from his right hand and white light from his left. Then he raised his palms to shoulder height and there was a momentary flash of red and white light before he extended his arms in front of him with his hands facing at a downward angle. Beams of light shone from his wounded palms upon the ground in front of him. I found myself standing in the converging beams of light. Inwardly I was consciously aware that I was receiving the unconditional mercy and love of God. As I savoured the experience I recalled a scripture text that seemed to encapsulate some aspects of the vision: 'His splendor was like the sunrise; rays flashed from his hand, where his power was hidden' (Hab 3:4).

Paying attention to the God of nature and art
Galileo Galilei once said in a letter: 'From the Divine Word, nature and the sacred scriptures did alike both proceed.'[16] Speaking of the natural world, St Antony the Great once wrote: 'My book is the nature of created things, and it is always at hand when I wish to read the words of God.'[17] When spiritual directors discover that their directees have rather joyless, formal ways of praying, they will sometimes ask them what leisure activities they most enjoy. It might be anything, from bird watching or gardening, to flower arranging and appreciating good music. If, for example, a male directee said that he really loved walking alone on mountain paths, the director might encourage him to express his heartfelt desire for a revelation of God. Then, ironically, he would encourage him to forget about saying any more prayers in order to pay undivided, self-forgetful attention to the natural things around him such as ferns, rocks, trees, streams and sky. He would do this in the belief that they could be the locus, not only of an enjoyable aesthetic experience, but also of a mediated awareness of the uncreated Origin of all created beauty.[18]

The religious literature of the world abounds in the testimonies of people who have received a revelation of God in and through their appreciation of nature. These experiences can range from what James Pratt referred to as mild to intense mysticism.[19] In their book, *Witnessing the Fire: Spiritual Direction and the Development of Directors*, Madeline Birmingham and Bill Connolly quote from the interchange between Bob, a director, and Phil, a directee. Recently, Phil went on a hike through a forest. He was fascinated by everything he saw. At one point he says: 'But what I became most aware of was the leaves, thousands of them around me and above me, all slightly stirring. Suddenly I was astonished at the abundance of all that life. I thought: I'm not alone.' Bob responds: 'All that abundance and you thought: I'm not alone.' Phil explains: 'Yes. I'm not alone. That's what I thought. I stopped and stood for a long time. I wasn't aware of the time. But I realised later it was a long time.' Bob responds: 'You stood there.' 'Yes,' replies Phil, 'I was listening.' 'Listening? 'inquires Bob, to which Phil replies: 'I know it's a strange thing to say, but I was listening to the silence.' Bob asks him to say more. Phil goes on to explain: 'It was as though the silence was full of life and was telling me something. As though something was being said that I couldn't make out. As though someone responsible for all that life was speaking.' 'As though someone was speaking?' inquires Bob. 'Yes,' says Phil, 'And telling me … well, after a while it sounded as though there was care for me. As though I were a swimmer immersed in care for me.'[20] This testimony illustrates the fact that God's presence can be mediated by wonder-filled appreciation of the beauties of nature.

Much the same dynamic can be at work when we pay sustained attention to a work of art of any kind. Many years ago I bought a long playing record of Beethoven's choral symphony. I can remember sitting on my own, in the living room, where I listened to it on a gramophone. It was a wonderful recording that absorbed my attention and moved me deeply. When the fourth movement was being played, a very clear image came spontaneously to mind. I could see the night sky. There was the plough constellation with its characteristic cluster of stars, and in the distance the dim light of the North Pole star. As I looked at them, I heard an inner voice saying, 'I am your heavenly Father, who lives beyond the stars.' It was a wonderful moment. I felt close to the Father and loved by him. Instead of evoking a lonely feeling as they had often done in the past, the sight of the stars now evoked a deep sense of belonging within me. As soon as the music ended I lifted the record sleeve and found that the words of Friedrich Schiller's *Ode to Joy* had been printed inside. I was more than surprised to find that they referred to God as the One who lives beyond the stars! This coincidence seemed to confirm, in a providential way, that the Father had revealed himself to me as I paid wrapped attention to Beethoven's masterpiece. Is it any surprise that Beethoven wrote in a letter to Louis Schlosser, 'Every real creation of art is independent, more powerful than the artist himself and returns to the divine through its manifestation. It is one with man in this; it bears testimony to the mediation of the divine in him.'

Paying attention to the God of human relationships
If God can be revealed through creation in general, this is pre-eminently true when it comes to the mediating power of human persons and their loving relationships, which are the 'highest' manifestation of created reality, so to speak. We can come into relationship with God through the love of our neighbour. The act of loving our neighbour has a transcendent dimension whereby we can come into an experience of God. There are many stories in the gospels which describe how people who met with Christ were suddenly enlightened and recognised to a greater or lesser extent who he was. Luke's account (cf. Lk 24:13-36) of the meeting between Jesus and the disciples on the road to Emmaus is a way of saying that if a believer wants to meet the risen Lord, he or she will do so in the eucharistic community where the word is read and explained as a preparation for the breaking of bread and holy communion. As Jesus himself said, 'Where two or three meet in my name, I am there among them' (Mt 18:20). St Paul realised something like this on the road to Damascus. To persecute the Christians was to persecute Christ himself. The community was the Lord's mystical body on earth. As Paul said: 'Christ's body is yourselves, each one of you with a part to play in the whole' (1 Cor 12:27) and 'Christ is the head of the body, that is, the church' (Col 1:18).

The implication is clear. Whenever there is a I-Thou relationship between two people as a result of contemplative knowing, the Lord can be revealed as the Hidden One, who is secretly present. As one prisoner in a concentration camp wrote, 'I sought my God, I could not find him. I sought my soul, it evaded me. I sought my neighbour, and found all three.' This sentiment is echoed in a verse of Gerald Manley Hopkins, 'God plays in ten thousand places, lovely in eyes and lovely in limbs not his, to the Father through the features of men's faces.' Jungian psychologist Irene de Castillejo has written, 'For there to be a meeting, it seems as though a third, a something else, is always present. You may call it Love or the Holy Spirit.'[21]

Those involved in the caring professions, such as spiritual directors, can have this kind of religious experience. Spiritual direction is the help given by one Christian to another which enables that person to pay attention to God's personal communication to him or to her, to respond to this God, to grow in intimacy with the Lord, and to live out the consequences of the relationship.[22] Directors are encouraged to develop a contemplative attitude. Having recognised the directee's religious experience they pay sustained, self-forgetful attention to it. This has a number of purposes. Firstly, it assists directees to pay attention to their own experience in such a way that they grow in conscious awareness of the One who has been revealed to them. Secondly, the director who listens with a contemplative attitude can end up by becoming so aware of the God of the directee's experience that the encounter becomes a religious experience in itself. The Lord is revealed to the director in and through the directee's sharing.

A personal experience

Many years ago I was directing a young man who was a student in a Protestant theological college. In the course of one of our many sessions together, this directee told me about an essay he had been writing. He had cause to look up many scripture quotations. He said that one of them had impressed him so much that he had stopped writing his essay and spent a period of time in reflection and prayer. I asked him about the words that had touched him so deeply. He said they were from Phil 3:8-11. They read: 'I consider everything a loss compared to the surpassing greatness of knowing Christ Jesus my Lord, for whose sake I have lost all things. I consider them rubbish, that I may gain Christ ... I want to know Christ and the power of his resurrection and the fellowship of sharing in his sufferings, becoming like him in his death, and so, somehow, to attain to the resurrection from the dead.' Having quoted these words, the student went on to talk in a sincere and eloquent way about them. He said that he had a growing desire to know the Lord and a willingness to get rid of anything in his life that was incompatible with such a relationship. He said that he had already talked to the girl he was living with and they had agreed to separate and to avoid having sexual intercourse. I was not only very interested in what this directee was telling me, I was also deeply touched by what he said. I had a strong sense that I was meeting with the God of his experience and sharing in his desire to know the Lord no matter what the cost.

Over the years I have also found that instances of genuine intimacy can become a real focal point for the revelation of the Lord's presence. They can occur, especially, in the context of marriage or friendship. For example, when Jewish psychiatrist Viktor Frankl was in Auschwitz he was separated from his wife who was in a neighbouring camp. One day as he was going to his work the luminous image of his spouse came to mind. Then he went on to observe: 'Love is the highest goal to which people can aspire. I grasped the meaning of the greatest secret that human poetry and human thought and belief have to impart – the salvation of man is in love and through love ... For the first time in my life I was able to understand the words: The angels are lost in perpetual contemplation of an infinite glory.' A little later he added: 'Love goes far beyond the physical person of the beloved. It finds its deepest meaning in his spiritual being, his inner self.'[23] It would seem that loving intimacy is an intimation of a greater Love in which it lives and moves and has its being (cf. Acts 17:28).

God within encountering the God without

Vincent de Paul was not a mystic in the classical sense like Teresa of Avila or John of the Cross. But he had a quasi-mystical sense that if Christians ministered to the needy and the marginalised with compassion, it was a matter of the compassionate Jesus within, ministering to the suffering Jesus without, in the person of the afflicted poor. For example, speaking to some Daughters of Charity about the immanence of God in the compassionate heart, Vincent said: 'We must open our hearts so that they become responsive to the sufferings and miseries of the neighbour. We should pray God to give us a true spirit of mercy and compassion, *which is in truth the Spirit of God within you.*' Speaking about the presence of the wounded Christ in the suffering poor, he said to Daughters of Charity: 'In serving the poor you are serving Jesus Christ. A sister may go to the sick ten times a day, and ten times a day she will find God there. Visit the poor convicts in the chain gangs and there you will find God. Oh Daughters, how gratifying it is! You go into poor homes and *you find God there.*'

I talked to a woman recently who told me about her affection for an eleven year old girl named Geraldine. She was suffering from a severe spinal problem which required a six hour operation during which a metal rod was inserted down her vertebrae. When the operation was complete, Geraldine had plaster of Paris put round her body. It reached from her neck to her buttocks. For some unknown reason she had to lie on her stomach for a few weeks. Unfortunately some of Geraldine's spinal nerves had been damaged in the course of the intricate surgery. As a result she periodically suffered from terrible stomach spasms. They were so severe that she used to scream out with pain. For medical reasons the nurses couldn't administer strong pain killers. They were so disturbed by Geraldine's afflictions and their own powerlessness to help her that they tended to avoid her when her suffering was particularly bad.

The woman who befriended her noticed this when she visited Geraldine in hospital. On one occasion when she was talking to her, the young patient went into another spasm and began to cry out in pain. The woman decided to sit with her as long as the pain lasted. She found that the screams were almost unbearable. At one point she said in prayerful anguish, 'Lord why does such an innocent young girl have to suffer so much?' The Lord seemed to reply to this *cri de coeur* when he said inwardly to her, 'It is I who am in an agony in this young girl and it is I who scream through her, and it is I too who am in a compassionate agony in you on her behalf.' As soon as the woman comprehended these words, a great peace came over her. Soon afterwards Geraldine stopped screaming and dozed off to sleep. As I listened to the woman tell this story I was deeply moved, so much so that I felt that I had vicariously experienced God's compassionate presence, even as I paid attention. As Jesus once said: 'I tell you the truth, whatever you did not do for one of the least of these, you did not do for me' (Mt 25:45).

Typical effects of prayerful religious experience
In a religious experience feelings are evoked by what is revealed about God. Following the initial emotional *response* to the revelatory awareness, a secondary emotional *reaction* occurs. It is sometimes referred to as resistance. As we noted in the preceding chapter, it is characterised by a sense of apprehension to do with possible implications of the experience, such as a need to change one's life.

Genuine religious experiences can have a number of predictable consequences. Firstly, they lead to a new recognition of who God is and what God is like. Secondly, they tend to expose, challenge, and displace false images of the Lord. Thirdly, they motivate the graced person to express his or her response in a prayerful way by means of thanks, praise and worship, and sometimes in the form of heartfelt sorrow for having failed to give due honour to God in the past. Fourthly, they revitalise beliefs already held, while at the same time activating the person's inner potential for a closer relationship with God. Fifthly, as a result of this growing intimacy, the person relates more deeply to his or her spiritual self. Pope John Paul II has written: 'the man who wishes to understand himself thoroughly, and not just in accordance with immediate, partial, often superficial and even illusory standards and measures, must … draw near to Christ. He must, so to speak, enter him with all his own self, he must 'appropriate' and assimilate the whole of the reality of the incarnation and redemption in order to find himself. If this profound process takes place within him, he then bears the fruit not only of adoration of God but also of deeper wonder at himself.'[24]

As growth in wholeness and holiness occurs, the person has an increasing sense of inner freedom. Genuine growth in relationship with God prompts the desire and provides the power to change one's behaviour. Religious experience, therefore, is the true source of ethics. They are a response to revelation, rather than being a substitute for it, as is often the case. This distinction captures the meaning of Paul's differentiation between living by the Spirit and living by the law (cf. Gal 5:16-26).

CHAPTER FIVE

Seeking God's will in prayer

There are two main stages in the Christian life. They are de-scribed in Heb 5:13-14: 'Anyone who lives on milk, being still an infant, is not acquainted with the teaching about righteousness. But solid food is for the mature, who by constant use have trained themselves to distinguish good from evil.' Those who feed on milk are motivated by what God can do for them. Their principal desire is for the graces and blessings God can give them such as mercy, love, peace, healing, material prosperity, etc. Of course in a secondary way they also desire to do the will of God. Those who feed on solid food are motivated by what they can do for God. Their principal desire is to discover and to carry out the divine will. As Charles de Foucauld wrote in his *Prayer of Abandonment,* 'Let your will be done in me and in your creatures. I wish no more than this, O Lord.' However, in a sec-ondary way mature Christians do ask for the graces and bless-ings of the Lord, many of which are necessary in order to carry out the divine purposes.

In the Old Testament faithful believers sought to do God's will. There is a threefold pattern evident in their lives. Firstly, in the words of Ps 143:10, they prayed: 'Let your good spirit lead me.' Secondly, the Lord responded by promising them: 'I will instruct you and teach you in the way you should go' (Ps 32:10). Thirdly, God fulfilled the promise. The prophet Isaiah acknowl-edged: 'You guided your people to make for yourself a glorious name' (Is 63:14). In the gospels, Jesus was the One, *par excellence,* who always did the will of God. In John 6:38 he testified: 'For I have come down from heaven not to do my will but to do the will of him who sent me.' In Heb 10:9 he declared: 'Here I am, I have come to do your will.' In chapter two we saw how, in gen-eral terms, Jesus felt called to show to others, especially the poor, the limitless love the Father was showing to him. In the course of his ministry Jesus 'was led by the Spirit' (Lk 4:1), and stated that his words and deeds, all of which were expressions of merciful love, were inspired by his Father (Jn 14:10; 5:19). In this way, he proclaimed in anointed words and demonstrated in deeds of power the coming of the kingdom.

The will of the Lord is expressed in many ways. Principal among them are the ethical teachings of the scriptures such as the ten commandments. Then there are the commandments of the church and the instructions of those who exercise rightful authority in so far as they are not sinful. But there are many other choices we have to make which are not necessarily covered by any of these guidelines. What if a person gets an internal impulse to do something, to write a letter to the paper or to end a relationship, how would he or she be able to discern whether the prompting came from himself or herself, the evil spirit or from the Lord? If a woman gets a proposal of marriage should she accept? Should a worker respond to a request to do overtime at the weekend when he could spend quality time with his wife and children? All such choices are important for a conscientious Christian. In this chapter I propose to indicate how difficult decisions can be made in accordance with the will of God. It is a large and complicated subject, but due to the constraints of space, the treatment here will not be as nuanced as it might otherwise be. Happily, more comprehensive treatments are currently available.[1]

Whether they feed on milk or solid food, Christians are urged by Paul in Gal 5:16 and 18 to be guided by the Spirit. Arguably this injunction is the key to New Testament spirituality and ethics. As George Montague has pointed out, the Christian life is not a list of do's and don'ts. It is the gift of being moved by the Spirit of God, and the key to life is to allow the Spirit to lead. Paul clearly speaks of an inspired ethic and of inspired action – and it is not reserved for the holy few but is the birth-right of all believers. A crucial point: When confronted with any moral decision, great or small, the Christian's first question should be 'Where does the Spirit lead me in this?'[2] In his near 1000 page book on Paul's teaching on the Spirit, Gordon Fee says of the phrase 'be guided by the Spirit': 'Even though this imperative occurs only here in the Pauline corpus, both the argument in which it occurs and the rest of Pauline theology indicate that this is Paul's basic ethical imperative.'[3] H. D. Betz concurs when he says that the injunction to walk by the Spirit sums up the apostle's ethic, and therefore defines Paul's concept of the Christian life.[4] Not surprisingly, therefore, the apostle to the gentiles says that it is important to 'find out what pleases the Lord' (Eph 5:10). He hopes that believers 'may abound more and more in knowledge and depth of insight, so that they may be able to discern what is best' (Phil 1:9). Finally, Paul reveals: 'since the day we heard about you, we have not stopped praying for you and asking God to fill you with the knowledge of his will through all spiritual wisdom and understanding. And we pray this in order that you may live a life worthy of the Lord and may please him in every way: bearing fruit in every good work, growing in the knowledge of God' (Col 1:9-12).

Conditions for discerning God's will

If Christians truly desire to discover and to do God's will, St Paul makes it clear that they can only receive the inspired insight if their lives are molded by the values and beliefs of Jesus. In Eph 4:23-24 he says: 'be made new in the attitude of your minds; and put on the new self, created to be like God in true righteousness and holiness.' In Rom 12:2 he adds: 'Do not conform any longer to the pattern of this world, but be transformed by the renewing of your mind. Then you will be able to test and approve what God's will is – his good, pleasing and perfect will.' Paul would have been familiar with the Greco-Roman practice of making statues by pouring molten metal into moulds so that it would assume their shapes. Analogously, Paul was saying to the people, don't let yourselves be molded by the values and beliefs of the pagan world.

St Ignatius of Loyola suggested that typically the evil One uses three loves or attachments to lead souls away from God. First is an inordinate love of riches and the things money can buy, such as material goods, pleasures, power, security, and earthly fulfilment. Second is an inordinate love of being noticed, a longing for things such as a good reputation, success, qualifications, status, and honours. Third, there is a desire for an exag-

gerated independence which can lead to such things as the pri-
vatisation of morality in the pursuit of personal pleasures. It is
not that all these things are necessarily wrong in themselves but
the devil can tempt us to change them from being possible objects
of legitimate choice into absolutes, and therefore idols, which
become substitutes for God. Paul says, be molded, instead, by
the values and beliefs of the gospel. If you do, you will be detached from earthly things, and thus will have the inner power
to seek and discover God's will in a single-minded way. But
wouldn't it be true to say that the lives of many of us are compromised? Unwittingly, they are molded by a false synthesis of
worldly and gospel values. Not surprisingly, therefore, we frequently lack the spiritual wisdom that is necessary to discern
God's will.

The gift of wisdom

Christians also need the gift of wisdom mentioned in Is 11:2 and
1 Cor 12:8 in order to discover God's existential will. In this context the word 'wisdom' does not refer to the theoretical specula-
tions of philosophers. Rather it refers to the intuitive insight that
is given to a person or group who are seeking God's will in the
particular circumstances of their lives. The Latin word for wisdom is *sapientia*. It is derived from the word *sapere*, meaning 'to
taste or to savour'. The gift of spiritual wisdom enables people,
who are closely united to God by means of faith and an experience of divine love, to have an experiential sense of God and
God's purposes. It is interesting to note that St Thomas Aquinas
says: 'Now perception of this kind, implies a certain experimental
knowledge; and this is properly called wisdom, as it were a
sweet knowledge.'[5] As a bee or a bird is directed by instinct so
the spiritual person is inclined to act, not principally through the
movement of his or her own will, but by the instinct of the Holy
Spirit.

Pope John Paul II speaks about this same gift in *Veritatis
Splendor*. 'It is the heart converted to the Lord and to the love of
what is good which is really the source of true judgements ...
knowledge of God's law in general is necessary, but it is not sufficient: what is essential is a sort of "connaturality" between
man and the true good.[6] Such connaturality is rooted in and de-

velops through the virtuous attitudes of the individual himself.'[7] The notion of connaturality, to which the Pope refers, is a medieval one which was often mentioned by St Thomas Aquinas. People who are closely united to the Lord are endowed with an instinctive ability to see things the way God does and to recognise those inspirations that are prompted by the Spirit and those that are not. They are like people who, having heard one syllable spoken on the phone by a person they know well, can distinguish his or her distinctive and familiar voice from every other voice in the world. People with this gift of wisdom may not be able to explain why they made the judgement they did, but they will usually be correct nevertheless.

It is the Spirit that imparts such practical wisdom. As Jesus promised: 'But when he, the Spirit of truth, comes, he will guide you into all truth' (Jn 16:13). As 1 Jn 2:27 explained: 'As for you, the anointing you received from him remains in you, and you do not need anyone to teach you. But his anointing teaches you about all things.' Presumably, this includes an inkling of what the Lord wants one to do in the here and now. So we need to pray for the spiritual wisdom to know the will of God. As James 1:5 says: 'If any of you lacks wisdom, he should ask God, who gives generously to all without finding fault, and it will be given to him. But when he asks, he must believe and not doubt, because he who doubts is like a wave of the sea, blown and tossed by the wind. That man should not think he will receive anything from the Lord.'

Prayerful discernment

On one occasion St Vincent de Paul said, 'Prayer is a conversation of the soul with God, a mutual communication in which God interiorly tells the soul what he wishes it to do.' In other words prayer is the place where we become consciously aware of God's providential plan for our lives. It has two main aspects. Firstly, there is our overall Christian vocation in life, e.g. marriage, priesthood, dedicated single life, etc. Secondly, there is the working out of that vocation in the specific choices of everyday living. Speaking to a younger colleague who had been appointed superior of a seminary in 1656, St Vincent said, 'An important point, and one to which you should carefully devote yourself, is to establish a close union between yourself and the Lord in prayer. That is the reservoir in which you will receive the instructions you need to fulfil the duties on which you are now about to enter. When in doubt, have recourse to God and say to him: "O Lord, you are the Father of light, teach me what I ought to do in this circumstance." I give you this advice not only for those difficulties which will cause you anxiety, but also that you may learn from God directly what you shall have to teach, following the example of Moses who proclaimed to the people of Israel only that which God had inspired him to say.'[8]

Mindful of the importance of divine guidance, one could say the following words which have been attributed to both Cardinal Mercier and to Cardinal Newman: 'Come, O Holy Spirit, soul of my soul, I adore you. Enlighten me, guide me, strengthen and console me. Show me what to do and help me to do it. Give me your inspirations. I promise to submit myself to all that you desire of me and to accept all that you permit to happen to me. Let me only know your will. Amen.' At this point we will take a brief look at some of the ways in which the Lord can respond to this prayer.

God leads through holy desires

In chapter three we mentioned the importance of being aware of our God-prompted desires for God. Down the centuries, great spiritual writers have agreed that they are of great importance in the Christian life. They have pointed to gospel texts which make it clear that Jesus focused on such desires in his ministry. For example, in Jn 1:35-38 John the Baptist tells two young men that Jesus is the Lamb of God. 'When the two disciples heard him say this, they followed Jesus. Turning around, Jesus saw them following and asked, "What do you want?"' (my italics). Jesus asked this all-important question because he realised that God reveals his providential purposes in and through such desires.[9] Thus St Augustine could write: 'The whole life of a good Christian is a holy desire.' Augustine went on to say: 'The things you desire you cannot see yet. But the desire gives you the capacity, so that when it does happen that you see, you may be fulfilled ... This is our life, to be motivated by holy desire. But we are motivated by holy desire only in so far as we have cut off our longings from the love of the world. I have already pointed out how it is necessary to empty that which is to be filled. You are to be filled with good, pour out the bad.'[10]

Perhaps one of the best examples of God's will being expressed through holy desires is to be found in the autobiography of St Ignatius of Loyola. When he was recuperating from a war wound he happened to read two religious books. The first was *The Life of Christ* by Ludolph of Saxony, the second a collection of saints' lives known as *The Golden Legend* by Jacopo de Voragine. As a result he found himself desiring to imitate the heroic lives and deeds of Jesus and the saints. But he tells us that he also had a second, more worldly desire. He often thought about a lady, perhaps Princess Catherine, the beautiful sister of King Charles of Spain. He imagined what he would do for the princess if he visited her. He described how 'this succession of such diverse thoughts either of the worldly deeds he wished to achieve or of the deeds of God that came to his imagination, lasted for a long time … yet there was a difference. When he was thinking about the things of the world, he took much delight in them, but afterwards when he was tired and put them aside, he found he was dry and discontented. But when he thought of going to Jerusalem … not only was he consoled when he had these thoughts, but even after putting them aside he remained content and happy … He began to marvel at the difference and to reflect upon it, realising from experience that some thoughts left him sad and others happy. Little by little he came to recognise the difference between the spirits that agitated him, one from the demon, the other from God.'[11] Ignatius says that God can lead us by means of wholesome desires that are associated with the consolation of the Spirit. He was so impressed by this realisation that it would be true to say that the *Spiritual Exercises* are, first and foremost, a means of discovering, by means of discernment of spirits, what it is that we most deeply want. He firmly believed that in doing this, people were discovering God's will for them.

In my experience, an inner desire which has been prompted in the heart with accompanying consolation, may be confirmed some time later by outward events of a providential nature. For example, a young nurse is thinking of doing voluntary service overseas. At about the same time she happens to meet a man who organises such projects in troubled parts of the world. He asks her whether she ever considered the possibility of offering her expertise to needy people abroad. Some time later she decides to go to Africa for two years as a result of the congruence of the inner prompting and the outer invitation. In my experience it is a mistake to make a decision on the basis of an external stimulus only. It needs to be matched by a free, spontaneous and independent inner prompting. As a general rule, the Lord acts first and foremost in and through our own inner selves.

Be for others what God is for you
We saw in the preceding chapter how the Lord can reveal the God-self to those who pay self-forgetful attention to divine revelation. Whenever a formal or informal prayer experience comes to an end, it is well worth while engaging in an examen of consciousness. The following four questions could be used to facilitate reflection.

1. When were you most aware of the Lord's presence?
2. What did you feel when the Lord's presence or word was revealed to you? Were your emotions positive, e.g. peace, joy, hope, or negative – anxiety, anger, worthlessness?
3. What did you notice about the Lord that evoked such positive, negative or mixed feelings? This is a key question as far as the religious experience is concerned. Try to find a few words to describe the God who was revealed to you.
4. How did you decide to respond to the Lord in a prayerful way, e.g. in thanksgiving, praise, or sorrow, and/or in a practical way?

The answer to the third question is the vital one as far as this chapter is concerned because the following ethical imperative is implicit in every genuine religious experience: 'Be for others what God is for you.' If you have found God to be loving, accepting, understanding, compassionate, or encouraging, be loving, accepting, understanding, compassionate, and encouraging yourself. We saw in chapter two how, at his baptism and afterwards, Jesus was immersed in the immense, inexhaustible and unfathomable love and favour of the Father. Not only did he discover his true identity in the light of that love, he felt called to be for others, especially the poor, what God was for him.

Some time ago I was conducting a healing service in northern Italy. At one point I was praying and seeking guidance when I saw an image of Jesus from behind. He looked very tall, about ten to fifteen feet in stature. Bright beams of red and white light were shining from his heart and they were moving to and fro in the audience like lively lasers. I had a sense that this image, which was charged with energy and vitality, was a symbol of the merciful love of Christ who brings salvation and healing to the needy. When I reflected on the experience afterwards I was aware that it reaffirmed many other experiences I have had down the years. I felt that God was saying, 'Show to others the merciful love I have shown to you.'

Since then I have been led to two texts in particular which articulate what this guidance might imply. The first from Rom 13:8-10 says: 'Let no debt remain outstanding, except the continuing debt to love one another ... The commandments, "Do not commit adultery," "Do not murder," "Do not steal," "Do not covet," and whatever other commandment there may be, are summed up in this one rule: "Love your neighbour as yourself." Love does no harm to its neighbour. Therefore love is the fulfilment of the law.' The second, from Mt 7:12, describes how to show that love: 'In everything, do to others what you would have them do to you, for this sums up the Law and the Prophets.' As I have reflected on these ethical injunctions I have come to realise that Christian love is a matter of two things, *benevolence*, i.e. wanting what is best for the other person, and *insight*, i.e. being aware of what the other person's unique needs might be. I have also come to appreciate that the necessary insight comes largely as a result of empathising with the other person by sensing in an understanding way what he or she desires and feels.[12] I have also come to recognise that by trying to contribute in this way to the up-building of a 'civilisation of love,' one is contributing to the up-building of God's kingdom on earth.

Conscience as the voice of God
God can reveal the divine will in and through the activity of conscience. Paul says in Rom 2:14-15, 'Indeed, when Gentiles, who

do not have the law, do by nature things required by the law, they are a law for themselves, even though they do not have the law, since they show that the requirements of the law are written on their hearts, their consciences also bearing witness.' Catholic theology has long maintained that the voice of an informed conscience is the voice of God. St Bonaventure wrote: 'Conscience is like God's herald and messenger, it does not command things on its own authority, but commands them as coming from God's authority, like a herald when he proclaims the edict of the king. This is why conscience has binding force.'[13] In par. 43 of *Lord and Giver of Life*, Pope John Paul II encapsulated these points when he wrote: 'For the conscience is the most secret core and sanctuary of a man, where he is alone with God, whose voice echoes in his depths. It can speak to his heart more specifically, do this, shun that.' It is clear that if we seek God's will in prayer, the Lord can respond by revealing the divine purposes in and through a well-informed conscience which is under the influence of the Spirit of truth.

I can remember reading a book many years ago by Gordon Zahn.[14] It was about an Austrian Catholic named Franz Jagerstatter who was happily married with three children. Following the Nazi invasion of his country he was the only person in his village to vote against the Anschluss, i.e. the political union of Germany and Austria in 1938. Like many others, Franz was enlisted into the army. However he refused to go because he believed that Hitler was fighting an unjust war. He was aware that the Fuhrer was the one who had said: 'I freed Germany from the stupid and degrading fallacies of conscience and morality.'[15] The army authorities said that if Jagerstatter objected to active combat he could serve in the medical corps. But he refused that offer as well. He also refused to co-operate in any way with the Nazi projects such as the Winter Relief Collection or the People's Welfare Fund. He opted instead to help the poor in a personal capacity so as to avoid making charity to others an excuse for tacitly supporting something unChristian.

Many people, including his wife, parish priest and bishop tried to prevail upon him to change his mind. But he could not be swayed by patriotic appeals, by reminders of his duty to his wife and children, nor by the accusation that he knew better than those in authority. He said he was not questioning the rightness or wrongness of what other Catholics had done. All he knew was that before God his conscience was telling him that it would be wrong to participate in any way in Hitler's corrupt regime. As a result of this decision, he was arrested, tried by a military court and sentenced to death. In prison he showed no bitterness towards the civil or the ecclesiastical authorities which had given him no support whatsoever. He derived comfort from the Eucharist which he was allowed to receive on rare occasions, and from the news that a year before a Pallotine priest named Fr Reinish had gone to the scaffold for being a conscientious objector. On 9 August 1943, Franz Jagerstatter himself was beheaded for refusing in the name of Christian conscience to compromise with evil. As a result of prayerful reflection, God had revealed his will to him and, like his Saviour, he was obedient, even to death.

Guidance through scripture

The bible can give guidance for right living. The Old Testament says in Ps 119:105: 'Your word is a lamp to my feet and a light for my path.' In the New Testament we read: 'All scripture is inspired by God ... it can judge the secret thoughts and emotions of the heart ... it is useful for teaching the truth, rebuking error, correcting faults *and giving instruction for living*' (2 Tim 3:1; Heb 4:12; 2 Tim 3:1). The history of the church is punctuated with stories about the way in which God's word of guidance had a major impact on the lives of devout Christians. For example, Francis of Assisi was one of the greatest saints the church has ever had. He tells us that during a time when he was seeking God's will he attended Mass in the little chapel of Portiuncula. It was the feast of St Matthias, February 1209. The gospel for the day was taken from Mt 10:7-13. Among other things it said: 'As you go, preach this message: "The kingdom of heaven is near." Heal the sick, raise the dead, cleanse those who have leprosy, drive out demons. Freely you have received, freely give. Do not take along any gold or silver or copper in your belts; take no bag for the journey, or extra tunic, or sandals or a staff; for the worker is worth his keep.' These words and the subsequent homily had a profound effect upon him. Francis was inspired and exclaimed, 'This is what I want, this is what I with all my soul want to do with my life.'[16] Francis the church builder and hermit was now to become Francis the evangelist, the announcer of the good news of conversion and peace.

Sincere Christians always seek the will of God in a general sense. But in the course of their daily lives they seek out God's will in the particular circumstances they face. This general desire informs the way they read scripture at times when they face specific choices. They seek God's will and they have a divine assurance that they will find (Mt 7:7). The Lord can respond either in the form of exemplary or specific guidance. Exemplary guidance occurs when people read about the lives of characters in the bible, especially those of Jesus and the first disciples. As they come to admire their virtues they may have a desire to imitate them by living in the same way. For example, a few days ago I was very struck by the following words of Jesus: 'My Father is always at his work to this very day, and I, too, am working' (Jn 5:17). I was struck by the fact that our God is not a God who merely exists, but rather one who is constantly working, constantly active in an energetic, creative and saving way. The word God is not so much a noun as a verb. Jesus is like God. He too is forever labouring to serve others with zeal and generosity. Implicit in this exemplary testimony is a word of guidance, an invitation to overcome laziness, apathy and selfishness in order to work tirelessly to build up the kingdom.

Specific guidance is received when the scriptures give instructions about the particular ways in which the Lord wants believers to live. The pages of the Old and New Testaments are peppered with such ethical instructions. Any one of them can jump alive off the page into the heart as a specific word of guidance for the here and now. For years I have been involved in inter-church activities. Needless to say, one needs guidance in such circumstances. In this connection one text in particular has often come to mind. In Phil 2:2-3 Paul says: 'Make my joy complete by being like-minded, having the same love, being one in spirit and purpose. Do nothing out of selfish ambition or vain conceit, but in humility consider others better than yourselves.' While the call to unity of mind and heart attracts me, it is the phrase 'in humility consider others better than yourselves' which really strikes me as a word of guidance. I interpret it in subjective terms as a matter of focusing on qualities of a personal kind rather than on matters of objective orthodoxy of a doctrinal kind. In other words, in a self-forgetful spirit of mutual deference, ecumenists should avoid competitive self-assertion or a desire to dominate. Instead, they should acknowledge and appreciate the virtues and gifts of others. In this way unity is nurtured. As Paul says in another place: 'Do not think of yourself more highly than you ought, but rather think of yourself with sober judgment, in accordance with the measure of faith God has given you … Honour one another above yourselves' (Rom 12:3, 10). I have tried to put this guidance into action, but I must admit that my idealistic aspirations still far exceed my actual performance.

Guidance in the form of inspired promptings

God commonly guides people by means of inner promptings. While they are similar to desires, they are different. God-prompted desires are rooted in our deepest spiritual needs, whereas God-prompted impulses are not. More often than not, they are to do with the needs of others. In many ways they are the opposite of temptations where the evil one prompts people to engage in sinful activities of one kind or another. Inspired urges are prompted by the Spirit and can come in the form of spontaneous impulses, thoughts, and images which are associated with on-going consolation of spirit. The history of Christianity is dotted with countless examples of this kind of guidance. For instance, at one point during his mission in Ireland, St Patrick desired to visit Britain in order to see his relatives. He says: 'God knows I greatly desired it, but I am bound by the Spirit, who protests to me that if I do this he will pronounce me guilty.'[17] While Patrick had a natural desire to visit Britain, the Spirit gave him a supernatural prompting to remain in Ireland.

A number of years ago I was sitting at my desk thinking of nothing in particular. Suddenly the following thought came into my mind, why not write a daily prayer to the Holy Spirit? My immediate reaction was to say yes. I felt it would be a relatively easy thing to do and wouldn't take long. So I set to work, thinking I'd complete the task in a day or two. In the event it proved much more difficult than I had anticipated. I wrote one draft after another. But none of them satisfied me. Pages were repeatedly crunched into a ball and thrown into the wastepaper basket. Many a time I thought to myself, 'Why am I putting myself through all this hassle? After all, no one asked me to do this!' Then I'd abandon the project for a while. But I would have no peace. So I'd have to go back to it again. This went on for months. I lost count of all the versions of the prayer I wrote. None of them really satisfied me. In 1986 I published a provisional version in *New Creation* magazine and asked the readers for their feedback. Later that same year I brought a revised version to the printer intending to get 500 copies. I was shocked when he told me how much each one would cost. Then he said that if I got 5,000 copies, the price per leaflet would be considerably cheaper. Although I thought it would take years to sell them, I ordered the larger number.

A few days later I collected the box of new leaflets and returned to All Hallows College where I was living at the time. As soon as I came through the front door I was greeted by a priest and a lay woman, who were standing in the foyer. They asked if I was Fr Pat Collins. I said that I was. 'We heard you were writing a daily prayer to the Holy Spirit,' the priest explained, 'and we have come to see if we could buy some.' I said that by a remarkable coincidence I was in fact returning from the printers and that the box in my arms was full of leaflets. 'How many copies would you like?' I asked. 'Well, to start with we would like 1,000 copies,' replied the priest. I nearly dropped the box with surprise. They wanted exactly twice the number of leaflets I had proposed to order originally. That was many years ago. Since then I have sold over a quarter of a million copies of the prayer. I learned something important from that experience. If one responds to a God-given prompting, it is not only associated with inner consolation, it is usually richly blessed. While it is true that 'unless the Lord builds the house, its builders labour in vain' (Ps 127:1), the opposite is also true. As Jesus said: 'No branch can bear fruit by itself; it must remain in the vine. Neither can you bear fruit unless you remain in me' (Jn 15:4). When our actions are prompted by God they are richly blessed.

Appropriately enough, the daily prayer to the Holy Spirit

contained the following request for guidance: 'Father in heaven, yours is a Spirit of truth and love. Pour that same Holy Spirit into my body, my mind and my soul. Preserve me this day from all illusions and false inspirations. Reveal your Presence, your word and your will to me in a way that I can understand. And I thank you that you will do this, while giving me the ability to respond, through Jesus Christ our Lord. Amen.'

Testing the spirits

Among other things, we need to engage in discernment of spirits in order to protect ourselves from the illusions and false inspiration mentioned in the morning prayer. This petition echoes the words of Jesus in the Lord's Prayer where we ask to be delivered from evil, i.e. the malign influence of the evil One. We have already adverted to the way in which St Ignatius discerned which of his two desires came from God. Later he went on to elaborate his rules for the discernment of spirits in great detail. However, St Vincent de Paul felt that they could be encapsulated in four main guidelines which he mentioned in a talk entitled 'True Inspirations and Illusions' on 17 October 1659.

- Firstly: is the prompting contrary to the commandments of God, the church or Sate law? Is it contrary to one's solemn obligations, e.g. marriage or priestly vows?
- Secondly: is there an element of superstition present, e.g. that an action has to be performed so often in such and such a way?
- Thirdly: is the prompting persistent and troublesome in such a way that it makes one uneasy? 'The Spirit of God,' observes St Vincent, 'is a Spirit of peace, a gentle light which infuses itself into the soul without doing it any violence. Its action is sweet and agreeable.' We will know an inspiration is from God 'if it instills itself gently into our souls and inclines us to seek whatever concerns the greater glory of God.'
- Fourthly: Vincent says, 'We should take advice. If a person is graciously, peacefully and quietly receptive to the advice given to him, e.g. by a confessor, spiritual director, or a person exercising legitimate authority, and takes account of it, that is a sign that there is no illusion whatever in what he does.' But if a person receives a prompting which he or she is

unwilling to share with anyone for discernment, it is a bad sign. St Vincent says, 'The Spirit of God inclines those it animates to docility. The Spirit of the gospel is a spirit of obedience.'

Vincent concluded his talk on discernment by saying that he had talked to experts, learned Jesuits perhaps, about the rules for the discernment of spirits. Others could be added, but he thought that these four would suffice. 'All the others,' he said, 'were connected with those I have mentioned.'[18] He felt that if one used a more elaborate method, one might be tempted to become overly introspective. St Vincent practised what he preached. In 1653 one of his priests wrote to him to say that he wanted to leave the Vincentians in order to join the Capuchins. In a letter dated 4 June, Vincent discerned that his desire had not been prompted by the Lord. Firstly, Vincent maintained that having put his hand to the plough in the Vincentians, it was unlikely that the Lord was directing the priest to join another religious community no matter how good it was. 'Another sign,' he wrote, 'which makes me think that God has not called you to the Capuchins, is that the desires which have come to you about this matter trouble and disturb you by their instance, as those suggested by the evil spirit generally do; while on the contrary the inspirations of God are gentle and peaceful, inclining us in a loving way to the good he desires of us.'

A choice between two good options
Even though Christians might try to follow God's will in the less important choices of daily life, they would make a particularly conscientious effort to discover God's will when making the more significant choices in life. This is particularly difficult when there are *pros* and *cons* no matter what decision the person makes. A number of years ago, while living in the US, a woman asked my advice when she was faced with such an invidious decision. Her father had died when she and her three brothers were young children. Her mother had made heroic efforts to raise the kids on her own. Apparently she had asked her teenage daughter to promise that she would never send her to an old folks home. Now some forty years later the mother was living

with her daughter. The strain of looking after her was beginning to have an adverse effect on her health. Recently, her husband had spoken to her about the situation. He pointed to the fact that his mother in law had reached the point where she needed around-the-clock medical supervision. She would receive it in a nursing home. He said that, although he knew about his wife's childhood undertaking, he thought it was time to break it as a promise that the mother should never have asked her daughter to make. He also pointed to the fact that his wife was spending so much time and energy caring for her mother that she was tending to neglect her relationship with himself and their two children. The woman felt caught between a rock and a hard place. She wanted to do God's will, but she didn't know how to be sure what it was.

I told her that I didn't know what the Lord wanted either. But I explained that there was a prayerful method of discovering God's purposes.[19] There were three preconditions. Firstly, she needed a genuine desire to discover God's will. Secondly, she needed to pray to the Lord for the wisdom to make the right decision. Thirdly, she needed to be detached enough not to have a prejudice in favour of one outcome more than the other. Then she should take out a piece of paper and begin by writing down the arguments for and against sending her mother to a nursing home. I explained that it is good to objectify the issues involved in this way. Then she could proceed to prayerfully savour the emotional implications of each course of action. I explained that no matter what she decided, it would have a down side. But whichever option evoked the deepest peace within her was probably the will of God because the Lord's inspirations are normally associated with the consolation of the Holy Spirit (cf. Gal 5:22). Some time afterwards the woman told me that she had followed the methodology, and that after prayerful reflection she felt it was God's will for her to keep her mother at home, at least for the time being. The methodology this woman used could be employed by anyone who is faced by a similar choice.

Charismatic forms of guidance
We will conclude this chapter with a brief look at charismatic

forms of guidance. They are pretty obvious in the Acts of the Apostles. God often revealed the divine will to the early disciples by means of such things as prophecy, dreams, visions, and words of knowledge. In recent years there has been a striking revival of the charisms in the teaching and life of the church. For example, par 25 of the instruction, *Some Aspects of Christian Meditation*, states: 'One has to distinguish between the gifts of the Holy Spirit and the charisms granted by God in a totally gratuitous way. The former are something which every Christian can enliven in himself by his zeal for the life of faith, hope and charity; and thus, by means of a serious ascetical struggle, he can reach a certain experience of God and of the contents of the faith … It is certain that a charism which bears fruit for the church cannot, in the context of the New Testament, be exercised without a certain degree of personal perfection, and that, on the other hand, every 'living' Christian has a specific task and in this sense a 'charism' 'for the building up of the body of Christ' (cf. Eph 4:15-16), in communion with the hierarchy whose job it is 'not indeed to extinguish the Spirit, but to test all things and hold fast to what is good' (*LG*, n. 12).'

Visions and dreams
The bible makes it clear that the Lord can reveal the divine will by means of dreams and visions. Job 33:14-15: 'For God does speak – now one way, now another – though man may not perceive it. In a dream, in a vision of the night, when deep sleep falls on men as they slumber in their beds.' The gospel of Matthew tells us that Joseph, like his Old Testament namesake, received messages from God in dreams, on no less than four occasions. They concerned his marriage to Mary (1:20), the exile of the holy family in Egypt (2:13), their return (2:19), and their decision to settle in Galilee (2:22). On each occasion the revelation enabled Joseph to protect the child Jesus. On Pentecost Sunday, St Peter quoted these words: 'In the last days, God says, I will pour out my Spirit on all people … your young men will see visions, your old men will dream dreams' (Acts 2:17). We find many examples in the lives of the apostles. St Peter was prompted to take the momentous step of preaching the gospel to the gentiles as a result of a vision (Acts 10:11ff). St Paul was led to take a similar

initiative when he came to preach in Europe as a result of a night-time vision or dream (Acts 16:6-11). How different the history of Christianity might have been if Peter hadn't preached to Cornelius and his household, or if Paul hadn't travelled to Greece and Rome.

The Emperor Constantine converted to Christianity as a result of a dream in which Christ appeared to him bearing the first two letters of his Holy Name in Greek. The Lord told Constantine to have these two letters emblazoned on the flags and shields of his army before the decisive battle of the Milvian Bridge in 312 AD. When victory was won, Constantine resolved to become a Christian, and Christianity replaced paganism as the official religion of the Roman Empire. It could be argued that two dreams played an important role in the conversion of the Irish people to Christianity. In his *Confessions* St Patrick tells us firstly how he escaped from captivity in Ireland. 'In my sleep one night I heard a voice saying to me, 'It is well that you fast, soon you will go to your own country. After a short time I again heard a voice saying to me, "Look your ship is ready." It was quite a distance away, about two hundred miles; I had never been to the place, nor did I know anyone there. I ran away and left the man with whom I had spent six years. The power of God directed my way successfully and nothing daunted me until I reached the ship.' When Patrick reached mainland Europe he was eventually ordained a priest. Subsequently, when he was on a visit to his relatives, probably in Britain, he had a second dream. 'It was there one night that I saw the image of a man named Victor, who appeared to have come from Ireland with an unlimited number of letters. He gave me one of them and I read the opening words which were: "The voice of the Irish." As I read the beginning of the letter I seemed at that moment to hear the voice of those who were by the wood of Vocult, which is near the Western sea. They shouted with one voice: "Young man, we ask you to come and walk once more among us." I was cut to the very heart and could read no more, and so I woke up. Thank God, after many years the Lord answered their cry.' Patrick died around the year 480 AD. In every century since then we find saintly Christians have experienced the inspiration of God in their dreams, much as the apostle to the Irish did.

Prophecy

The English word prophecy is derived from the Greek, and refers to 'the speaking forth of the mind and counsel of God' (cf. 1 Cor 12:10; 14:1). It is the declaration of that which cannot be known by purely natural means. It is often the forth-telling of the will of God. It is an inspired word which is directed to a particular person or group at a particular time. Over the years I have seen the gift of prophecy being exercised in a number of ways that reveal the purposes of God. Firstly, a preacher, whether clerical or lay, may be giving a homily or talk. At a certain point s/he seems to speak in a particularly inspired and inspiring way about God's desires (cf. 1 Pt 4:11). It is the kind of word that calls for a response, the Amen of faith and a change of heart and life. Something similar can occur at a meeting where people are discussing some important decision they have to make. At one point a person attending the meeting will make a contribution which is rooted in the gifts of wisdom and knowledge and anointed by the Spirit. It judges the secret thoughts and emotions of the heart, thereby enabling the group to make the correct choice.

Secondly, a person may utter a prophecy at a prayer meeting. It will often begin with the words, 'My people ...' and end with the phrase 'thus says the Lord' or something similar. Over the years I have heard many prophetic utterances. But I suspect that most of them were not genuine. The majority of them were non-prophecies, as opposed to false prophesies, pious sentiments mistakenly expressed in prophetic form. But occasionally I have heard the genuine article, and like the surgeon's scalpel it cuts to the core of one's inner being. More often than not, these prophecies say something about the Lord's attitude to those listening while calling for some specific response. For example, on 23 Aug 1989 I heard someone speak the following prophetic words while attending a bible course: 'My people, I have loved you beyond all imagining. I have chosen you to be here. Just as a shepherd gathers his lambs in his arms, so I have gathered you to myself in this place. I have pitched my tent among you. I am here among you. I am dwelling with you to heal your anxieties and to respond to the cry of your hearts. I am here to satisfy your deepest desires. And then, my people, in the knowledge and strength of my love for you, you will go forth. You will go forth, but not alone, for I myself will take you by the hand. I will lead you to the doors on which you are to knock. And when you knock, my people, just wait patiently. I will raise the latch and lead you across the threshold.'

Thirdly, when a person asks for ministry, such as prayer for inner healing, the one ministering sometimes receives a prophetic word for the other. A few years ago when I asked a Protestant woman to pray for me, she uttered such a word. Part of it said: 'My son, too long you have remained imprisoned by the thoughts and traditions of men and your fear of them, but I am calling you forth into a new place with me. The training I have given you, the dark places through which I have led you, have been but a preparation for far greater things yet. You praise me because of the blessings I have already given you, but this has been but a paddling in the shallows compared with what I wish to do through you, as I call you out to walk on the water with me. It will not be an easy walk my son, but I know your commitment to me and your desire to serve me, so all I ask of you is that you trust me.'

Fourthly, a person can receive a prophetic word of guidance which is addressed to himself or herself rather than to others. I got one such message in 1984 when I was living in the United States. I was travelling by train to a prayer meeting when the Lord said to me in graphic words I have never forgotten: 'Leave the city with its proud flags and go to the breach in the wall. Go and stand in the breach, the place of insecurity. Stand in the breach where the wind blows, where the jackal cries and where the enemy enters under the cloak of darkness. Stand in the breach and listen to my word. Stand in the breach and pray for yourself and the people. Then call my people to the breach to re-build the walls of Jerusalem.' I reflected a great deal on this prophetic word and interpreted it in symbolic terms as a call to recognise the diabolic origin of the present church crisis and to allow myself to experience my vulnerability while relying on the word and power of God. Finally, I felt that the Lord was calling me to work for a new springtime in the church.[20] Of course one could doubt whether this or the other prophecies were genuine. However, they illustrate the fact that God's anointed word usually has a directive dimension, one that reveals the divine will.

Words of knowledge

We will look at this form of revelation in the chapter on the prayer of command. So there is very little need to share much about it here. Suffice it to say that words of knowledge seem to be a supernatural form of infused understanding of an intuitive kind. Charismatics who conduct healing services, or who engage in the ministry of intercessory prayer, are sometimes aided by this gift. I can recall an occasion when the Lord revealed the face of a woman I had met many years before. As I looked at her in my mind's eye, the spirit gave me to understand that her husband had died that day and that I should pray for him and his wife. As I didn't know her married name or address I couldn't check whether the intuition was correct or not. But a few weeks later, a mutual acquaintance told me that the woman's husband had indeed died on the very day I had prayed for him.

Words of knowledge can also assist those who are involved in praying for inner healing. They can receive guidance, in the form of images or factual knowledge, which reveals the root problem, such as a repressed or forgotten memory that may be causing the person's inner suffering.[21] I can recall praying for a woman in her sixties whose presenting problem was arthritis. As I ministered to her I got a sense that her mother had died when she was eleven, that she had been mourning since, and that she was afflicted by a spirit of grief. When I asked her whether this was true, her two daughters who were with her replied in the affirmative. Their grandmother had died when their mother was eleven. She had often said that she had never got over the loss. As a result of that word of guidance I was able to pray in a very specific way for her.

Conclusion

The subject of divine guidance is a very large one. In this chapter we have looked at some, but by no means all, of the ways in which Christians can seek God's will in prayer. I hope you can see that the Christian life is not a matter of cheerless obligation but rather one of joyful conviction. It avoids a purely notional approach which says 'because such and such is objectively true then I ought, must, should, have to do such and such'. Rather it is motivated by love of God and led by the Spirit. Mature

Christians do take objective truths and obligations seriously, but because they are growing in inner freedom they do God's revealed will because they want to. As Augustine observed: 'Love God and do what you will.'

CHAPTER SIX

Prayer as Petition

In the Christian life a pre-eminent way of expressing trust in God is by having a childlike confidence in the power of the prayer of supplication. It can take two forms. Firstly, there is the prayer of petition whereby people pray for their personal needs, and secondly, the prayer of intercession where they pray about the needs of others. One could argue that supplicatory prayer is the fundamental religious act. In the beatitudes Jesus says: 'Blessed are the poor in Spirit, theirs is the kingdom of heaven' (Mt 5:3). In other words, blessed are those who are aware that, as creatures, they ultimately depend on God for all things. This sense of dependence is rooted in a feeling of contingency. It is normally encountered, indirectly, through the experience of material or psycho-spiritual need. Closely related to this creature feeling is a trusting reliance on the providence of God. It is an acknowledgement that God has a benevolent plan for our lives. It also believes that the Lord provides for us and the whole world through secondary causes, as God does for the birds of the air and the lilies of the fields, so that we can all fulfil the divine plan. St Vincent de Paul encapsulated this evangelical attitude when he wrote: 'We ought to have confidence in God that he will look after us since we know for certain that as long as we are grounded in that sort of love and trust we will be always under the protection of God in heaven, we will remain unaffected by evil and never lack what we need, even when everything we possess seems headed for disaster.'[1]

Petition in the Christian teaching
It is also clear from the gospels that petition plays a central role in Jesus' teaching on prayer. It is a striking fact that he says more about the prayer of supplication than any other. It would be a

114

mistake to think that asking prayer, of a truly Christian kind, focuses primarily on human need and only in a secondary way upon the Lord. Instead of looking at God from the point of view of human needs, authentic Christian supplication looks at human needs from the point of view of trusting relationship with a loving and benevolent God. Some books give the mistaken impression that because the prayers of thanksgiving, praise and worship focus on God, they are superior to petition and intercession, which seem to focus primarily on human needs. Although they are distinct, the other forms of prayer are rooted in a creaturely dependence that is expressed in petition. In other words, prayerful appreciation of God is rooted in an appreciation of the gifts of God. It acknowledges that many of them were granted in response to prayers of petition and supplication.

People who have a trusting relationship with God try to become consciously aware of their deepest desires. It could be argued that there are different kinds. First and foremost, from a theological, if not always an experiential, point of view, there is a need for a deeper more personal relationship with God. It can express itself in a heartfelt longing, one which was clearly articulated by St Anselm of Canterbury who wrote: 'Lord, teach me to seek you and reveal yourself to me when I seek you. For I cannot seek you unless you teach me, or find you except you reveal yourself. Let me seek you in longing, let me long for you in seeking: let me find you in love and love you in finding.'[2] Secondly, we can desire all kinds of spiritual and temporal gifts for ourselves, such as inner peace, emotional healing, success in an exam, a well paid job, etc. Thirdly, we can have desires for others, for relatives, friends, neighbours and needy people around the world. As a result we can pray for such things as healing, justice, an end to war, food for famine victims, etc. This will be the focus of attention in the next chapter.

Say what you mean, mean what you say
As was suggested in the chapter on prayer as self-disclosure, it is important to express to God, not just what we want, but also the deep feelings that these needs arouse within us. For example, the father of a sick child would not only ask God to heal her, he would pour out his feelings of anxiety, protectiveness, and love

to the Lord. There is a good example of this kind of heartfelt petition in the Old Testament. Hannah was married to Elkanah. Unable to bear children, she suffered ridicule from her husband's second wife Peninnah, who bore the priest several offspring. On one occasion Hannah went to the temple to implore God for a son. 'As she kept on praying to the Lord, Eli observed her mouth. Hannah was praying in her heart, and her lips were moving but her voice was not heard. Eli thought she was drunk and said to her, "How long will you keep on getting drunk? Get rid of your wine." "Not so, my lord," Hannah replied, "I am a woman who is deeply troubled. I have not been drinking wine or beer; *I was pouring out my soul to the Lord*. Do not take your servant for a wicked woman; I have been praying here out of my great anguish and grief." Eli answered, "Go in peace, and may the God of Israel grant you what you have asked of him."' (1 Sam 1:12-17). Hannah's prayer was answered sometime later when Samuel was born.

It is also important to sense, in a prayerful way, what the Lord feels about the needs and emotions we have talked about, such as compassion, sadness, understanding, etc. This awareness can come through a scripture text or directly in prayer. It enables us to begin to tune into God's attitudes and desires. It may be that, instead of granting our petition as we would wish, the Lord would invite us through on-going neediness, of one kind or another, to 'fill up in our flesh what is still lacking in regard to Christ's afflictions, for the sake of his body, which is the church' (Col 1:24). In doing so, the Lord would give us the inner assurance that we would be enabled to cope, no matter what happened. In Is 41:10 God says: 'Fear not, for I am with you, be not dismayed, for I am your God; I will uphold you with my victorious right hand.'

Thy will be done
One has only to reflect on the passion of Jesus to see what this means. 'During the days of Jesus' life on earth, he offered up prayers and petitions with loud cries and tears to the one who could save him from death' (Heb 5:7). God the Father did not send a legion of angels to shield his charismatic Son from a cruel death. Instead, 'he learned obedience through what he suffered'

(Heb 5:8). Paul had much the same experience. He tells us that he prayed on three separate occasions that the Lord would remove a thorn from his flesh. Scripture scholar Gordon Fee suggests in a tentative way that it may have been an eye complaint (cf. Gal 4:13-15).[3] In any case the Lord said to him, '"My grace is sufficient for you, for my power is made perfect in weakness." Therefore I will boast all the more gladly about my weaknesses, so that Christ's power may rest on me. That is why, for Christ's sake, I delight in weaknesses, in insults, in hardships, in persecutions, in difficulties. For when I am weak, then I am strong' (2 Cor 12:9).

We can get a sense in prayer that, although God is not going to alter the circumstances of our lives, the Lord will use them to develop our characters and to help others. St Paul expressed these sentiments when he wrote: 'We rejoice in our sufferings, because we know that suffering produces perseverance; perseverance, character; and character, hope' (Rom 5:3-4). On another occasion he said: 'Praise be to the God and Father of our Lord Jesus Christ, the Father of compassion and the God of all comfort, who comforts us in all our troubles, so that we can comfort those in any trouble with the comfort we ourselves have received from God' (2 Cor 1:4). Finally, in certain instances, the Lord might give a sense in prayer that sooner or later the Spirit will mysteriously answer our petitions, even to the point of healings and miracles.

The promises of God

Most people ask God for graces and favours. Some do so with great intensity and sincerity. Yet despite Christ's many promises to answer prayer, they often experience disappointment. The ailing child eventually dies. The unemployed relative fails to get a job. The woman enduring arthritic pain continues to suffer. The terrible war continues year after year. Not surprisingly the question is asked: 'Why doesn't God seem to respond to our requests?' Ultimately only the Lord knows (cf. Rom 11:34). That said, Jesus repeatedly promises in the gospels that our petitions will be answered.

To come to terms with this problem we need, firstly, to look at what the bible has to say about the promises of God in general and those to do with petitionary prayer in particular. According to the *New Shorter Oxford English Dictionary* a promise is 'a declaration or assurance by which a person undertakes a commitment to do or refrain from doing a specified act or gives a guarantee that a specified thing will or will not happen, be done, etc'. Promises are usually associated with specified conditions, e.g. 'If you make a down payment of $35,000 by Friday next, and a further payment of $380,000 by 10 May next year, then I promise to sell you my house even if I get a better offer in the meantime.' There are two main reasons why promises are not kept. On the one hand, either the person who made the promise had no intention of carrying it out, or he or she was unable to do so. On the other hand, the person to whom the promise was made may have been either unwilling or unable to meet the stated conditions.

When God makes a promise, God is both willing and able to fulfil it. As Heb 10:23 reminds us: 'He who has promised is faithful.' The author of 2 Tim 2:13 adds: 'God remains faithful for he cannot deny himself.' But, like human promises, the ones God makes are usually associated with conditions. For example, in Ireland we have often prayed for peace. In 2 Chr 7:14 we read this relevant and reassuring promise: '*If* my people who bear my name humble themselves and pray and seek my presence and turn from their wicked way, *then* I will listen from heaven and forgive their sins and restore their country.' In this verse the Lord undertakes to fulfil three promises if and when the people, for their part, fulfil four designated conditions. It is no different in the gospels. In Mt 11:28-30 Jesus promises: 'Come to me, all that are weary and are carrying heavy burdens, and I will give you rest.' Understandably many hassled people stop short at this point by focusing on the reassuring promise. But in the next verse the Lord mentions two conditions. 'Take my yoke upon you, i.e. the great commandment of love, and learn from me; for I am gentle and humble of heart. *Then* you will find rest for your souls.' It is my firm belief that one of the principal reasons why we experience disappointment in petitionary prayer is the fact that while we hear what God promises to do in response to our requests, we often fail either to notice or to fulfil the associated conditions. In the New Testament many overlapping conditions are connected with God's repeated promises to answer prayers of supplication. We will look at ten of them.

Praying in the name of Jesus
Jesus made it clear that prayers of petition had to be offered in his name. In Jn 14:13 we read: 'I will do whatever you ask in my name, so that the Father may be glorified in the Son. If in my name you ask me for anything, I will do it.' Again in Jn 16:23 we read: 'In that day you will no longer ask me anything. I tell you the truth, my Father will give you whatever you ask in my name. Until now you have not asked for anything in my name. Ask and you will receive, and your joy will be complete.' A question arises. What exactly did Jesus mean when he said that we should pray in his name? One thing is sure. He didn't mean that if people added the holy name to their prayers of petition, as an afterthought, as a sort of magic formula, they would automatically receive what they asked for.

A person can only pray in the name of Jesus when he or she does so in the light of a heartfelt awareness of the unconditional mercy and love of God. Normally, this will only come about as a result of a spiritual awakening. There is a growing agreement nowadays that although Catholics have been sacramentalised, many of them have not been fully evangelised. They need an outpouring of the Spirit so that, like Jesus at the Jordan, they may come to know and trust in the incomprehensible love that God has for them. The Irish bishops have observed: 'Perhaps only a minority of people experience this conversion as something sudden; for most people it seems it is more gradual, occurring over a period of time.'[4] Whether sudden and dramatic or slow and incremental, this kind of religious experience inaugurates a heartfelt awareness of the loving presence and power of God in one's life. It is then, and only then, that one can truly pray in the name of Jesus.

What Jesus and, later, the apostle Paul said about petitionary prayer was informed by a vivid awareness of the generosity and faithfulness of God the Father. Those who, like Jesus, enjoy the Abba experience,[5] are consciously aware that the Lord wants what is best for us. This powerful intuition is the key to an understanding of Christian petition. It is expressed in a number of texts. In Lk 15:31 the Prodigal Father says to his elder son: 'You are with me always, *all I have is yours.*' In other words, 'If you related to me, your loving father, in a trusting rather than a dutiful way, you would realise that there is no good gift I would withhold from you. You could have claimed the ring of my authority, worn the cloak of honour, the shoes of freedom, and killed the fatted calf whenever you liked.' On another occasion Jesus said: 'If you parents, who are evil, know how to give good gifts to your children, *how much more will your Father who is in heaven give good things to those who ask him?*' (Mt 7:11). If imperfect parents often go to great lengths to help their children, how much more will a perfect Father in heaven be willing to do what is best for the children of God? Later St Paul echoed those sentiments in Rom 8:32 when he observed: 'If God has given us his Son *would he not give us all things in him?*' If, in his unimaginable goodness, God the Father has given us Jesus as his greatest gift, why should he withhold any lesser gifts? As St Paul said in another place: 'My God will supply every need of yours according to his riches in glory in Christ Jesus' (Phil 4:19). Clearly, St John had personally experienced the unbounded generosity of God promised in the scriptures. He wrote: 'From his fullness have we all received grace upon grace' (Jn 1:16).

Abiding in Christ
This point follows directly from the first. Jesus promises that our prayers of petition will be granted if we abide in Christ and hear his word. In John 15:7 he says: 'If you remain in me and my words remain in you, ask whatever you wish, and it will be given you.' What does Jesus mean by saying we must remain in him? As soon as people experience the incomprehensible mercy and love of God, which was first given in the sacraments of initiation, it is as if the Risen Jesus appears to them and then passes through the walls of their bodies to live within them. As a result they can say with St Paul: 'I no longer live, but Christ lives in me. The life I live in the body, I live by faith in the Son of God, who loved me and gave himself for me' (Gal 2:20). I think that this is what Paul meant when he prayed that Christ might live in our hearts through faith (cf. Eph 3:17). In the seventeenth century St Vincent de Paul gave eloquent expression to this awareness

when he wrote: 'We live in Jesus Christ through the death of Jesus Christ, and we die in Jesus Christ through the life of Jesus Christ. In order to die as Jesus Christ, we must live as Jesus Christ.'[6] Speaking about the immanence of the Lord in a Godly person, Pope John Paul II observes: 'God is present in the intimacy of man's being, in his mind, conscience and heart; an ontological and psychological reality, in considering which St Augustine said of God that he was closer to us than our inmost beings.'[7]

Jesus goes on to add that he will answer our prayers if his words remain in us. What does he mean? If Christ abides in people, they, like him, have to be attentive to the revelatory word of God. In the Ezech 3:3 the Lord said in a symbolical way to the prophet that he should eat and digest the word of God. St Paul had something similar in mind when he said: 'Let the word of Christ dwell in you richly' (Col 3:16). We can chew on and digest the word of God in different ways, such as paying attention to the liturgical readings and praying the scriptures on a regular basis by means of *lectio divina*. In Jn 14:25 Jesus says that he will continue to abide in those who keep his word: 'If anyone loves me, he will obey my teaching. My Father will love him, and we will come to him and make our home with him.'

Regular reception of the Eucharist, the sacrament of God's love, also nourishes the life and expression of Christian charity. As Jesus says in Jn 6:56: 'Those who eat my flesh and drink my blood abide in me and I in them.' John makes it clear that Christ will only continue to abide in people if, having received him in the Eucharist, they love one another in the way Jesus loves them. He wrote: 'No one has ever seen God; but if we love one another, God lives in us and his love is made complete in us. We know that we live in him and he in us, because he has given us of his Spirit' (1 Jn 4:12-13).

Praying without resentment
While it is true that Jesus lives in believers and that God's unconditional mercy is always available to us, it can only be accepted and experienced, in an on-going manner, to the extent that we are willing to extend it to those who have hurt us in one way or another. If we hold on to unforgiveness, the sanctuary

lamp of God's loving presence is quenched in the heart. This is so because resentment is so contrary to God's divine nature. Therefore, it is not surprising to find that, having made a mighty promise about the Father's willingness to answer prayers of petition, Jesus went on to add: 'And when you stand praying, if you hold anything against anyone, forgive him' (Mk 11:25). In another place he said: 'First go and be reconciled to your brother' (Mt 5:24), then come and offer your prayer. The author of 1 Tim 2:8 adds: 'I want men everywhere to lift up holy hands in prayer (e.g. of supplication), without anger or disputing.'

Let's face it, many of those who offer fervent prayers to God, in times of personal, familial or social crisis, often fail to deal with their conscious and unconscious resentments. As a result they can neither consciously abide in Christ or truly pray in his name. Their God is not the God who is experienced inwardly as the One who offers unconditional mercy and love to them, and through them to those who hurt them, but rather the apathetic God of the philosophers. Those who offer prayers of petition to God need to ask the Spirit of truth to search and know them. They do this in order to discover if there is anyone who hurt them in the past who still needs their forgiveness. Because they recognise that to err is human and to forgive divine, they ask God to give them the divine power to forgive over a period of time. As soon as it is sincerely done, there can be such a Spirit-given witness to God's loving presence in the heart, that hesitant faith becomes firm and mountains of difficulty begin to move.

A few years ago I visited Ethiopia. While I was there I heard of a Christian tribe which was vividly aware of the connection between the efficacy of petitionary prayer and reconciliation. If the tribe needed to ask God for a favour they would come together to pray. If an individual was at peace with everyone present he could put a stick upon the ground. However, the villagers could only make their request known to God if and when every person present was able to put his or her stick in a continuous line. If someone had fallen out with a family member or neighbour the onus was on him or her to sort it out. Otherwise the prayer couldn't be offered. Clearly, they had grasped an important aspect of the teaching of Jesus on petitionary prayer.

Praying in harmony with others

This point follows directly from the last. The New Testament makes it abundantly clear that, ideally, the Christian community should be united in mind and heart. In Phil 2:2; 5 St Paul wrote: 'Be of the same mind, having the same love, being in full accord and of one mind ... Let the same mind be in you that was in Christ.' This ideal was echoed in many other epistles, e.g. Rom 15:5-6; 1 Cor 1:10 and 1 Pt 3:8.

When Jesus spoke about petitionary prayer, he wanted it to be offered by individuals and groups who were united with their fellow believers. St Ambrose added: 'Many insignificant people, when they are gathered together and are of one mind, become powerful, and the prayers of many cannot help being heard.'[8] On another occasion Jesus said: 'I tell you that if two of you on earth agree about anything you ask for, it will be done for you by my Father in heaven' (Mt 18:19). Commenting on these verses, Origen (185-254) wrote: 'And this also is the reason why our prayers are not granted, because we do not agree together in all things upon earth, neither in doctrine, nor in conversation. For as in music, unless the voices are in time there is no pleasure to the hearer, so in the church, unless they are united God is not pleased therein, nor does he hear their words.'[9]

I have long believed that good ecumenical relationships are of particular importance in this regard. We need to pray together that inter-church unity will grow. Pope John Paul II has written: 'Along the ecumenical path to unity pride of place certainly belongs to common prayer ... If Christians meet more often and more regularly before Christ in prayer, they will be able to gain the courage to face all the painful reality of their divisions, and they will find themselves together once more in the community of the church which Christ constantly builds up in the Holy Spirit.'[10] The psalmist observes: 'How good and pleasant it is when people dwell in unity ... it *commands* the blessing of the Lord' (Ps 133:1; 3). When Jesus speaks of believers uniting to make a request what is intended here is not so much an agreement in the flesh, the kind that comes about as a result of discussion, as an agreement in the Spirit, the kind that comes about as a result of similar God-prompted inspirations.

Praying with a good conscience
The spiritual reality of points one to four can be jeopardised by a
bad conscience. Not surprisingly, prayers of petition will only
be heard if they are offered by a person with a good conscience.
'Dear friends, if our hearts do not condemn us, we have confidence before God and receive from him anything we ask' (1 Jn
3:21). Again we read: 'We know that God does not listen to sinners, but if anyone is a worshipper of God and does his will,
God listens to him' (Jn 9:31; 1 Pt 3:12). This implies that it is only
when people acknowledge their secret, unconfessed sins, in a
spirit of contrition and a firm purpose of amendment that they
can pray with inner assurance. C. S. Lewis has made the perti-
nent observation that: 'We have a strange illusion that mere time
cancels sins ... But mere time does nothing either to the fact or
the guilt of sin. The guilt is washed out not by time but by repentance and the blood of Christ.'[11] This is so because as soon as they
have made their peace with God their hearts are once again
warmed by the inner assurance of the Holy Spirit who witnesses
to the incomprehensible goodness and benevolence of God.

Associated with this condition is the repeated assertion that
if people keep the commandments their prayers will be answered. As 1 Jn 3:22 says: 'We receive from him whatever we
ask, because we keep his commandments and do what pleases
him.' John makes it clear that the commandments are encapsulated in the great injunction to love one another as God in Christ
has loved us (1 Jn 3:23). It would be a mistake to think that St
John is saying that if we keep the commandments we earn God's
approval and generous response. What he is actually saying is
that those who keep the commandments have a good conscience
and enjoy, in an unimpeded way, the witness of the Holy Spirit
within them.

Praying in accordance with God's will.
Petitions should be in conformity with God's loving and benevolent will. St John comments: 'We have this assurance in approaching God, that if we ask anything according to his will, he
hears us' (1 Jn 5:14). Conversely, Jas 4:3 says: 'When you ask,
you do not receive, because you ask with wrong motives, that
you may spend what you get on your pleasures.' On a number

of occasions the New Testament writers ask God, to reveal the divine will to people. We have examined how the Lord does so in chapter five. Jesus promised: 'Whatever you ask for in prayer, believe that you have received it, and it will be yours' (Mk 11:24). But in Gethsemane he said: 'Abba, Father, everything is possible for you. Take this cup from me. Yet not what I will, but what you will' (Mk 14:36). There are three striking points here. Firstly, Jesus states his belief that God can do all things. He has no doubts about that. Secondly, he states what he himself would want from a human point of view. He would like to avoid his impending passion. Thirdly, he is not sure whether his human desire is in accord with the will of his Father in heaven. In a resigned way that acknowledges his confidence in the inscrutable goodness and benevolence of a loving God, Jesus submits himself, in a spirit of blind faith, to the unfolding of God's will through events, no matter what suffering they might entail.

Ideally, faithful Christians should share in these dispositions when faced by need or adversity of any kind.[12] As Karl Rahner once observed: 'A petitionary prayer which is not thoroughly imbued with Jesus' words before his death: "Let your will be done, not mine," is not a petitionary prayer, not a prayer at all, but at most the projection of a vital need into the void, or the attempt to influence God as if it were by magic, which is senseless.'[13] It should be noted that Rahner's words only apply in cases where God's specific will has not been revealed to the person praying. Not surprisingly, therefore, people attending the Jesuit Novena of Grace are encouraged to offer their petitions to God. But mindful of the importance of praying in accordance with God's purposes, they say: 'If what I ask is not in accordance with your will, or for your greater glory, grant me whatever is in conformity with both.'

Praying in a spirit of humility

On a number of occasions in the Old Testament we are told that Yahweh listens to the prayers of the humble, i.e. those that are realistic and down to earth about their need of God's gratuitous grace and blessings. For example we are told that when Manasseh, the longest reigning king in Israel, was a captive of the King of Assyria he prayed fervently for deliverance: 'In his distress he sought the favour of the Lord his God and humbled himself greatly before the God of his fathers. And when he prayed to him, the Lord was moved by his entreaty and listened to his plea and restored him again to Jerusalem and to his kingdom. Then Manasseh knew that the Lord is God' (2 Chr 33:12-13). It is interesting to note that in many ways Manasseh was the most flawed of the Israelite kings.

In the New Testament we are told in Jas 4:6 that: 'God opposes the proud but gives grace to the humble.' By telling the parable of the Pharisee and the Publican, Jesus made it clear that God hears and answers petitions which are offered in a humble rather than a self-righteous spirit (cf. Lk 18:9-14). The tax collector is clearly a public sinner, but he is a humble one. St Peter endorses his Master's teaching when he says: 'God resists the proud, but shows favour to the humble. Humble yourselves, therefore, under God's mighty hand, that he may lift you up in due time. Cast all your anxiety on him (by means of petitionary prayer) because he cares for you.' (1 Pet 5:5-7)

Praying in a persevering way
On a number of occasions Jesus pointed out that petitions have to be offered in a persevering way. He says in a generic way in Mt 7:7-8: 'Ask and it will be given to you; seek and you will find; knock and the door will be opened to you. For everyone who asks receives; he who seeks finds; and to him who knocks, the door will be opened.' The implication of the Greek is that if we persistently keep on asking, seeking and knocking we will receive. Jesus illustrates what he meant in his parables. Firstly, there is the story of the man whose guest comes visiting at midnight. Because he has no bread to give him, he calls to a friend's house, knocks repeatedly at his door and asks for the loan of some bread. Jesus says that if he persists in asking his neighbour for help, 'I tell you, though he will not get up and give him the bread because he is his friend, yet because of the man's boldness he will get up and give him as much as he needs' (Lk 11:8). Secondly there is the story of the widow and the judge. She keeps on pestering him until he agrees to deal with her son's case. 'And the Lord declared, "Listen to what the unjust judge says. And will not God bring about justice for his chosen ones,

who cry out to him day and night? Will he keep putting them off?"' (Lk 18:6-7). Some years later, St Peter added: 'The Lord is not slow in keeping his promise, as some understand slowness. He is patient with you' (2 Pet 3:9).

Praying with expectant faith

Prayers need to be offered in a spirit of expectant faith. Mark 11:24 says: 'Therefore I tell you, whatever you ask for in prayer, believe that you have received it, and it will be yours.' Sharyn Echols Dowd suggests that this verse could be more accurately translated as 'Keep on believing that you have received everything that you are praying and asking for, and it will be done for you.'[14] In many ways this is a vitally important condition. Verse 24 can only be properly understood in the light of verses 20-23. They are examined in the chapter on the prayer of command. Christopher Marshall points out that in Mark the degree of expectancy referred to in this verse is not the unvarying prerequisite for all answered prayer. 'Rather he affirms that *when* prayer is made with such certitude, it is *always* answered.'[15] The conviction of the person praying goes beyond wishful thinking and merely notional certainty. Such unhesitating faith is firm evidence that the petition is being offered in accord with God's revealed will. As Marshall points out: 'The certainty of faith, in other words, presupposes *revelatory insight* (my italics) into the divine intention, though this must be actualised by the believer's willing commitment to refuse doubt and seek undivided faith (cf. Mk 5:36; 9:22-24).'[16]

There are two forms of trust, hesitant and expectant. A person with hesitant trust accepts God's promises at a notional level, believing them to be true. However, when faced by a particular problem such as an illness, he or she may not be quite sure whether God is going to act, right now, in these specific circumstances. Typically the person prays a prayer of petition in the *hope* that God *may* do something in the *future*, *if* what is asked is in accordance with God's will. As Kathryn Kuhlman, the well known healer, once observed: 'The word of God teaches that faith is a gift ... One of the chief difficulties is the failure to see that faith can be received only as it is imparted to our hearts by God himself. You cannot manufacture it. You cannot work it up.

You can believe a promise and at the same time not have the faith to appropriate that promise ... But we have formed the habit of trying to appropriate by belief, forgetting that belief is mental – while faith is from God.'[17] A person with expectant faith accepts that the promises of God are true at a notional level. But as a result of a divine inspiration, an experiential awareness of God's will in a particular situation of need, s/he has no inner doubt about them, and confidently believes that God is acting in the here and now. The seed of God's response has been planted. Having taken invisible root in the present it will go on to bear visible fruit in the future. Instead of having to see evidence in order to believe, this kind of confident faith believes in order to see.

Praying in a spirit of thanksgiving
We will deal with the prayer of thanksgiving in chapter ten. Suffice it to say in this context that when people pray with expectant faith they can anticipate God's response by means of thanksgiving. St Paul alludes to this aspect of petitionary prayer in Phil 4:6. He says: 'Do not be anxious about anything, but in everything, by prayer and petition, with thanksgiving, present your requests to God.' Paul reiterated this point when he wrote: 'And whatever you do, (including prayers of petition) whether in word or deed, do it all in the name of the Lord Jesus, giving thanks to God the Father through him' (Col 3:17). Paul could look to Jesus as an example of what he meant. When he was standing before the tomb of Lazarus he said: 'Father, *I thank you that you have heard me.* I know that you always hear me, but I said this for the benefit of the people standing here, that they may believe that you sent me' (Jn 11:41-42). Evidently, Paul did much the same. He revealed that: 'We always thank God, the Father of our Lord Jesus Christ, when we pray for you' (Col 1:3).

An example of petitionary prayer in the New Testament
There are numerous examples of effective petitionary prayer in the New Testament. One has only to think of the many needy people who asked Jesus for help. I have thought for a long time that the story of the cure of blind Bartimaeus in Mk 10:46-52 is an archetypal model of petitionary prayer. A fourfold structure is

often evident in gospel healing accounts.[18] There is an acknowledgement of need; a nascent awareness of the good news; a response of expectant trust; and finally a confession of faith. Let's
look at the text. 'Then they came to Jericho. As Jesus and his disciples, together with a large crowd, were leaving the city, a blind
man, Bartimaeus (that is, the Son of Timaeus), was sitting by the
roadside begging. When he heard that it was Jesus of Nazareth,
he began to shout, "Jesus, Son of David, have mercy on me!"
Many rebuked him and told him to be quiet, but he shouted all
the more, "Son of David, have mercy on me!" Jesus stopped and
said, "Call him." So they called to the blind man, "Cheer up! On
your feet! He's calling you." Throwing his cloak aside, he
jumped to his feet and came to Jesus. "What do you want me to
do for you?" Jesus asked him. The blind man said, "Rabbi, I
want to see." "Go," said Jesus, "your faith has healed you."
Immediately he received his sight and followed Jesus along the
road.'

It is quite obvious that Bartimaeus was well aware of his
need. He was materially poor and had no means of support
other than begging. He was marginalised by his physical dis-
ability and by the fact that the Jewish authorities considered him
to be unclean and one of the accursed. His blindness was wrongly
interpreted as a sign of God's displeasure. As a handicapped
person he was often on the receiving end of people's indiffer-
ence, condescension and hostility. Evidently his sufferings
hadn't made him bitter or hopeless. Instead, they had humbled
him and strengthened his desire to be well again. As soon as he
heard that Jesus was passing, he expressed his pent up feelings
by urgently crying out to him for mercy. Implicit in the Greek
text there is the notion of a scream. One is reminded of the
words of the psalmist: 'Out of the depths I cry to you, O Lord; O
Lord, hear my voice. Let your ears be attentive to the voice of my
pleading' (Ps 130:1). Because of his single-minded desire,
Bartimaeus was undeterred by the rebukes of the bystanders.
Instead he shouted even more loudly. Jesus heard him above the
noise of the crowd. He had been anointed by the Spirit to bring
the Good News of God's unconditional and unrestricted mercy
and love to poor people like Bartimaeus and to give sight to the
blind (cf. Lk 4:18). He instructed the apostles to bring the blind

man to him. As soon as he received the Lord's request, Bartimaeus responded immediately. He cast off his cloak, which was symbolic of his willingness to cast off anything that might impede his relationship with Jesus. Then he ran, without being able to see, toward the Lord. In doing this he epitomised what Paul meant when he said years later, 'walk by faith not by sight' (2 Cor 5:7).

He did so because in all probability he had already heard that Jesus had a reputation as a prophet, healer and man of God. Presumably Bartimaeus' faith was strengthened by the fact that instead of presuming to heal him, Jesus made it clear with exquisite sensitivity, that he was there to serve him. He expressed his attitude of empathy and respect by asking Bartimaeus what he wanted. He reverenced that fact that God the Father was already active in this poor man, by his grace. As Jesus himself had said on another occasion, 'No one can come to me unless the Father who sent me draw him' (Jn 6:44). It seems clear that Jesus discerned that ultimately Bartimaeus's petition was the articulation of a holy, God-prompted desire to see Jesus. By relating to Bartimaeus in this way, Jesus not only boosted the blind man's self-esteem, he also revealed to him something of the loving kindness of the heart of our God. This revelation strengthened the blind man's trust in Jesus.

Unlike the man at the pool with five porticos in Jn 5:7, Bartimaeus expressed his growing confidence when he responded without hesitation, 'I want to see.' One could interpret this faith-filled reply in a literal and a metaphorical way. Of course he wanted to see with the eyes of his body, but there is also reason to believe that he also wanted to see Jesus with the eyes of his heart (cf Eph 1:18).

As have already suggested, Jesus discerned that Bartimaeus' desire for healing was the expression of God's will. This recognition evoked firm faith within him, so that he could unhesitatingly address the metaphorical mountain of the man's blindness with an authoritative prayer of command. With the restoration of his sight, the longings of Bartimaeus' heart were satisfied. As Jesus had once observed: 'The lamp of the body is the eye. It follows that if your eye is sound, your whole body will be filled with light' (Mt 6:22). As Bartimaeus' body and soul were illumined, the very first person he saw was the Lord of life standing right in front of him. With the psalmist he could have proclaimed: 'This poor man called, and the Lord heard him and delivered him out of all his troubles' (Ps 34:6). He immediately confessed his faith in Jesus by becoming his disciple and following him along the road.

Elsewhere in the New Testament there are many examples of different forms of petitionary prayer. For example, there are prayers of contrition where people ask God to forgive their sins (cf. Lk 18:13). Others pray for such things as good weather (cf. Jas 5:16-19) or the conversion of an errant sister or brother in the community (cf. 1 Jn 5:16).[19] In each case the fourfold structure is either explicit, or implicit in the account.

A personal example

My first remembered experience of answered prayer occurred when I was nineteen. I had failed Latin in my Leaving Certificate. When I entered the seminary I studied the language for a year as it was a requirement for entry to the university. Although I gave it my best shot I made very little progress. When the university entrance exam was drawing near I was very anxious indeed. I prayed fervently to God asking for help. I reminded Jesus of the adage, 'God helps those who help themselves.' I said, 'Lord, you know that I did the best I could. But I have a mental block as far as Latin in concerned. You are aware that I want to go to university and that I have the ability to get a degree, so please help me now in my moment of need.' Having offered this prayer I added, 'By the way, Lord, if you guided me to revise at least half the exam questions, I would pass.' Then I thought to myself, how will God help me to revise the right questions? After a time it occurred to me that I should stick a pin in my Douai-Reims bible. Whatever page number it opened would be the first of the twenty lines of Virgil we would have to translate the following day. Then I would stick it in a second time, it would land on the first of twenty lines of the Livy we would also have to translate. After that, I would stick the pin into my Roman history book and study the subject matter that chapter dealt with. When I had pondered this apparent inspiration, I got an inner sense that if I asked God to help me, the

Lord would do so. Therefore, I prayed, and stuck a pin into my two Latin texts and history book. Then I memorised the relevant subject matter.

The next day I headed off to do the exam. When I opened the paper, there were the very twenty lines of Virgil I had learned off by heart the night before. As for the Livy, I never did find out where it came from. But the history question was OK, it was the very one I had revised. Subjectively I was quite convinced that the Lord had answered my prayer. I was admitted to the university and three years later I got my degree. Although others might think I had a magical mentality, I don't think so. It was more a naïve and youthful case of wholehearted trust that the Lord would act (cf. Ps 37:5). Over the many years that have elapsed since then, the Lord has continued to answer my prayers, some of them in a remarkable way.

Conclusion

Some time ago I gave a talk on the New Testament's teaching on petitionary prayer. Afterwards I asked the audience for comments. One man said, 'If you are right about the conditions that must be met before petitionary prayers are answered, I can see why so many of us experience disappointment. They are well nigh impossible to fulfil.' I can identify with those sentiments. Jesus' teaching on petitionary prayer is idealistic and demanding. But as many committed Christians have discovered, it is by no means impossible. I have little doubt that when Jesus taught his disciples about the nature, motives and means of offering petitions, he was describing his own way of prayerfully depending on God the Father in his life and ministry. When we strive to fulfil the same conditions we become one in mind and heart with him as he was with the Father. In a very real sense, this enables the Lord who lives within us, by his Spirit, to pray in and through our petitions.

CHAPTER SEVEN

Prayer as Intercession

While there is a good deal of overlap between petitionary and intercessory prayer they are distinct. In the former, people pray about personal needs. In the latter, they pray about the needs that others are experiencing. There are two interrelated forms of intercessory prayer, conventional and charismatic. In this chapter we will deal with both. We will reflect on the nature of biblical intercession and the reasons we have for engaging in it, while suggesting practical ways in which individuals and groups can engage in this important form of prayer.

Intercession in the Old Testament
Many of the great religious figures of the Old Testament, such as Abraham, Moses and Jeremiah, were intercessors. The Hebrew words used to describe this type of prayer means 'to annoy someone with importunate requests.' Intercessors are those who persistently ask God's help for others. The key image used to describe this ministry is that of standing in the breach.[1] In Ezech 22:30, the Lord says: 'I have been looking for someone among them ... to man the breach in front of me, to defend the country.' As the book of Nehemiah illustrates so graphically, a breach in the walls of a city is the place of greatest danger and vulnerability. The intercessor stands in that place of weakness, where the winds of adversity blow, where the jackal of unbridled instinct cries and where the evil one can try to enter under the cloak of darkness. The intercessor prayerfully strives to repel them with the shield of faith and the two-edged sword of God's word.

This kind of intercession is mentioned in a number of texts. For example, in Gen 18:16-33, Abraham acted as a mediator between God and the people by pleading with Yahweh on Sodom's behalf. He implored the Lord not to destroy the city if

even ten just people lived there. Moses was another great model
of intercession on behalf of the people. Jethro, his father in law,
encapsulated the purpose of his role when he said: 'You should
represent the people before God and bring their cases before
God' (Ex 18:19). The *Catechism of the Catholic Church* cites Moses
as the greatest intercessor of the Old Testament, the one on
whom Jesus would later model his intercessory role. Speaking
about him it says: 'He does not pray for himself but for the people whom God made his own. Moses already intercedes for
them during the battle with the Amalekites and prays to obtain
healing for Miriam ... The arguments of his prayer – for intercession is also a mysterious battle – will inspire the boldness of the
great intercessors among the Jewish people and in the church.'[2]
The prophet Jeremiah was another outstanding intercessor. We
are told in a number of texts that he felt called to represent the
cause of his ungrateful people before the Lord.[3] In Jer 42:2 the
people approached the prophet and asked him to pray to God
on their behalf: 'Let your God show us,' they said, 'where we
should go and what we should do.' Jeremiah replied: 'Very well,
I am going to pray to the Lord your God as you request and
whatever the Lord answers, I will tell you.'

Jesus our intercessor

The ministry of intercession in the New Testaments centres
around two great advocates, namely Jesus and the Holy Spirit.
We will look at each in turn. Before doing so we can make three
introductory points. Firstly, it is clear in the gospels that Jesus
admired and modelled his ministry on that of Abraham and
Moses. Secondly, Jesus' intercessory prayer was motivated by
compassion.[4] He was so moved by the sufferings and vulnera-
bilities of the people he met that they evoked a deep-seated emotional response within him. It was this visceral sense of empathy
for the afflicted that motivated his heartfelt prayers on their behalf. Thirdly, as intercessor, Jesus is our advocate. The word has
a legal background. It refers to the way a lawyer acts on a client's
behalf, by expertly and effectively pleading his or her cause.
Jesus is our advocate, our definitive mediator before the Father.
There are a number of examples of his intercessory prayer. We
will look at three of them.

As his passion drew near, Jesus anticipated that although they were full of good intentions, Peter and the apostles would have to cope with strong temptation and disillusionment. In Luke 22:31-32 he declares: 'Simon, Simon, Satan has asked to sift you as wheat. But I have prayed for you, Simon, that your faith may not fail. And when you have turned back, strengthen your brothers.' These are very moving sentiments. Jesus speaks with the kind of knowledge that is rooted in real intimacy, but he does so without any hint of judgement or condemnation. His prayer is suffused with the confidence that it will be heard by the Father because he knows that he is praying in the Spirit in accordance with the benevolent will of God.

The second example is to be found in Jn 17:20-21. It occurred at the last supper when Jesus prayed his high priestly prayer on behalf of the apostles and all those, down the ages, who would trust in him. He said: 'My prayer is not for them alone. I pray also for those who will believe in me through their message, that all of them may be one, Father, just as you are in me and I am in you. May they also be in us so that the world may believe that you have sent me.' It is obvious from this prayer that Jesus had a passion for unity, a yearning that all those who believed in him would be so united in mind and heart that they would be a credible witness to his presence in their midst. As he said: 'For where two or three come together in my name, there am I with them' (Mt 18:20).

The third example of the intercessory prayer of Jesus was uttered on the cross. In Is 53:12 we read, in prophetic words that referred to the messiah to come: 'For he bore the sin of many, and made intercession for the transgressors.' The author of the letter to the Hebrews comments: 'Every high priest is selected from among men and is appointed to represent them in matters related to God, to offer ... sacrifices for sins' (Heb 5:1). That intercession reached a high point when Jesus prayed while we were still his enemies through sin: 'Father, forgive them, for they do not know what they are doing' (Lk 23:34).

Following his death, resurrection and ascension into heaven, Jesus' role as advocate continues. This is made clear in three texts. As 1 Jn 2:1 says: 'We have one who speaks to the Father in our defence – Jesus Christ, the Righteous One.' Heb 7:25 adds that Jesus 'is able to save completely those who come to God through him, because he always lives to intercede for them.' In Rom 8:34 St Paul asks the rhetorical question: 'Who is he that condemns? Christ Jesus, who died – more than that, who was raised to life – is at the right hand of God and is also interceding for us.' 'For those who are in Christ Jesus,' declares St Paul, 'there is now no condemnation' (Rom 8:1). What a consoling thought! No matter how cut off, miserable and misunderstood we may feel, there is always One who prays for us, night and day, 'with loud cries and tears' (Heb 5:7), before the Father in heaven. Mary and the saints are intimately associated with this compassionate intercessory prayer of their glorified Lord. We will return to this topic in a later chapter.

The Holy Spirit and intercession
During his ministry Jesus promised that he would send the Holy Spirit to be our go-between-God. 'I will ask the Father,' he said, 'and he will give you another Advocate to be with you always, the Spirit of truth' (Jn 14:16). Acting in and through our compassionate concerns, the Spirit bears witness to the intercession of the heavenly Jesus. So whenever we pay empathic attention to the sufferings of others, near or far, with feelings of tenderness, protectiveness, understanding, etc., we can become aware of another Presence who sanctifies and transforms our natural emotions in such a way that we share in Christ's concern for others. In this way our hearts become a point of intersection between the travail of the body of Christ on earth, and the intercessory travail of the risen Lord in heaven, through the action of the Holy Spirit.

When people are interceding on behalf of others they will often be able to express their longings in articulate ways in the form of remembered, written, vocal and mental prayers. But there will be times when the pre-conceptual longings of our hearts cannot be put into words. As St Paul said in a memorable passage in Rom 8:26-27: 'In the same way, the Spirit helps us in our weakness. We do not know what we ought to pray for, but the Spirit himself intercedes for us with groans that words cannot express. And he who searches our hearts knows the mind of the Spirit, because the Spirit intercedes for the saints in accordance with God's will.'

Sometimes these inarticulate longings can only be expressed in the form of tears and sighs. One is reminded in this regard of the travail of Jesus at the tomb of Lazarus. John says that he not only wept, 'He was deeply moved in spirit and troubled' (Jn 11:33). Those who have received the gift of praying or singing in tongues – which is a form of pre-conceptual prayer expressed in unintelligible words – can intercede with the lips even when their understanding is shrouded in a cloud of unknowing.[8] They know and believe that the Spirit within them is praying to God beyond, in accordance with the mind and heart of the risen Jesus. It is a form of prayer that is offered without the aid of concepts and images, to the God who lives in light inaccessible. It conforms to the adage in Prov 3:5: 'Trust in the Lord with all your heart and *lean not on your own understanding.*'

When St Paul wanted to describe this form of prayer, he compared it to the travail of childbirth. It is an apt image. The word 'compassion' in the Old Testament is derived from the Hebrew *rachamim* meaning 'womb'. Compassionate intercession is a painful movement of the spiritual womb which longs to give birth to new life in others. As St Paul says: 'We know that the whole creation has been groaning as in the pains of childbirth right up to the present time. Not only so, but we ourselves, who have the first fruits of the Spirit, groan inwardly' (Rom 8:22-23). In the light of this passage, it doesn't surprise me that women I have known over the years seem to have had a particularly deep insight into the nature, purposes and dynamics of compassionate intercession in the Spirit.

Many years ago I attended a charismatic conference in the Royal Dublin Society in Ballsbridge. At one point a priest spoke about the troubles in Northern Ireland. When he had finished he recalled something that John Paul II had said during his visit to Ireland in 1979. 'I ask you for a great, intense and growing prayer for all the people of Ireland, for the church in Ireland, for all the church which owes so much to Ireland. Pray that Ireland may not fail in the test. Pray as Jesus taught us to pray: Lead us not into temptation, but deliver us from evil.'[6] Then he invited the large audience of over two thousand people to spend some time in prayer for the healing of our nation. At one point people began to sing quietly in tongues. They did so spontaneously in a minor key. It was quite haunting to hear a large crowd singing a lament in perfect harmony. It seemed to express the inexpressible sadness and longings of the people in unintelligible words, to a melody that was taking spontaneous shape as they sang it. The whole experience sent shivers up and down my spine. Not only was it beautiful in a strange and poignant way, I had a profound impression that the Spirit was anointing our compassionate desires and that God was doing immeasurably more than we could ask or think, according to his power that is at work within us (cf. Eph 3:20).

Aids to intercessory prayer

In the previous chapter, on petitionary prayer, we examined ten conditions associated with the Lord's repeated promises to answer prayer. Needless to say they are equally relevant where intercessory prayer is concerned. At this point I would like to highlight the importance of two other aids to effective prayer for others, namely, discernment of spirits and fasting.

Discernment of spirits

Those who are familiar with the prayer of intercession stress the fact that anyone who wants to get deeply involved with this form of supplication needs to appreciate the fact that it takes place within a context of spiritual conflict. There is a struggle going on between the kingdom of God and the prince of this world.[7] As St Peter once wrote: 'Be alert, be on the watch! Your enemy, the devil, roams around like a roaring lion, looking for someone to devour' (1 Pt 5:8).

I'm aware of the fact that many modern Christians feel uncomfortable with this worldview which they consider to be anachronistic, an echo of a pre-scientific age. I have argued elsewhere,[8] that while we should reject a simplistic emphasis on the devil and evil spirits, the church teaches that they exist as perverted and perverting beings who are adamantly opposed to God's purposes. For example, Pope Paul VI said in an address: 'The question of the devil and the influence he can have on individual persons as well as communities, whole societies or events, is a very important chapter of Catholic doctrine ... It is a departure from the picture provided by biblical and church teaching to refer to the devil's existence ... as a pseudo reality, a conceptual and fanciful personification of the unknown causes of our misfortunes.'[9] The Pope's views were echoed in *Christian Faith and Demonology*, published by the Vatican in 1975. It states: 'We repeat ... that though still emphasising in our day the real existence of the demonic, the church has no intention ... of proposing an alternative explanation which would be more acceptable to reason. Its desire is simply to remain faithful to the gospel and its requirements.' Those who engage in intercessory prayer need to test everything in order to ascertain what spirit is at work in the situation. As St John says: 'Do not trust every spirit but test the spirits to see whether they belong to God' (1 Jn 4:1). There are two overlapping ways of discerning spirits.

Firstly, there is the charismatic gift mentioned in 1 Cor 12:10. Scripture scholars incline to the view that it is principally an ability to distinguish true from false prophecy. Secondly, there is the art of discernment. It is an ability to establish whether an inspiration was prompted by the human spirit, the evil spirit or the Spirit of God. As we have noted already, it all depends on whether the inspiration was associated with inner desolation or the consolation of the Holy Spirit (cf. Gal 5:22). St Ignatius of Loyola's rules for the discernment of spirits are probably the best-known method of discernment in the contemporary church. In the chapter on seeking God's will in prayer we cited St Vincent de Paul's four point summary of Ignatius' teaching.

Because the evil one knows that intercession is so effective in advancing God's cause, it is not surprising that he attacks intercessors in one way or another through misfortune, ill-health, false inspirations, temptations, etc. Sometimes he will do this as an angel of light, i.e. under the appearance of an apparent good (cf. 2 Cor 11:14). One way or another he will try to undermine their authority. Intercessors need to become aware of these possibilities and to pray for protection against the devil. In Eph 6:16 Paul assures us that 'the shield of faith puts out *all* the fiery darts of the evil one.' In other words, if the person under attack nestles in the Lord through faith, e.g. by means of praise, instead of trying to wrestle with the evil spirit, s/he will be freed from the harmful effects of such things as illusions, false inspirations and temptations.

Discernment of spirits also enables intercessors to become aware of what to pray against in external situations of need. So if they are praying about some issue, such as a war in another country, they need to recognise that the murderous, lying spirit of the Accuser may well be at work. In this context the following New Testament text is particularly helpful. It states: 'For though we live in the world, we do not wage war as the world does. The weapons we fight with are not the weapons of the world. On the contrary, they have divine power to demolish strongholds (of Satan). We demolish arguments and every pretension that sets itself up against the knowledge of God, and we take captive every thought to make it obedient to Christ' (2 Cor 10:3-5). With this assurance in mind, it is advisable to pray a deliverance prayer, one that opposes the oppressive power of whatever evil spirits may be at work in the problematic area the intercessors are concerned about, in order to deliver the people from oppression.[10] Intercessors can silently command them, in the name of Jesus Christ, to yield to the liberating power of God. As St Paul testified in 1 Cor 4:20, 'The kingdom of God is not a matter of talk but of power', i.e. in the Holy Spirit.

Fasting and intercession
It is a striking fact that when Jesus was led into the wilderness to be tempted by the evil spirit, he fasted for forty days. In all probability this kind of mortification not only heightened his awareness of the presence and malign purposes of the devil he would have to contend with throughout his ministry, it also helped him to recognise his false inspirations and to reject them. It is not surprising, therefore, that when the apostles asked Jesus why they hadn't been able to expel an evil spirit from an epileptic boy, Jesus replied: 'This kind can only come out through prayer and fasting' (Mk 9:29). In par. 26 of his encyclical, *Some Aspects of Christian Meditation*, Pope John Paul II has written: 'The Christian fast signifies, above all, an exercise of penitence and sacrifice; but, already for the Fathers, it also had the aim of rendering man more open to the encounter with God and making a Christian more capable of self-dominion and at the same time more attentive to those in need.' Realising this to be true, many people who engage in intercessory prayer become involved in

discreet and prudent fasting. Some live on bread and water on a designated day, while others abstain from all food for part of a day, or for a few days.[11] Many of those who fast in these ways find that they are not only more alert and perceptive from a spiritual point of view, their physical hunger acts as a symbol of their radical need for God's help. As the Magnificat says: 'He fills the hungry with good things' (Lk 1:53).

Interceding as an individual

In Eph 6:18 St Paul says: 'Pray in the Spirit on all occasions with all kinds of prayers and requests. With this in mind, be alert and always keep on praying for all the saints.' The same exhortation is made in 1 Tim 2:1. In my experience there are two ways of interceding as an individual: conventional and charismatic. Non charismatic intercession is the norm. It can occur in a number of ways:

- As a spontaneous prayer which is evoked by some situation of need, e.g. a story on TV.
- As a response to some situation of need one has experienced oneself, e.g. a colleague at work who is a victim of alcoholism.
- Or because someone has asked one to pray about some urgent need, e.g. a marriage that is on the rocks.

Personal prayers of intercession may take the form of short aspirations. They might be offered during a designated part of a person's regular prayer time, e.g. the final fifteen minutes. Occasionally, people may decide to devote all of their personal prayer time to intercessory prayer. Whether regular or irregular, short or long, it is important that intercessors tell God how they feel about the situation and what it is that they desire. If at all possible they should try to tune in to God's feelings and desires about the matter. During quiet moments like these, intercessors can get an inspired sense of God's presence and purposes in a manner that assures them that God will respond to their intercessions in one way or another.

St John illustrates the potential efficacy of intercessory prayer by saying it can bring about repentance in the lives of sinners. He writes in 1 Jn 5:16: 'If you see your brother or sister committing what is not a mortal sin, you will ask, and God will give life to such a one – to those whose sin is not mortal.' The reference, here, to mortal sin, is not to 'ordinary' grave sins but to some extremely deadly sin such as the sin against the Holy Spirit or apostasy. For example, in Heb 6:4-6 we read: 'It is impossible for those who have once been enlightened, who have tasted the heavenly gift, who have shared in the Holy Spirit, who have tasted the goodness of the word of God and the powers of the coming age, if they fall away, to be brought back to repentance, because to their loss they are crucifying the Son of God all over again and subjecting him to public disgrace.' The Johannine author is speaking about intercessory prayer. He hasn't intercessions in general in mind, but rather prayer for a non-schismatic member of the community who has fallen into some kind of public sin, e.g. robbery or sexual promiscuity. If members of the community pray with the kind of expectant faith already mentioned, 1 John 5:16 promises that the prodigal will eventually come to his or her senses, and will repent.

There is a good example of this kind of intercession in St Augustine's *Confessions*. His mother Monica prayed for years for her brilliant but wayward son. He was young, lustful and interested in heretical beliefs. She was so upset by his behaviour that she would not even dine with him. In book nine of his *Confessions*, he tells us that his mother prayed from the heart with many tears, sometimes with her face pressed to the ground. He also informs us that during this period of fervent intercession she had a prophetic dream. In retrospect, he was convinced that the dream had been prompted by God. 'She dreamed that coming toward her in a halo of splendour she saw a young man who smiled at her in joy, although she herself was sad and quite consumed with grief. He asked her the reason for her sorrow and her daily tears, not because he did not know, but because he had something to tell her, for this is what happens in visions. When she replied that her tears were for the soul I had lost, he told her to take heart for, if she looked carefully, she would see that where she was, there also was I. When she looked, she saw me standing beside her.'

Monica told Augustine about the dream. He tried to interpret it to mean that she would stand beside him by sharing his theological point of view. She replied at once and without hesitation

'No, he did not say "Where he is you are," but, "where you are, he is".' As a result of the dream she was prepared to eat with him again. But nothing happened for nine years. In the mean-time Monica continued to pray. She was a model of persistence in intercessory prayer. Augustine tells us, 'All the time this chaste, devout, and prudent woman, a widow such as is close to your heart, never ceased to pray at all hours and to offer you the tears she shed for me. The dream had given new spirit to her hope, but she gave no rest to her sighs and her tears. Her prayers reached your presence and yet you left me to twist and turn in the dark.' But nine years later, Monica's prayers were finally an-swered. One day Augustine heard a child skipping and singing, 'take and read, take and read.' When he looked at his open bible he read a passage from Rom 13:13-14: 'Let us behave decently, as in the daytime, not in orgies and drunkenness, not in sexual im-morality and debauchery, not in dissension and jealousy. Rather, clothe yourselves with the Lord Jesus Christ, and do not think about how to gratify the desires of the sinful nature.' Augustine was converted. He says: 'I went in to my mother and told her, to her great joy, how it had come about. She was filled with triumphant exultation.' The impossible had actually hap-pened; the professor had finally found his master. A short time later he was baptised by St Ambrose in Milan.

Charismatic intercession

There are other individuals who rely on the charisms of revela-tion, such as wisdom, knowledge, prophecy, dreams, visions and inspired scripture readings, to guide their intercession. I tend to use the following simple method.

1. Become aware of the presence and power of God.

2. Ask the Holy Spirit to fill you and to guide your time of in-tercession.

3. Spend some time in worship by thanking, praising and adoring the Lord.

4. Allow the issues and concerns that are in your heart to sur-face. Express your feelings and desires to the Lord.

5. Then blank your mind and ask the Spirit to guide your prayer by means of the charisms of revelation such as an in-spired thought, a vision, word of knowledge, or scripture reading.

6. If no charismatic guidance seems to be forthcoming, intercede in an agnostic way in tongues, in the belief that the
Spirit within is praying to God above.

7. As the time of intercession comes to an end, thank God for
the graces received.

I can remember an occasion when my intercession was guided
in a charismatic way. A number of years ago I met a doctor
named Kenneth McAll. He was the author of a well-known book
entitled *Healing the Family Tree*.[12] We talked for hours about his
belief that the unresolved problems of ancestors can continue to
afflict the living. He maintained that healing can come as a result
of having a Requiem Mass offered for the deceased. I told him
that I was sceptical about the notion that troubled spirits can impinge on the minds and wills of their descendants. At the end of
our conversation Dr McAll suggested that I spend a quiet time
in intercessory prayer for the dead. He urged me to have no
fixed agenda and to allow the Spirit to lead. Shortly afterwards I
did what he recommended. I can recall that as soon as I turned
to the Lord a vivid image came to mind. I could see the surface
of the ocean. Sad sighs seemed to be released from its watery
depths. I felt as if I were hearing the still, sad lamentation of
thousands of Africans who had been dumped into the sea by the
crews of slaving ships in the past. I was deeply moved by this
experience, and prayed for all those forgotten people, asking the
Lord to enable them to rest in peace. I also prayed that the Lord
would forgive those who so cruelly mistreated them. Although
that time of prayer failed to convince me that the spirits of the
restless dead can affect the living, I was convinced that the Spirit
can reveal God's will to our hearts, so that we may pray in
accordance with God's compassionate purposes.

Group intercession
In Heb 10:25 we read: 'Let us not give up meeting together, as
some are in the habit of doing.' One of the motives for such gatherings is to pray for others. There are conventional and charismatic ways of doing this. Conventional group intercession is the
norm. The best-known form is the prayer of the faithful which
follows the readings and homily at the Eucharist. It is introduced and concluded by the celebrant. Par. 45-46 of the *General*

Instruction of the Roman Missal has this to say about it. 'In the general intercessions or prayer of the faithful, the people, exercising their priestly function, intercede for all humanity. It is appropriate that this prayer be included in all Masses celebrated with a congregation, so that petitions will be offered for the church, civil authorities, those oppressed by various needs, all young people, and for the salvation of the world. As a rule the sequence of intentions is to be:

    a) For the needs of the church
    b) For public authorities and the salvation of the world
    c) For those oppressed by any need
    d) For the local community.

In particular celebrations such as confirmations, marriages, funerals, etc., the series of intercessions may refer more specifically to the occasion.' Conventional prayer groups, and there are many of them, would do well to keep these guidelines and the promises of scripture in mind when offering prayers for others.

Charismatic guidance

Charismatic prayer groups seem to have a deep understanding of the importance and dynamics of intercessory prayer. To a greater or lesser extent they devote time to it. Sometimes a period is set aside at the end of a meeting for intercession. On other occasions a whole meeting may be devoted to this form of prayer. Then there are intercessory groups, such as Women Aglow, and the Lydia Fellowship, which specialise in intercession. Audrey Merwood has described their method of praying in her book *The Way of an Intercessor*.[13] There are sites on the Internet where intercessors from all over the word can communicate.

    I have found that many of those who are involved with intercessory groups are female. They consist of a relatively small number of people who feel called by God to become involved in the difficult and demanding ministry of intercessory prayer. The members need to be mature from a human and spiritual point of view, with an experiential grasp of discernment of spirits and spiritual combat. Many of them will have prayer partners, soul friends who support them emotionally and spiritually. In this way they try to shield one another from the wiles of the evil one. By and large, when they come together to pray, they follow an outline similar to that which is used by individuals. They high-light the importance of vigorous praise, receiving charismatic guidance and praying in tongues.

Sometimes a group will feel that they are being called to pray for some particular intention on an on-going basis, such as a particular political leader (cf. 1 Tim 2:1), for reconciliation in a particular community, for revival and renewal in the churches,[14] etc. They will try to find out what they can about the issues that concern them, and to discern what kind of prayer is needed. For example, they may feel that they have to pray against evil spirits of pride, resentment, hatred, condemnation and the like which may be oppressing people's minds and wills. It takes great faith to pray like this, because frequently the group will not be sure whether they are praying for the right intentions or whether their prayers are being granted. They simply trust in the Lord. However, every now and then they may discover just how well directed and effective their prayers have been.

For example, I attended an ecumenical conference in the North of Ireland a few years ago. Toward the end of one of our days together a small group met to intercede. One of them was led to pray for a very specific area in Belfast. She felt that a bomb was going to be planted there in the near future. When the group completed their time of intercession they invited the rest of us to pray about the problem. The following day we read in the newspapers how, the night before, a family in Belfast had been hosting a prayer meeting in their home when a number of paramilitaries knocked at the door. When it was answered, they brushed the man of the house aside, rushed in and held every-one captive. They took the householder's car keys and stole his vehicle which they later used to plant a bomb in the very area of Belfast that the intercessors had been led to pray about the night before. The newspaper reported, however, that, inexplicably, the primed bomb had failed to go off. Joyfully, we thanked the Lord. We knew why it had not exploded.

Conclusion

Many of those who are involved in the ministry of intercessory prayer will testify that it is one of the deepest, most demanding and mysterious forms of prayer. A number of years ago I attended

an ecumenical conference in Belgium. The late Cardinal Suenens
gave a memorable homily during which he spoke about the importance of intercession. To illustrate his point he cited a text in
Is 62:6-7 which reads: 'I have posted watchmen (i.e. intercessors)
on your walls, O Jerusalem (i.e. the people of God); they will
never be silent day or night. You who call on the Lord, give
yourselves no rest, and give him no rest till he establishes
Jerusalem and makes her the praise of the earth.' In the Old
Testament, therefore, the Lord called on intercessors to pray urgently and unceasingly that the breaches would be repaired.
This metaphor symbolically signified the restoration, revival
and renewal of God's people in and through the Lordship of
Jesus Christ.

CHAPTER EIGHT

The Prayer of command

In the last two chapters we noted how the prayers of petition and intercession are rooted in a creaturely sense of dependence on the providential plan and provision of God. That same sense of dependence can find expression in a related but distinct form of prayer. When faced by the needs of others, this kind becomes so identified with the love and will of God that supplication expresses itself in the form of the prayer of command. It is usually, though not always, uttered in ministry situations in order to move metaphorical mountains of difficulty, either physical, such as an illness, or spiritual, such as demonic oppression. In the name of Jesus the praying person orders the problem to yield to the will and the power of God. This form of prayer tends to be overlooked in many books on prayer. This is surprising in view of the fact that not only did Jesus pray in this way on many occasions, he authorised those who believed in him to do the same in his name. We will look at each of these points in turn.

Jesus and the prayer of command
There are many instances of the prayer of command in the ministry of Jesus. Instead of looking at an exhaustive list of examples, we will mention three representative texts which illustrate how Jesus used the prayer of command to heal, exorcise and to perform miracles. In Mk 1:41 a leper came to ask Jesus for help. We are told that Jesus was moved with compassion and 'stretched out his hand and touched him and said to him … *Be made clean.*' On another occasion a distraught father brought his epileptic son to Jesus. Having expressed his frustration and disappointment at the apostles' lack of faith, Jesus said: 'Bring him here to me. And Jesus *rebuked the demon*, and it came out of him, and the boy was cured instantly' (Mt 17:18). Finally, the gospels

indicate that Jesus performed many miracles. For example, on one occasion the apostles woke up Jesus who was fast asleep in the stern of a boat. 'Master, master, we are perishing,' cried the apostles. And he woke up *and rebuked the wind and the raging waters*. They ceased and there was calm' (Lk 8:24). Speaking to Cornelius, Peter summarised the ministry of Jesus when he said: 'You know what has happened throughout Judea, beginning in Galilee after the baptism that John preached – how God anointed Jesus of Nazareth with the Holy Spirit and power, and how he went around doing good and healing all who were under the power of the devil, (by means of the prayer of command) because God was with him' (Acts 10:37-38).

Jesus commissioned and authorised the apostles, and those who believed in him to pray the word of command in his name. In Jn 14:12 he makes this astounding promise: 'I tell you the truth, anyone who has faith in me will do what I have been doing. He will do even greater things than these, because I am going to the Father.' Although some writers, such as Rudolf Bultmann, interpret this promise in a reductionist way to refer only to effective preaching, Raymond Brown and others have suggested that it should be interpreted in a more literal way to include possible deeds of power such as healing and exorcism.[1] We will look at some corroborative texts, in which Jesus spelt out what he meant. Then we will go on to comment on their meaning and implications.

In Mk 11:12-14 we are told how Jesus cursed a fig tree. Then in Mk 11:20-23 we are informed that: 'In the morning, as they went along, they saw the fig tree withered from the roots. Peter remembered and said to Jesus, "Rabbi, look! The fig tree you cursed has withered!" "Have faith in God," Jesus answered. "I tell you the truth, if anyone says to this mountain, 'Go, throw yourself into the sea,' and does not doubt in his heart but believes that what he says will happen, it will be done for him."' There are a number of related texts which can be added to this foundational one. In Mt 17:20 Jesus says: 'I tell you the truth, if you have faith as small as a mustard seed, you can say to this mountain, "Move from here to there" and it will move. Nothing will be impossible for you.' Later he promises: 'I tell you the truth, if you have faith and do not doubt, not only can you do

what was done to the fig tree, but also you can say to this mountain, "Go, throw yourself into the sea," and it will be done' (Mt
21:21). In Lk 17:6 we read: 'If you have faith as small as a mustard seed, you can say to this mulberry tree, "Be uprooted and
planted in the sea," and it will obey you.' Finally, before ascending into heaven Jesus gave the believers the commission to
preach the Good News to the whole of creation. Then he encapsulated his teaching on the prayer of command when he indicated
how it could be used, in different forms of ministry, as a demon-
stration in deeds of the coming of the kingdom which had already been proclaimed in the Good News: 'And these signs will
accompany those who believe: In my name they will drive out
demons … they will place their hands on sick people, and they
will get well' (Mk 16:17-18).

The prayer of faith and deeds of power
At this point we will concentrate on Mark's teaching in 11:12-14
and later in 11:20-23 because of its central importance. In the first
episode we are told that: 'The next day, as they were leaving
Bethany, Jesus was hungry. Seeing in the distance a fig tree in
leaf, he went to find out if it had any fruit. When he reached it,
he found nothing but leaves, because it was not the season for
figs. Then he said to the tree, "May no one ever eat fruit from
you again." And his disciples heard him say it.' This was a
prophetic action which was intended to express divine displeasure with the people's lack of fruitfulness, their manifest failure
to either repent or to accept Jesus or his teaching. The saying
about the withered fig tree foreshadowed the destruction of the
temple and the manifestation of the power of God. The believing
community would eventually replace the temple as God's
'house of prayer.'[2] One is reminded in this context of the words
of Paul, which echoed those of Jesus in Jn 4:2-23: 'Do you not
know that you are God's temple and that God's Spirit dwells in
you?' (1 Cor 3:16).

Many scripture scholars agree that the phrase 'have faith in
God,' in the succeeding episode, is the interpretative key to the
Lord's extravagant promise in Mk 11:20-23.[3] It emphasises the
necessity of expectant faith in uttering effective prayers of command. However the scholars are not agreed about the way in

which it should be translated. Having considered the different possibilities, Christopher Marshall says that this phrase represents a summons to participate in the activity of God as a result of having firm trust in the Lord.[4] Speaking about the same verse Sharyn Dowd has observed: 'Faith is the worldview that attributes to God the power to do the impossible.'[5] Central to this understanding is the counter-cultural belief that God can do all things, and that the Lord will indeed perform mighty deeds in and through those who have firm confidence in the promises and power of God. Dowd has clearly demonstrated that in the New Testament era some people, such as the Epicureans and Academics, denied that all things were possible to God. This view has become even more widespread in modernist and post-modernist culture which tends to deny the possibility of divine influence in the laws of nature.

What exactly did Jesus mean when he stated: 'I tell you the truth, if anyone says to this mountain, "Go, throw yourself into the sea," and does not doubt in his heart but believes that what he says will happen, it will be done for him' (Mk 11:23)? In Jewish thinking the notion of moving mountains was used as a metaphor for feats of an exceptional, extraordinary or impossible nature. It is probable that the mountain Jesus had in mind was the stubborn unbelief of the Jewish people of his day. His teaching was rooted in the Old Testament conviction that to establish or to move a mountain was the work of God alone. In this passage, however, Jesus says that God's power will be active in and through believers who pray with even a mustard seed of unhesitating faith.

Hesitating and unhesitating faith
For many years now I have been intrigued by the particular phrase which speaks about the believer 'who does not doubt in his heart, but believes that what he says will happen.' St Cyril of Jerusalem (c. 315-386) pointed out in one of his catechetical sermons that the word 'faith' had two meanings. 'First of all, it is concerned with doctrine and it denotes the assent of the soul to some truth.' Then he added, 'The word "faith" has a second meaning: it is a particular gift and grace of Christ.'[6] He went on to explain that this gift is a form of firm trust which reaches its

most intense form in mountain moving faith. Typically, Christians experience two degrees of trust, hesitant and unhesitating.

A person with hesitant trust accepts God's promises at a notional level, believing them to be true. However, when faced by a particular problem such as an illness, s/he may not be quite sure whether God is going to act, right now, in these particular circumstances. So the person prays a prayer of *petition* in the hope that God may do something in the future, if what is asked is in accordance with the divine will, e.g. 'Lord I know that nothing is impossible to you. I ask you, if it is your will, to heal this person whom you love.'

A person with expectant faith accepts that the promises of God are true at a notional level. But as a result of a divine inspiration in a particular situation of need, e.g. as a result of a living word from scripture, a graced intuition, or an interior picture, he or she has no lingering doubts about the promises of God (1 Jn 5:14-16), and confidently believes that the Lord is acting, or soon will act. Often such a person prays a declaratory prayer of *command* rather than a supplicatory prayer of petition (Mk 11:23; Lk 17:6). Instead of having to see evidence in order to believe, this kind of confident faith believes in order to see. For example, the person might pray as follows. 'I say to this sickness, in the name of the Lord Jesus Christ, be healed. May the light of God's power so shine within you that your immune system may be enabled to overcome this disease. And I thank God that even now this prayer is being answered. Amen.' The future hope of a prayer of command like this is rooted in present conviction. As the letter to the Hebrews 11:1 puts it: 'Faith is the assurance (in the present) of things hoped for (in the future), the conviction (in the present) of things not seen (in the future).'

Speaking of St Paul's reference to faith in 1 Cor 12:9, scripture scholar James Dunn writes: 'Paul presumably has in mind that mysterious surge of confidence which sometimes arises within a man in a particular situation of need or challenge and which gives him an inspired certainty and assurance that God is about to act through a word or through an action.'[7] I would suggest that the gift of expectant faith can be defined in the following way. It is not a sanctifying grace. It is freely granted to some people, by the Holy Spirit, for the sanctification of others. It is rooted in the revelatory gifts of wisdom, knowledge and discernment of spirits (cf. 1 Cor 12:8:10). It enables believers in particular situations to know with trusting conviction, of a heartfelt and expectant kind, that in answer to either a prayer of petition, intercession or command, the unconditional mercy and love of God will be manifested through a deed of power such as an exorcism, healing or miracle. Such manifestations of God's glory are anticipations, in the present, of the future transformation of all things in the Second Coming of Christ.

An anatomy of expectant faith

The following ten-point analysis examines the gift of unhesitating faith in greater detail.

1. The gift of unhesitating faith is not granted for self-sanctification, but for the sanctification of others. It is not necessarily a sign of personal holiness.

2. Instead of focusing on the *existence* of God, this form of faith focuses on the saving *activity* of God in accordance with the divine nature and promises.

3. The Holy Spirit gives the gift to *some* people. In my experience it is more likely to be granted to those who have experienced a spiritual awakening, an in-filling of the Holy Spirit (Eph 5:18). It pre-disposes them to receive the gifts mentioned by Paul in 1 Cor 12:8-10, including the gift of unhesitating faith.

4. No one can presume to have the gift of unhesitating faith in every demanding situation. It is given in accordance with the providence of God in *particular* situations. The Jesus of Mark's gospel understands faith to mean that the community is persistent in maintaining its worldview even when their prayers seem to be unanswered. Like Jesus in Gethsemane they say on the one hand, 'Abba, Father, *all things are possible to you*' (Mk 14:36), while saying on the other hand, 'yet not what I will, *but what you will*' (Mk 14:36).[8]

5. Implicit in point four are two notions of time: secular, unredeemed time in which we experience our on-going problems of a chronic nature, and the sacred time of the Lord, in which we experience the manifestation of God's salvation and healing.

6. Heartfelt faith is evoked by inspired knowledge rather than being directly willed. For example, one can receive a graced inward awareness of what God wants to do. Revelations of this kind *evoke* trust of a convinced and expectant kind, which is quietly and effortlessly certain about what is happening or is soon going to happen. This volitional certainty often involves an associated form of emotional conviction. It can vary in intensity from weak to strong feelings of certainty. Reference to the mustard seed of faith seems to imply that even expectant faith of a relatively weak kind can be enough to utter an effective prayer of command.

7. We noted that trusting faith of the wishful kind prays in the *hope* that something *may* happen in the *future*, if it is in accord with a notional knowledge God's will, whereas expectant faith of an unhesitating kind, offers either a prayer of petition (Mk 11:24), supplication or command (Mk 11:23), with the *conviction* that God *is* acting in the *present* in accord with divine inspirations and promises.

8. It is God who responds to the prayer of petition, supplication or command, and performs a deed of power, either by granting the petition – perhaps in a remarkable way, for instance, by converting a sinner – or by performing a deed of power, such as an exorcism, healing or miracle.

9. Epiphany situations of this kind manifest the loving kindness of God in two encouraging ways. Firstly, they demonstrate in deed what has been proclaimed in word. Secondly, those who exercise the gift of faith in their ministry almost invariably relate in a compassionate way to needy people. That compassion not only prompts a heartfelt desire to see a deed of power occur – often of a therapeutic kind – it animates such deeds when they do occur. The person who prays or ministers is closely united to the compassionate heart of the Lord, and 'has that mind which was in Christ Jesus' (1 Cor 2:16). We will return to this notion later in the chapter.

10. According to Cyril of Jerusalem, deeds of power, of whatever kind, are forms of realised and final eschatology. In other words, they are fleeting but real anticipations, firstly, of the victory of Jesus over Satan, sin, suffering and death. Secondly, they are intimations of the transformation of all

things in the Second Coming of Christ. As Peter says, 'According to his promise we wait for new heavens and a new earth, in which righteousness dwells.' (2 Pt 3:13).[9]

Praying within one's measure of faith

When uttering prayers, whether of petition, supplication or command, we need to do so within 'the measure of faith' (Rom 12:3) that God has given us. If it is a hesitant, notional kind of believing faith, we need to pray in a more tentative way. If, however, one is granted the gift of unhesitating, trusting faith either of a weak or a strong variety, then one can venture to pronounce a prayer of command. It is important that whatever prayers are said, we avoid presumption. Over the years I have found that one can say a prayer of command that lies half way between hesitant and unhesitating faith. For example, one might say something like this. 'Lord, nothing is impossible to you. In your name I say to this sickness, yield to the healing power of God at work within you. May the Holy Spirit, the Lord and giver of life, hasten to accomplish God's loving and life-giving purposes within you. And I thank you, Lord, that even now divine grace is at work in this situation. Amen.' Notice that such a prayer is non-specific. While affirming in a *general* sense that God is at work in the situation it does not directly address a *particular* illness, e.g. cancer, by telling it with thanksgiving to go. The beauty of a prayer like this is twofold. Firstly, it allows one to go to the limit of the measure of faith one currently experiences. Secondly, it disposes the heart to receive a revelation of God's will in this particular situation of ministry. This could authorise the praying person to utter a more specific command with the new measure of expectant faith which has been prompted by God.

The propensity to pray beyond the measure of faith one has actually received from the Lord can have two possible roots. Firstly, the person praying may have a messianic complex. Instead of desiring to bring glory to God, this kind of religious egotism secretly wants to bring glory to itself. As renowned American healer, Kathryn Kuhlman, once wrote: 'There are many who mix the ingredients of their own mental attitude with a little confidence, a little pinch of trust, a generous handful of religious egoism, quote some scripture, add some desire – then mix it all together and label it faith.'[10] Secondly, presumption can have its origins in a fundamentalist approach to the promises of God. It maintains that because God has promised such-and-such in scripture it *has* to happen. Again as Kathryn Kuhlman observed: 'Mind belief is nothing more than deep desire combined with mental assent. Heart belief is faith. It's warm. It's vital. It throbs. Its power is absolutely irresistible when it is imparted to the heart by the Lord.'[11] Instead of manifesting a strong faith in the heart, perhaps this almost desperate need to see deeds of power actually belies a lack of trust. Not surprisingly, these misguided forms of prayer, more often than not, fail to produce the desired results. But instead of admitting their own shortcomings, people who pray in these presumptuous ways often blame those they are praying for, for lacking faith. So instead of relieving their present problems, they add to them by stimulating feelings of guilt.

Promises fulfilled: A personal experience
In my late twenties I experienced a spiritual awakening. As a result Jesus became very real for me. My God was no longer the remote God of the philosophers, but rather the God of the bible, the loving One who is near and always active. This notion of God's dynamic activity is encapsulated in Goethe's well-known poem. When Faust was translating the first verse of John's gospel he began by writing: 'In the beginning was the Word!' Then he tried, 'In the beginning was the Thought!' Then he went on to, 'In the beginning was the Power!' Finally he wrote: 'The Spirit is helping me! I see now what I need and write assured: In the beginning was the Deed.'

Some time after my spiritual awakening I became intrigued by the words of Jesus in Mark 11:20-23. For months I read that amazing promise over and over again and prayerfully pondered its meaning. I wondered why I hadn't seen any obstacles move as a result of my own prayer or the prayer of anyone I knew. After a while, one point began to stand out. I noticed that there were conditions attached to Christ's promise. God would respond to my prayers if I had no doubt or hesitation in my heart and believed that I was already receiving what I was seeking.

But when I reflected on this point I realised that, while I had no problem believing at an intellectual level that God could respond to my prayers of command, or intercession, I found that at an experiential level I was always troubled by doubts. I was never quite sure that God wanted to respond to this particular prayer, in this particular situation, for this particular person. I was praying with hope about what God might do in the future rather than with firm conviction about what God was doing in the present.

Over the following months I also noticed that my ability to firmly believe in the promise of Christ was compromised by vague, unresolved feelings of unworthiness. This problem became apparent when I was asked to speak to a group about the in-filling of the Holy Spirit. After the talk, I was expected to pray for the people that they might experience such an out-pouring of the Spirit in their lives. I was confident enough that I could give a reasonably good teaching, but I was really apprehensive about the time of ministry. What if nothing happened? The people might think I was a man of words but devoid of spiritual authority. As St Paul said in 1 Cor 4:20: 'For the kingdom of God does not consist in talk but in power.'

The day before I was due to give the talk I had a vivid dream. I found myself standing in the sanctuary of a small church. I could see that a badly crippled boy was lying in the corner. Then the door burst open and in leaped St Francis of Assisi with some of his companions. He was radiant with joy and my attention and admiration was rivetted on him. Then Francis saw the handicapped boy and gestured to me and to the others to join him in praying for the lad. He told me to put my hands on the victim's knees, while he put his hands on his head. As we prayed I kept looking at Francis. I saw him as the reincarnation of the presence of Jesus. I was confident that his prayers would be effective. I was thrilled when I could feel the boy's bones moving beneath my fingers. I glanced downwards and thought to myself, 'Thank God Francis is here; this boy will soon be healed.' Then I looked up and, to my dismay, Francis and the others had disappeared. I thought to myself, 'What a terrible pity. The healing isn't complete yet.' Then I woke up.

When I reflected on the meaning of the dream I could see that it illustrated the dilemma I was facing the following day. I felt that the Lord could only act through extremely holy people like St Francis, but not through a flawed person like myself. Incidentally, it has since occurred to me that the crippled boy was an image of myself, the one who is in need of inner healing. Later that same day I happened to be teaching a scripture class. We were studying Philippians, chapter two. Eventually we reached verse thirteen, which reads: 'For it is God who works in you to will and to act according to his good purpose.' Spontaneously I banged the desk and said, 'That is it, that is the assurance I have been looking for!' My pupils didn't know what I was talking about. I apologised, and explained that for personal reasons verse thirteen meant a lot to me. I knew that the Lord was telling me that God was indeed acting in and through me to do two things, to know the Father's will and to carry it out. I was re-assured. The Lord would be with me that evening, helping me not only to give a good talk, but also to pray effectively for the people.

In the event I gave a reasonably good talk, but when it came to the time of ministry, I lacked confidence. Afterwards, when I reflected on the situation, I realised that I found it hard to affirm the fact that God was at work within me, because I felt unworthy of divine grace. Clearly, I was unable to appropriate the power of Phil 2:13 because of unresolved feelings of guilt. Shortly after this realisation I happened to come across Rom 8:1 which says: 'Therefore there is now no condemnation for those who are in Christ Jesus.' These words leaped off the page into my heart, alive with meaning. I thought to myself, 'In spite of all my faults, by baptism and by personal faith, *I am in Christ*. Therefore by God's mercy I am not condemned. I am declared got guilty and acquitted by the grace of God. It is not a matter of personal merit, but of God's free undeserved gift to me.' This new found awareness proved to be a memorable moment of liberation. From then on I was deeply convinced that, although I had fallen short of what God expected of me, my shortcomings were for-given and God was truly working in me to will and to do his good pleasure. This was an important breakthrough, which pre-pared me for situations where prayer for others was required. It enabled me to pray the prayer of command with the authority that comes from expectant faith.

Back to the main story. During this time when I was wrestling with the passage in Mk 11:20-23, a pupil of mine – a fine footballer – injured his back. He was in considerable pain, found it hard to sleep or study, and was unable to play on the College team. It had reached the semi-finals of the Mc Crory Cup that particular year. At one point a number of the sixth formers approached me. 'Father, we need Neil for the cup match,' they said, 'we have heard you preaching about God's willingness to answer prayer. Will you pray for him?' I said I'd consider it, if Neil asked me himself. Secretly I was hoping he wouldn't. Then the headmaster approached me and made a similar request. I gave him the same evasive answer. Finally, Neil himself came to see me and requested prayer. I arranged to meet him after school. When we got together I read the passage from Mark 11:20-23. 'Do you believe what the Lord promises?' I asked. 'Well, let's put it this way, Father, I believe that what the Lord says is true, but I find it hard to believe it will be true in my case.' 'I'm much the same,' I said, 'but we will pray and see what happens.' I put my hands on Neil's back while imagining that the light of God's healing love was shining upon it and within it. As my concentration deepened, I found myself telling the injury to yield to the power of God at work in all the cells. As I was doing this I became convinced that what we were praying for was being granted. I concluded by thanking the Lord for what he was doing and would continue to do in Neil's back. When the prayer was over I asked Neil how he felt. 'To tell the truth, Father, the pain is worse now!' 'Take no notice,' I said, 'Imitate St Peter when he was walking on the water. Keep your mind on Jesus; forget about your symptoms. We were praying for a healing, not a miracle. It is a process; it will take time.'

When I returned to my room I stormed heaven. 'Don't let me down Lord,' I prayed, half joking and whole in earnest, 'otherwise your reputation and mine will be in tatters in this school.' By the following morning my faith levels were weakening. When I got into class I asked Neil how he was. 'I had a great night's sleep,' he said cheerily, 'for the first time since the accident. My back is fine now,' and he did a number of twists and bends to prove the point. There was an addendum to the story. The next week a teacher in another school rang me. She said that she was suffering from a bad back and that Neil's girlfriend had encouraged her to contact me. I wasn't keen to see her. But I did so reluctantly. And to my amazement she got better as well, as a result of a prayer of command. That was the first time I prayed such a prayer and saw the healing power of God at work.

The prayer of command and deliverance from evil
Besides healing the sick, Jesus delivered those who were oppressed by the power of evil spirits. Speaking of Jesus, St Peter attested: 'He went around doing good and healing all who were under the power of the devil, because God was with him' (Acts 10:38). Jesus gave the same power to those who would make him known after his death and resurrection. Nowadays, many men and women consider that traditional references to the Evil One can best be understood as either symbolic references to the sum of human evil, the unjust and oppressive structures of society, or the dark and destructive potential of the human unconscious. As guardian and interpreter of divine revelation, the church has repeatedly restated its belief in the Devil's existence. At the launch of the revised *Rite of Exorcism* at the beginning of 1999, Cardinal Estevez, of the Congregation of Divine Worship, reiterated the church's teaching: 'The existence of the devil is not an opinion … It belongs to Catholic faith and doctrine … but the strategy of the devil is to convince people that he does not exist.'[12]

Catholic theology makes a distinction between oppression and possession by the devil. Possession is a form of spiritual psychosis where the entire personality seems to be under the control of evil influences. While possession is theoretically possible, in actual fact it is extremely rare. The vast majority of the cases that are presented as cases of possession are in fact manifestations of profound psychological problems. If, however, there is a suspicion that a person is possessed, only a priest appointed by the local bishop can deal with the problem.

Oppression is a form of spiritual neurosis where only an aspect of the personality seems to be under the influence of evil. In other words, the evil one, the accuser, the liar and opponent of God's kingdom, may exploit the person's psycho-spiritual vulnerability in some negative way or other, e.g. by prompting a compulsive and irrational desire to commit suicide. In my experience, besides suffering from psychosomatic difficulties, a minority of people are also victims of spiritual oppression.

Clearly discernment of spirits is essential when dealing with people who suspect that they are either oppressed or possessed by evil. To do so effectively, Christians need to have a knowledge of abnormal psychology as well as spirituality. If they don't have sufficient knowledge themselves they need to consult those who have. If it is established that, besides having psychological problems, a person seems to be oppressed by evil, any priest or lay person can pray silently but confidently in the name of Jesus by commanding the oppressive spirit to go, knowing that this kind of prayer is always within the will of God. Francis McNutt proposes that pray-ers use something like the following formula of words: 'In the name of Jesus Christ I command you, you spirit of (name), to depart without doing harm to (name of the person being prayed with) or anyone else in this house, or in his or her family, without making any noise or disturbance, and I command you to go straight to Jesus Christ to dispose of as he will. Furthermore, I command you never to return again.'[13]

The subject of deliverance is a large and controversial one which this author and others have dealt with elsewhere.[14] Suffice it to say that Mary Ann Fatula has made the interesting suggestion that if an individual Christian had reason to believe that s/he was oppressed by an evil spirit s/he could say the following prayer of deliverance: 'Be gone evil spirits of lust, or addiction, or depression, or despair, etc ... in the name of Jesus Christ. I renounce you. Most Holy Spirit, possess me, fill me and fill those whom I love with your joy and with your peace.'[15]

The anointing of the sick and the prayer of command
In Jas 5: 14-15 we read: 'Is any one of you sick? He should call the elders of the church to pray over him and anoint him with oil in the name of the Lord. And the prayer offered in faith will make the sick person well; the Lord will raise him up.' I have come to believe that the promise contained in this verse can only be properly understood if the phrase 'prayer offered in faith' is interpreted as unhesitating faith of the expectant kind.[16] Eminent scripture scholar Martin Dibelius supported the belief that the type of prayer mentioned in Jas 5:15 refers to expectant faith. He

wrote: 'The promise of healing is stated totally without qualifi-
cation; the possibility of a failure is not mentioned … the faith
referred to here corresponds to the gift of faith with which we
are familiar from the stories in the gospels, a faith which looks
for an answer to prayer, even expects miracles.'[17] If this is the
case, and I believe it is, then the gift of unhesitating faith of the
expectant kind would be evoked in one or other of the two main
ways mentioned above. As a result, instead of saying the words
of anointing in a hesitant way, the minister of the sacrament
would be able to utter them as a veritable prayer of command. In
my experience the words of anointing are likely to be effective
when they are spoken in this authoritative way.

I can recall a typical example. A few years ago I was a member of a team that had conducted a parish mission in a city in the
North of Ireland. On the last day a man approached me. He told
me that he was suffering from a disease of the bladder. It was so
severe that he had to go to the toilet every twenty minutes or so.
On some occasions he would suffer from such severe spasms of
pain that he would fall on the floor writhing in agony. His doctor thought that the problem was so bad that he had made
arrangements to have his patient operated on in a local hospital.
To prove his point the man produced a letter from his consultant,
giving all the details. When I read it, I noticed that the surgery
was supposed to have taken place a few days previously. When I
mentioned this, the man explained that he had cancelled the operation in order to attend the parish mission. He said that he had
felt that if he did, the Lord could cure him. Then he asked me if I
would pray for him and anoint him. I said that I would. When I
administered the sacrament he went off. About three months
ago I was in that city in the same church. A man introduced himself and explained that he had approached me some years before
during another mission and had asked to be anointed because
he was suffering from a bladder disease. As he spoke I recalled
all the details. How are you now? I asked. He explained with joy
and gratitude that he had completely recovered from his complaint, so much so that there was no need for any surgery.

Revelations of God's will
Over the years I have learned a good deal about the many ways

in which the Lord can reveal the divine will in such a way that one is empowered to utter the prayer of command with expectant faith. We will look at a number of them while illustrating them with practical examples. For more on this subject see chapter five, entitled 'Seeking God's will in prayer.'

An inspired word from scripture

Although faith is a key concept in the bible, it is surprising to find that there is only one verse in the scriptures which tells us how it is nurtured. In Rom 10:17 St Paul says: 'Faith comes from hearing the message, and the message is heard through the word of Christ.' One could add that the promises of Christ are particularly important in this regard, especially those to do with the prayer of supplication and the prayer of command. The word of God can be looked at either as a *noun* which is objectively true in itself, or as a *verb* which is spoken to a particular person so that it becomes subjectively true for him or her. This is the alive and active word of revelation which is referred to in a number of places in scripture. For example, in Is 48:6-8 we read: 'From now on I will tell you of new things, of hidden things unknown to you. They are created now, and not long ago; you have not heard of them before today. So you cannot say, "Yes, I knew of them." You have neither heard nor understood; from of old your ear has not been open.'

I have discovered that although a particular verse that one reads or hears may immediately jump alive with meaning into the heart, more often than not one has to ponder it like Mary. When God's living word finally makes its home in a person's inner self it evokes trusting faith of the expectant kind. Not only that, we have the scriptural assurance that the revelatory word contains the God-given power to effect what it says. As the Lord assures us in Is 55:11: 'So is my word that goes out from my mouth: It will not return to me empty, but will accomplish what I desire and achieve the purpose for which I sent it.' I discovered these realities when I was praying for Neil. The truth of the promise of Christ in Mk 11: 20-23 fell from head to heart even as I prayed. It was spoken into my innermost self as a verb that was subjectively true for me at that specific moment. It evoked unhesitating faith and found expression in a prayer of command.

Words of knowledge

This point expands on the previous one. In one of his many writings, St Thomas Aquinas describes how God can reveal his word and his will to people. The Lord can illumine the mind either by means of an intellectual message or a subjective image. God can illumine the mind externally by means of an audible word or a more objective vision. Thomas says: 'From these presentations, by the light internally impressed on the mind, people receive a knowledge of divine things.'[18] Pentecostals and charismatics talk about 'words of knowledge' (cf. 1 Cor 12:8), which are forms of revelation which can be experienced in the ways St Thomas describes. This gift can be defined in these words. It is a supernatural revelation of facts about a person or situation, which is not learned through the efforts of the natural mind, but is revealed through an inspired thought, a mental picture or a spiritual intuition. These words from the Lord, whatever form they may take, not only reveal God's here and now purposes, they also evoke an unhesitating faith, of greater or lesser intensity, which enables a person to utter a prayer of command.

Many well-known figures that are involved in the healing ministry rely on this gift for their effectiveness, notably the late Kathryn Kuhlman. At her large gatherings she would begin announcing healings as soon as she believed that she had received a special anointing from the Holy Spirit. The following words are taken from a transcript of one of her services. 'There is a heart condition disappearing. Wonderful Jesus, I give you praise and glory. There is a case of sugar diabetes … the sugar is draining from your body … an ear has been opened completely. Someone hears me perfectly. In the balcony. Check on that someone. Up there in the top left balcony is a man with a hearing aid. Check that ear, sir. Hold your good ear closed tight; you hear me perfectly … Arthritis of the feet down here to my left. Go quickly, Maggie; she is in the fifth or sixth row. Praise to you wonderful Jesus!'[19] Speaking about her experience of this remarkable gift, Kathryn said: 'My mind is so surrendered to the Spirit that I know the exact body being healed, the sickness, the affliction, and in some instances the very sin in their lives. And yet I do not pretend to tell you *why* or *how*.'[20] Many other people engaged in the healing ministry, such as Sr Briege Mc Kenna,

Ralf Di Orio, Bob de Grandis and Emilien Tardif, have received similar guidance. Often they utter a prayer of command which is accompanied with the laying on of hands. Dr David C. Lewis of the Religious Experience Research Project, Nottingham University and the Alister Hardy Research Centre, Oxford, has written an interesting evaluation of this phenomenon from a social anthropologist's point of view.[21]

Indignant compassion

I have described elsewhere how any Christian can experience three interrelated forms of compassion,[22] namely fellow feeling, wounded wonder and indignant compassion. Fellow feeling refers to the ability to identify with the suffering of another person because one has endured something similar. Wounded wonder refers to the fact that the perception of another person's value evokes a sense of wonder. But the extent to which he or she is wounded is the extent to which one's sense of wonder is wounded also. Indignant compassion refers to the fact that a person who is aware of the innermost value of another resists anything that might detract from that value. It is my conviction that Jesus experienced these forms of compassion when he met with afflicted people. When he did so, he knew inwardly that his affective attitude was a participation in the feelings of God the Father and that his desire to alleviate their sufferings was also a sharing in the saving and healing will of the Lord. This inner awareness authorised him to utter an authoritative prayer of command to either heal or deliver. We have already adverted to par. 521 of the *Catechism of the Catholic Church* towards the end of chapter two. Quoting some words from St John Eudes, the same paragraph says: 'We must continue to accomplish in ourselves the stages of Jesus' life and his mysteries and often to beg him to perfect and realise them in us.' This general principle applies to compassion. When loving Christians who have experienced either fellow-feeling or wounded wonder are moved to indignant compassion by the sufferings of others, they desire to resist all that afflicts the person. As they do so, they may become inwardly aware that they are participating in the very feelings and desires of Jesus himself. As a result of this experiential revelation of God's loving will, they know that they were being authorised and empowered to utter a therapeutic or liberating prayer of command.

I can remember a woman who came to see me many years ago. She shared the embarrassing fact that she suffered from chronic menstrual problems. Each month she bled heavily, suffered a lot of pain and had to endure blinding headaches. If she was at work when ovulation began, she would be so badly affected that her colleagues would call a taxi to take her home. There she would have to draw the blinds and lie in darkness for a day or two. As I listened, I was moved with compassion by her story and had a strong desire to see her well. As I experienced these feelings and desires I had the distinct impression that Jesus felt the same, only more strongly so. With this realisation, I felt my faith strengthen to the point that I could utter a prayer of command which ordered the woman's reproductive organs to return to their proper functioning. Thanks be to God, the prayer was effective. Afterwards, the woman told me, on more than one occasion, that her periods had returned to normal and that she experienced no more sharp pain or headaches.

Conclusion

With the restoration to the church of the more remarkable charisms mentioned in 1 Cor 12:8-10, there has been a welcome revival of the prayer of command. The commission to spread the good news to the whole of creation will be fulfilled when we demonstrate the truth of the gospel proclamation, not just by the witness of transformed lives, charitable deeds and action for justice, but also by the performance of 'signs and wonders' such as healings and miracles, which depend on the prayer of command. This view seems to be in accord with the teaching of the Second Vatican Council. It could be added, in the light of the Pauline theology of ministry, that evangelists are more likely to receive the gift of faith than others. There is an on-going need in the contemporary church to identify and affirm those who are gifted with this important ministry.

CHAPTER NINE

Praying to the Mary
and the Saints

Contrary to what some Protestants think, Catholics neither worship Mary or the saints. Rather they venerate them as men and women who were outstanding disciples of Christ, people who were exemplary in holiness and Christian virtue. We believe that those who have been saved by the Blood of the Lamb belong to the church triumphant. In heaven they praise and worship God in union with the angels and archangels. But we also believe that we can pray to them. But we do not believe that they are mediators, because scripture teaches 'There is one mediator between God and men, the man Jesus' (1 Tim 2:5). However, we do believe that because Mary and the saints are perfectly conformed to the person, will, and prayer of Christ, we can pray to them in virtue of that unity. In Rev 8:4 we are told that in heaven: 'The smoke of the incense, together *with the prayers of the saints*, went up before God.' Speaking of the role of the saints, the *Catechism of the Catholic Church* says: 'Their intercession is their most exalted service to God's plan. We can and should ask them to intercede for us and for the whole world.'[1] As philosopher Eleonore Stump has written: 'The official Catholic position regarding prayer to the saints is that they are to be petitioned only for their prayers to God, who alone is to be petitioned for what is being sought directly in the prayer.'[2] In this chapter I will concentrate on prayer to Mary as the greatest of all the saints. As theologian M. J. Scheeben has observed, the title of advocate 'is used almost exclusively for Mary, and not for the saints.'[3]

A memorable experience
A number of years ago I saw a memorable image in prayer. It was a medieval scene. I could see people streaming from all directions toward a distant valley. Some were walking, others

riding horses or being transported on carts. They were dressed in the distinctive clothing characteristic of the time. The valley they were travelling towards was surrounded by hills and guarded by four giant angels. In their hands they held swords with crooked, snakelike blades which were pointed upwards. When all the people had finally gathered, the angels bent down, caught the valley in their hands and carried it upwards into the heavens. In the next scene I saw that all the people were assembling in what I understood to be the court of heaven. One by one, they were taking their seats. Then Our Lady appeared. She was dressed in a dark blue, full length, velvet dress. She was beautiful, unpretentious and graceful. She was so homely and warm-hearted that she immediately put everyone at their ease. After a short while she said softly, 'He will be here soon.' I knew in my spirit that she was referring to her son Jesus. Sadly, the vision ended before I saw the glorified Lord. But ever afterwards I have had a strong sense that Mary is our go-between, our advocate with Jesus.

The biblical roots of Mary's intercessory role
The roots of Mary's intercessory role are to be found in the Old Testament. At one time in Israel the king could have many wives. In order to avoid rivalries and disputes, the queen mother was honoured as the first lady in the land. In Hebrew she was referred to as *gebirah*, which literally meant 'great lady'. She assisted the king in ruling the kingdom. The queen mother had two interrelated roles. Firstly, she was the king's counsellor. She would advise him about administrative matters (cf. Prov 31:8-9; 2 Chr 22:2-4). Secondly, she had the role of advocate. The ordinary people could approach her with their requests, and she would present them to her son, the king. She was their intercessor, who pleaded on their behalf. There is an instructive example of what was involved in 1 Kgs 2:19-20. It is about the relationship that existed between King Solomon and his mother Bathsheba. In the text we are told: 'And the king rose to meet her, and bowed down to her; and he sat on his throne, and had a seat brought for the king's mother, and she sat on his right. Then she said, "I have one small request to make of you, do not refuse me." And the king said to her, "Make your request, my mother, for I will not refuse you".'

On an other occasion we are told that Esther, a Jewish woman, was 'lovely and beautiful' (Esth 2:3). She was married to king Ahasureus, who is generally identified with Xerxes I. Sometime later the queen heard that Haman, one of her husband's advisors, had hatched a vindictive plot to kill all her fellow Jews. As a result she interceded with her husband. She 'pleaded with the king, falling at his feet and weeping. She begged him to put an end to the evil plan of Haman the Agagite, which he had devised against the Jews. Then the king extended the gold sceptre to Esther and she arose and stood before him. "If it pleases the king," she said, "and if he regards me with favour and thinks it the right thing to do, and if he is pleased with me, let an order be written overruling the dispatches that Haman son of Hammedatha, the Agagite, devised and wrote to destroy the Jews in all the king's provinces. For how can I bear to see disaster fall on my people? How can I bear to see the destruction of my family?"' We are told that the king granted her request, sentenced Haman to death, and gave Esther his authority to write to the people on his behalf. He said: 'Now write another decree in the king's name in behalf of the Jews as seems best to you, and seal it with the king's signet ring – for no document written in the king's name and sealed with his ring can be revoked' (Esth 8:3-8).

In the story of the marriage feast of Cana we have an outstanding New Testament example of the spiritual relationship between the mother and the king. When a shortage of wine was immanent, Mary interceded with a confidence greater than that of queens Bathsheba and Esther. We are told in Jn 2:3-5: 'When the wine failed the mother of Jesus said to him. "They have no wine." And Jesus said to her, "O woman, what have you to do with me? My hour has not come yet." His mother said to the servants, "Do whatever he tells you."' Although up to that moment Jesus had no reason to believe that the Father was authorising him to perform deeds of power, he discerned in Mary's request that the hour had finally arrived. He recognised that her spontaneous impulse of loving concern was inspired by the Spirit and therefore an expression of the Father's will. Just as she had given birth to Jesus as a result of her obedient faith at the annunciation, so now she was giving birth to his public ministry, as a result of the same docile trust.

Mary as advocate in Catholic tradition

Our Catholic faith tells us that we have two divine advocates in the persons of Jesus and the Holy Spirit. However, our Blessed Lady, who is mother of Jesus and spouse of the Spirit, is our third advocate. She is the only human being who has been assumed body and soul into heaven. There she intercedes with her Son on our behalf. St Bernard said of her: 'Our heavenly Father who wants to show all possible mercy, gives us Jesus Christ as our principal advocate, and then gives us Mary as our advocate with Jesus.' St Bonaventure added: 'It is the great prerogative of Mary to be all powerful with her Son. What good would such a prerogative be as far as we are concerned, if she did not bother about us? No. Let us have no misgivings about it, and let us thank our Lord and his Blessed mother. As she is far more powerful than all the saints, to the same degree she is more tender and solicitous for our happiness.'

When Our Lady appeared to Catherine Laboure in the Rue du Bac, in 1830, she saw her holding a golden ball, which represented the world and every person in it, surmounted by a little golden cross. Mary was wearing many rings on her fingers. Each one was set with gems, some of which were more beautiful than others. Brilliant rays of light of varying degrees of intensity were streaming from most of these precious stones. Catherine was given to understand that they represented the many different graces our Lady was willing to dispense on her Son's behalf. Afterwards she said: 'This made me realise how right it was to pray to the Blessed Virgin and how generous she was to those who did pray to her, what graces she gave to those who asked for them, what joy she had in giving them. The gems from which rays do not fall are the graces which souls forget to ask.'[4] Around the figure of the blessed Mother were written the words: 'O Mary conceived without sin, pray for us who have recourse to you.' This well known apparition was the prelude to the solemn definition of the doctrine of the Immaculate Conception in 1854. It also implied that Mary was the Mediatrix of all graces. This theological notion implies that all prayers and petitions, whether addressed specifically to Mary or to her Son, are presented to the Lord by her, and that all graces whether answers to prayer or gifts unsought, pass through her hands to God's children. Like Queen Esther of old she acts in the name of the delegated authority of the King of heaven.

The Second Vatican Council acknowledged and endorsed what Catholic tradition had repeatedly said about Mary's intercessory role when it declared: 'The Blessed Virgin is invoked in the church under the title of Advocate … By her maternal charity, she cares for the brothers and sisters of her Son, who still journey on earth surrounded by dangers and difficulties, until they are led into their blessed home.'[5] This role is expressed in a number of our beautiful Marian prayers. In the *Hail Mary*, Catholics pray, 'Holy Mary mother of God, pray for us sinners now and at the hour of our death.' In the *Hail Holy Queen* we say, 'Turn then, most gracious advocate, your eyes of mercy towards us, and after this our exile show unto us the blessed fruit of your womb, Jesus.' In the *Memorare*, which dates back to the third century, we say, 'Remember, O most gracious Virgin Mary, that never was it known that anyone who fled to your protection was left unaided.'

Although Mary prays for all kinds of graces and blessings, arguably she has priorities. We will mention four of them here. Firstly, she prays that all God's people will experience divine mercy. Pope Pius XII wrote: 'Our advocate, placed between God and the sinner, takes it upon herself to invoke clemency of the Judge so as to temper his justice, touch the heart of the sinner and overcome his or her obstinacy.'[6] Secondly, Mary prays, as she did in the upper room before Pentecost, that the church will be filled, especially at times of special need, with the same Spirit that overshadowed her at the annunciation. Thirdly, the Blessed Mother prays for the unity of the church. As John Paul II has written: 'The church recognises in Mary a mother who keeps watch over its development and does not cease to intercede with her Son to obtain for Christians more profound dispositions of faith, of hope and of love. Mary seeks to promote the greatest possible unity of Christians, because as mother she strives to ensure accord among her children.'[7] Fourthly, Mary prays for the consummation of all things in Christ, by asking for the second coming. As Pope John Paul points out: 'If as Virgin and Mother she was singularly united with him in his first coming, so through her continued collaboration with him she will also be united with him in expectation of the second … when all those who belong to Christ "shall be made alive" (1 Cor 15:26).'[8]

Three images of Mary's role

Pope Pius VII summed up all that we have said so far when he declared in 1805: 'While the prayers of those in heaven have, it is true, some claim on God's watchful eye, Mary's prayers place their assurance in a mother's right. For that reason, when she approaches her divine Son's throne, as Advocate she begs, as Handmaid she prays, but as Mother she commands.' We will look at examples of what these three images imply.

The advocate who begs

Some time ago I went to the National Concert Hall in Dublin, to hear a performance of Henryk Gorecki's *Symphony of Sorrowful Songs*. This popular work was written by a Polish Catholic to lament the murder of so many Jewish people in Auschwitz. I was deeply moved by the performance. At one point I became so aware of a vivid mental image that I was no longer conscious of the orchestra or the voice of the Polish soprano who was singing a haunting melody. I could see a railway line that led to the front gates of the concentration camp. Then the gates opened and inside I could see the emaciated form of pathetic inmates who were wandering around like ghosts. My attention rested on one particular woman. I could see her from behind. For some reason I thought to myself, 'That is the Blessed Virgin.' Then she turned around. Tears were streaming down her sad but beautiful face. She said in a low, sorrowful voice 'I too am a Jew.' These almost unbearably poignant words made a profound impression on me. Tears flowed down my cheeks. I realised that not only was Mary a Jewess like Queen Esther, she was the compassionate mother of all those who suffered, Jewish or not, such as refugees, the survivors of natural disasters and the victims of wars. I realised that it was this sense of compassionate solidarity that motivated her, as advocate, to beg God for help.

The handmaid who prays

Back in the early eighties I had another experience which deepened that appreciation. I attended an extraordinary prayer meeting on a Thursday evening. From the outset a special anointing of the Spirit was upon it. At one point, early in the proceedings a woman gave a powerful utterance in tongues. Subsequently we were told by Cardinal Ó Fiaich's secretary, a nun who had once ministered in Africa, that the woman had recited parts of the litany of Loretto in Swahili. Apparently, she had repeated the phrase, 'Mary is Queen of peace' a number of times. It is interesting to note that this occurred a few months before the first of the apparitions in Medjugorje, where Mary was to be revealed as Queen of Peace.

Some time later in the meeting, two women were granted the same image at the same time. They saw Our Lady holding a baby in the air as if she were interceding on its behalf. Minutes later the door opened and a women rushed in. She was crying in a distracted way. Then she addressed the whole meeting and said, 'My baby is dying in Belfast. Please pray for her.' I encouraged her to sit down. We all began to pray fervently through the intercession of Mary. Then one of the people present got a prophetic word which suggested that the baby would get well, but not immediately. Meantime the mother would experience other adversities. She should not loose heart, but rather trust in the Lord. In the event that inspired word was fulfilled to the letter. A short time later the mother was involved in a car accident and received minor injuries to one of her legs. A few weeks after that, the doctors who were caring for her daughter discovered that she was allergic to milk. As soon as she was weaned from it, she recovered completely, as the Lord had foretold. In a sense that incident taught me that as handmaiden of the Lord, Mary prays with confidence.

The Queen who commands

I know a priest who, in the late seventies, preached an eight day retreat for the Daughters of Charity in Dublin. Incidentally, it is the order to which Catherine Laboure belonged. During the retreat many of the sisters came to see him for a chat. One of them told him that she was in the grip of a severe depression. She also told him that she suffered from a congenital spinal defect which meant that every morning she had to endure a severe headache. Apparently he encouraged her to focus in faith on the final Eucharist when he intended to have an anointing of the sick.

On the last day of the retreat the healing Mass was said as planned. Throughout the celebration the celebrant had a strong sense of Our Lady's love for these women who were generously devoting their lives to the service of the poor. He was also aware that Mary had told Saint Catherine Laboure that she had a special care for the Daughters of Charity. Following the gospel and homily, he administered the sacrament of anointing. Many infirm sisters came forward, but to his surprise the woman who was suffering from depression failed to do so. For his part he respected her decision and continued with the Mass.

After the distribution of communion he closed his eyes, raised his arms, and uttered a spontaneous prayer of thanksgiving. As he was doing so, he began to experience a tingling sensation in his left arm, rather like pins and needles, and a burning sensation in the palm of his hand. At first he thought that someone must have foolishly placed the candles on the near, left hand side of the altar. But when he opened his eyes to check, he saw that the two candles were on the right hand side of the altar, as far from his left hand as was possible. As he prayed he was thinking that he must have pinched a nerve in his arm, so he moved it about under his vestment, but to no avail.

When the Mass was over, the depressed sister approached him in an agitated state. She said that she got confused at the time of the anointing and had failed to come forward. The priest encouraged her not to fret. He anointed her with the oil of gladness and put his left hand on the back of her neck with the intention of praying about her complaints. Apparently he can clearly remember turning to our Lady. He was aware that in the biblical era there were two concepts of time. Firstly, there was secular unredeemed time, where people suffered their 'chronic' problems. Secondly, there was sacred time in which the power and glory of God was revealed. Was this the timeless moment of grace for this Sister? He prayed to Mary. 'I don't know if this is God's appointed hour, but it would need to be. Ask now, as you once asked at Cana in Galilee, that the Lord's timetable may be changed.' The instant he spoke those words, he felt a surge of energy pass through his arm, and the sister fell to the ground under the power of the Holy Spirit. With difficulty he lifted her into a chair. Another sister joined him in the prayer. The woman they were ministering to cried out, 'Stop praying. I'm on fire!' They continued to pray, however, believing that fire was reminiscent of the purifying flames of Pentecost and could do nothing but good.

During that memorable experience of the numinous, the priest said that he had the most vivid sense of God's presence he had ever known. He was palpably aware of the holiness of God. On the one hand he wanted to run away as someone who was unworthy to be in the awesome presence of the good Lord, while on the other he was drawn to the divine mystery as by a magnet. He can remember that he whispered, with more naïvete than realism: 'Lord, you are holiness itself. I promise I will never sin again!'

At the end of the prayer, he could see that many of the sisters, who were still sitting in the chapel, were frightened by what had been happening. He said to them, 'There is no need to be scared. We often talk about the power of the Holy Spirit but now you have seen it at work.' They left the woman who had been prayed with, sitting on her chair. Some twenty minutes later she staggered into the dining room and sat in an empty seat beside the retreat master. 'What on earth happened to me in there?' she asked. He said, 'Sister, I have no doubt that God has blessed you today. I wouldn't be a bit surprised to find that your depression will go and that your back will be strengthened. Please contact me in a month's time to tell me how you are getting on.' She did so, and explained in a joyful letter that her depression had indeed lifted, and that her headaches had almost disappeared. Ever since coming to know about that memorable experience, I have had a greater appreciation of the fact that, as Queen of Heaven, Mary prays with great authority, and that in a real sense her word is tantamount to God's command.

Conclusion

As the testimonies demonstrate, when we experience any kind of need we can turn to our Lady, and by extension to the saints, with confidence. She is the mother of the church and our mother. As Queen of Heaven she prays ceaselessly that each of her spiritual children will be worthy of the mighty promises of her divine son. As we have seen, her intercession is uniquely powerful with God. You can turn to her with confidence. As one Irish prayer puts it succinctly: 'Mary, because you are God's mother you can't say you can't. Because you are my mother you won't say you won't. So you will, won't you?'

CHAPTER TEN

The prayer of appreciation

The twin bibles of creation and the scriptures can elicit a child-like sense of wonder. It is the state of mind produced by some-thing new, unexpected or extraordinary such as a marvel, prodigy or miracle which evokes a sense of awe or admiration. The most basic form of wonder is the recognition that it is simply amazing that something rather than nothing exists and that I am part of that something. There is an English folk story that captures that sense of creature feeling.

In AD 625 a monk named Paulinus visited King Edwin in the North of England. He wanted to persuade him to accept Christianity. The king was unsure, so he summoned his advis-ers. One of them said to him: 'Your majesty, imagine you are sit-ting at table with your courtiers. It is winter and the fire is burn-ing brightly. Outside a storm is howling. Snow is falling. Then someone opens the door. A small bird flies in and soon after-wards it flies out again. For the few moments it is in the bright banqueting hall it doesn't feel the cold. But as soon as it leaves your sight it returns to the dark of winter. It seems to me that the life of man is much the same. We do not know what went before and we do not know what follows. In truth, life is a sigh between two mysteries. If the monk Paulinus can throw light on these mysteries, you would do well to listen attentively.' Perhaps sometime later Paulinus quoted the following words from St Paul: 'For even if there are so-called gods, whether in heaven or on earth, yet for us there is but one God, the Father, from whom all things came and for whom we live; and there is but one Lord, Jesus Christ, through whom all things came and through whom we live' (1 Cor 8:5-6).

When I was in my early twenties I endured a painful crisis of faith. For a time I doubted the existence of God and of ultimate meaning. For years I anxiously tried to resolve these issues by means of personal reflection, discussion with others, and philosophical reading. No matter how hard I tried, convincing answers seemed to elude me. Then unexpectedly I experienced a welcome and grace-filled breakthrough. I was studying for an exam. Not for the first time, I happened to doze off at my desk. As I emerged into full consciousness there was a fleeting moment when I was aware, but not of anything in particular. There was no idea or image in my mind. Instead, I had what seemed like a vivid and unmediated awareness of my own existence and by extension of the existence of all things. It was accompanied by a strong conviction that my existence was *good* and *meaningful* in itself, while at the same time not being the adequate explanation of its own existence or meaning. In that moment I had an intuitive assurance that God existed as the One who sustains in being all the good and meaningful creatures that exist, including myself. If that were not so, my being, like the rest of the universe, would have been ultimately absurd. But I was certain that this was not the case. Therefore God existed. My conviction was not *logical*, but an *experiential* certainty; and since it rested on subjective grounds, I was not able to say: It is morally certain that there is a God, but rather I am morally certain there is a God. I may say that this form of creature feeling, and its associated belief, has remained in the background of my consciousness ever since.

Over the years I have come to realise that there is a related but subordinate form of wonder. Rather than being evoked by the fact of existence, it is evoked by the perception of the particular qualities of specific objects, such as their beauty, goodness, and essences. These intuitions tend to leave everyday perceptions behind as one becomes aware of the surprise of the real/Real. Poet William Blake once wrote: 'I assert for myself that I do not behold the outward creation, and that to me it is a hindrance ... it is as the dirt upon my feet, no part of me. "What?" it will be questioned, "When the sun rises do you not see a round disk on fire, something like a gold coin?" Oh no, no. I see an innumerable company of the heavenly host crying: "Holy, holy, holy is the Lord God Almighty".'[1]

I can recall a journey I made some time ago. I was travelling to Dublin airport on the upper deck of a bus. The traffic was heavy and so we stopped many times along the way. At one point we spent a few minutes beside a roadside tree. When I looked out the window I could see the rich canopy of its varie-gated leaves. There were tens of thousands of them, each of which was perfectly shaped, with a stem, lighter coloured veins, shiny green tops and silvery green under sides. I thought to my-self, 'How beautiful each and every leaf is in itself. Although many of them are invisible, and go unnoticed they are happy nevertheless to be their charming selves in the presence of the One who created, sustains and beholds them in love.' I was humbled by that awareness. Why had I such an anxious desire, at times, to be noticed and appreciated by others? Better to be like the leaves, content to rest in the awareness of the Father's favour and to live for the glory of God alone. In spite of the fact that we were stuck in a traffic jam, this experience filled me with a sense of well-being and inner peace. I have come to the conclu-sion that a sense of wonder is the birthplace of religious experi-ence. It can put a person into heartfelt contact with the 'Beyond Who is in the midst' of everyday existence in such a way that the fundamental anxiety which was evoked by the threat of non-existence is permanently replaced by a joyful sense of ultimate belonging.

Appreciative wonder as a form of love
Over the years I have come to see that the examples of wonder I have described are forms of love, when love is understood as the will to approve the perceived and potential inner value of peo-ple and things. It is interesting to note that the etymology of the word 'love' supports this point of view. It is related to the Old High German word *gilob* meaning 'precious' and the word *lob* meaning 'praise'.[2] In other words, the sense of wonder enables attentive men and women to perceive what is precious and praiseworthy in people and things. As they become aware of the value of being in general, and the qualities of specific people and things in particular, they approve of their intrinsic worth, in a manner that desires that they realise their full potential by be-coming what they are. They esteem them as created gifts of God. From a religious point of view, this deep-seated sense of appre-

ciative love is expressed in three interrelated forms of prayer, thanksgiving, praise and worship.

The word to 'thank' in English is taken from the Old English *thonc* which is a cognate with the German *dank*, meaning 'to think', literally, 'to be mindful, to be aware of'. Appreciation as thanksgiving means that one is mindful of, and grateful for, the gifts of God. The word 'praise' in English is derived from the Latin *pretiare*, to prize, which is derived from *pretium* meaning price. Appreciation as praise acknowledges the value of the God of the gifts. The word 'worship' in English is derived from the Old English *weorth*, meaning 'worth'. Appreciation as worship is a heartfelt awareness of the glory of the Lord. Ps 95:6 shows how the prayer of appreciation as thanksgiving and praise reaches its point of highest intensity in the form of worship: 'Come, let us bow down in *worship*, let us kneel before the Lord our Maker.' Worship is commonly expressed in bodily gestures such as the ones described by the psalmist, together with prostrations, raising of arms, clapping, etc.

As was mentioned in chapter six, appreciative prayer is built on the foundation stone of a sense of absolute dependence on God for existence, life and talents. St Thomas Aquinas says: 'Prayer is an act of reverence for God, which subjects us to him and professes that we need him as a source of our blessings; so clearly it is an act of religion.'[3] This sense of reliance also expresses itself in a heartfelt acknowledgement that God has given us countless gifts and graces in response to our petitionary prayers. It could also be said that, from an experiential point of view, the prayer of appreciation is like a bridge that enables us to cross over from the visible to the invisible, the natural to the supernatural, from this needy world into the presence of the all-sufficient God. Praise is a keystone in that bridge, flanked on the one side by thanksgiving, and on the other by worship. We will look at each interconnected form of prayer in turn.

Appreciation as thanksgiving
While gratitude for existence is the ever-present subliminal form of appreciation informing the prayer of thanksgiving, it usually focuses in a more precise and conscious way upon particular gifts and graces. In Tob 12:6; 22, the messenger Raphael says to

Tobit and his son Tobias: 'Praise God and give thanks to him; exalt him and give thanks to him in the presence of all the living for what he has done for you. It is good to acknowledge God and to exalt his name, worthily declaring the works of God. Do not be slow to give him thanks ... they stood up ... and confessed the great and wonderful works of God.' We can thank God for an endless list of blessings, such as salvation, health, special abilities, education, financial security, etc.

Reading St Paul, it is evident that he saw thankful appreciation as an act of fundamental religious importance. By contemplating the existence and beauty of the created world a rational human being could perceive the existence and character of its Maker. As 2 Mac 7:28 says: 'Look at the heaven and the earth and see everything that is in them, and recognise that God did not make them out of things that existed. Thus also mankind comes into being.'[4] Paul echoed that sentiment when he wrote: 'For since the creation of the world, God's invisible qualities – his eternal power and divine nature – have been clearly seen, being understood from what has been made.'

Then Paul goes on to make an all-important observation about unbelievers: 'For although they knew God, *they neither glorified him as God nor gave thanks to him*' (Rom 1:21). In other words, in Paul's mind lack of appreciation of the gifts of God is indicative of a culpable lack of reverence for the God of the gifts. For him, therefore, ingratitude and unbelief are virtually synonymous. Not only that, irreligion has dire consequences from a moral and social point of view. Paul echoes an observation of Judg 17:6: 'In those days Israel had no king; everyone did as he saw fit.' Instead of honouring God, unbelievers idolise created things and either re-write or ignore the commandments to suit themselves:[5] 'Because of this,' he says, 'God gave them over to shameful lusts ... Furthermore, since they did not think it worthwhile to retain the knowledge of God, he gave them over to a depraved mind, to do what ought not to be done. They have become filled with every kind of wickedness, evil, greed and depravity. They are full of envy, murder, strife, deceit and malice. They are gossips, slanderers, God-haters, insolent, arrogant and boastful; they invent ways of doing evil; they disobey their parents; they are senseless, faithless, heartless, ruthless' (Rom 1:26-31).

Surely Paul's indictment continues to have relevance in our secular culture where lack of grateful reverence of a religious kind is evident in moral permissiveness and social fragmentation.

Thanksgiving always for everything

In marked contrast, St Paul not only thanks God repeatedly himself, he says to people of faith: 'Pray continually; give thanks in *all circumstances*, for this is God's will for you in Christ Jesus' (1 Thess 5:17-18). In Eph 5:20 he adds: 'Always give thanks to God the Father *for everything*, in the name of our Lord Jesus Christ'. In Phil 4:6 he says: 'Do not be anxious about anything, but *in everything*, by prayer and petition, with thanksgiving, present your requests to God'. Finally in Col 3:17 we read: 'And *whatever you do*, whether in word or deed, do it all in the name of the Lord Jesus, giving thanks to God the Father through him'.

It is clear that we should thank God for the graces and blessings of life. It is good not to take them for granted, but rather to call them to mind with gratitude. But St Paul implies that we should also thank God for the bad things, like illness and personal sin. He says that it is God's will that we do so. How can we thank God for the misfortunes and sins in our lives? It is not that we thank God for these evils in themselves, but because we believe that they have been embraced by God's providence. Over the years I have come to realise that no matter what misfortunes I endure or what mistakes I make, they are integrated into God's plan for my life, and embraced by divine providence. So I firmly believe that, strange as it may seem, sin and suffering can become the birthplace of grace. Evil does not have the last word. That word belongs to God and it is a redeeming word of blessing and victory.

An Old Testament example

There is an outstanding biblical example of what I mean. In the book of Genesis we are told that Joseph was the first child of Rachel and his father's favourite son. This is most clearly shown by the special coat that Jacob gave to Joseph. His ten older brothers hated him because he was their father's pet and because Joseph had dreams that he interpreted to his brothers in a rather conceited way. Joseph and his family were shepherds in the land of

Canaan. One day Jacob sent Joseph to search for his brothers, who were tending the flocks. When Joseph found them, they seized upon the chance to kill him. The only opposing voice was Reuben's, so they compromised and sold Joseph into slavery.

Joseph was taken to Egypt. Ps 105:17-21 tells us that he was sold as a slave. His good conduct soon earned him the highest position in the household of Potiphar. His wife became infatuated nevertheless with Joseph and tempted him to commit adultery with her. When he refused, she accused him of the crime and Joseph was sent to prison. While incarcerated, Joseph met the Pharaoh's baker and his butler. When each of them had a dream, Joseph interpreted them.

Sometime later the butler was released. When the Pharaoh had dreams that none of his counsellors could interpret, the butler remembered Joseph and mentioned him to the Pharaoh. Then Joseph was called to appear before the ruler of Egypt. He interpreted his dreams, predicting seven years of plentiful food, followed by seven years of famine. He also advised the Pharaoh to appoint a commissioner to store up supplies during the plentiful years. To Joseph's surprise, the Pharaoh appointed him as minister of food. This was a position of great prestige. Under Joseph's care, many supplies were stored and the land prospered. When famine struck, Joseph was second only to the Pharaoh in power and prestige. People from all the surrounding lands came to buy food from him.

Many years elapsed between Joseph's arrival in Egypt as a slave and his rise to power in the nation during the famine. The famine also struck Canaan, and Joseph's brothers eventually came to Egypt to buy grain. When they met Joseph he recognised them, but they failed to recognise him. He decided to test them to see if they had changed. He accused them of being spies. Then he sold them grain on the condition that Simeon stay as a hostage until they bring Benjamin, the youngest brother.

When they arrived some time later, Joseph treated them royally, weeping openly at the sight of his youngest brother. Simeon was returned to them. After purchasing their grain, they headed home. On their way, however, they were stopped by one of Joseph's servants, who accused them of stealing Joseph's silver cup. The cup was found in Benjamin's bag, where Joseph

had placed it. The brothers returned to face Joseph, who declared that Benjamin must stay in Egypt. At this point Judah
pleaded with Joseph, saying that it would break their father
Jacob's heart if Benjamin failed to return with them. Judah's
offer to stay in Benjamin's place is one of the most moving passages in the Old Testament.

Joseph was overcome with emotion. He revealed himself to
them as their brother, whom they had sold into slavery years
earlier. And he wept so loudly that the Egyptians heard him,
and ... Joseph said to his brothers, 'I am Joseph! Is my father still
living?' But his brothers were not able to answer him, because
they were terrified at his presence. Then Joseph said to his brothers,
'Come close to me.' When they had done so, he said, 'I am your
brother Joseph, the one you sold into Egypt! And now, do not be
distressed and do not be angry with yourselves for selling me
here, because *it was to save lives that God sent me ahead of you* ... to
preserve for you a remnant on earth and to save your lives by a
great deliverance. So then, it was not you who sent me here, but
God' (Gen 45:2-8).

Joseph's statement is a remarkable one when you think about
it. God used the heartless treachery of his brothers as the providential source of their future blessing. There is an intimation in
this story of the way in which another brother would be delivered into the hands of the chief priests and the Roman authorities
who would cruelly murder him. And just as Joseph's suffering
became a source of blessing for those who inflicted it, so Jesus'
suffering and death would become the providential source of
salvation and healing for those who had caused it. We see that
same paradoxical dynamic at work in the life of St Peter.

A New Testament example
St Peter, the leading apostle, clearly loved the Lord. He was full
of good intentions and expressed a willingness to die with Jesus.
For his part, Jesus knew that Peter was, in fact, incapable of carrying out his resolution. His lack of self-awareness and spiritual
presumption closed his personality to the power of God. Hence
the strange prayer of Jesus in Lk 22:31-34 which was referred to
in the chapter on the intercessory prayer. He said: 'Simon,
Simon, Satan has asked to sift you as wheat. But I have prayed

for you, Simon, that your faith may not fail. And when you have turned back, strengthen your brothers.' There are two notable points about this remarkable prayer. Firstly, Jesus knows that the power of evil will exploit Peter's vulnerability during passion week. Secondly, he doesn't pray that Peter will resist in the day of temptation. He knows that, given his spiritual immaturity, presumption and lack of self-awareness, his fall is inevitable. So he prays instead that the disillusioned Peter will not loose trust in him, as Judas did, and that afterwards he will be strengthened by the Holy Spirit. Clearly, Jesus had Pentecost in mind here.

Jesus' prayer was answered after his death, resurrection, and ascension. The apostles met in the upper room. There they had time for reflection. No doubt each one looked into his own heart and remembered the shameful way in which he had deserted the Lord in his hour of need. Peter more than any of them would have had reason to weep bitter tears of sorrow, on account of his own cowardly behaviour. As one saint has said, 'Knowledge of self without knowledge of God can lead to despair.' I imagine that Mary tried to encourage Peter. For example, she could have recalled the beatitude which says, 'Blessed are those who mourn; they shall be comforted.' (Mt 5:4). This saying is not so much a reference to mourning for a human loss, as mourning on account of sin. The reference to comfort is another intimation of the coming of the Holy Spirit, the Comforter. As Jean Vanier has said, 'The Holy Spirit, the Paraclete, is God's answer to the cry of the broken human heart' (cf. 2 Cor 7:10). After a time of repentance, Pentecost followed and the apostles were filled with the Spirit. At this time Peter could have cried out, 'Oh happy fault, oh necessary sin of betrayal, that won for me such an outpouring of the Holy Spirit.' He could have quoted what Paul was to say – God has made us 'prisoners of disobedience in order that God might show mercy' (Rom 11:32).

A personal example

Surely this principle can be extended not only to our sins but also to our sufferings. We can thank God in all circumstances, rather than for all circumstances, in the knowledge that they can become the springboards to God's grace either sooner or later. I can remember an occasion that occurred many years ago. I was

due to attend a conference for priests. I travelled to it by motor-
bike. As I went along the road I was singing hymns. At one point
I prayed: 'Lord if you have any message for the conference
please speak to me.' Then I felt inwardly that the Lord was saying, 'Tell your fellow priests about the pearl of great price.'
While I was glad to get that word, I didn't really know what it
meant. When I got to the conference there was a preparatory
prayer session. During a quiet time the image of an oyster came
to mind. It was on the mud of the sea floor surrounded by water.
I understood that the sea floor was the world, the sea the Spirit,
and the oyster, the human person. Then I felt that the Lord was
saying: 'Think of how a pearl is formed. Grit and dirt from the
sea-bed get into the oyster. It cannot expel it. So it secretes a
milky liquid which surrounds the grit over a seven year period.
The greater the irritation the greater the pearl that is finally
formed. It is the same with the human heart. The sin of the
world makes an entry. But in my compassion I weave the pearl
of mercy around it. The greater the sin the greater the pearl that
is finally formed. Tell the priests not to be disheartened by their
weaknesses. I will bring good from evil, blessing from failure.'
As St Paul proclaimed: 'Where sin increased, grace increased all
the more' (Rom 5:20).

Over the years I have found that the following prayer exercise is very beneficial. I think either of the greatest sin or the
greatest misfortune in my life, or in the life of the community,
e.g. church scandals. Then I express my negative feelings such as
shame, humiliation, anger, guilt, etc., but then I go on to express
my faith conviction in prayers of thanksgiving. Like many others I have found that thanksgiving of this kind opens up my
heart to the liberating power of God. I'm not surprised that
Anthony de Mello said that if he had to choose the one form of
prayer that made Christ's presence most real in his life it would
be the prayer of thanksgiving. He explained: 'The prayer consists quite simply in thanking God for everything. It is based on
the belief that nothing happens in our life that is not foreseen
and planned by God – just nothing, not even our sins.'[6] I'm sure
that Merlin Carothers is correct when he says in his books, such
as *Prison to Praise* and *Power in Praise*, that if, in adverse circumstances, we thank God in an unconditional way, the circumstances themselves can change in a remarkable manner.[7]

Why not try this suggestion: Think of something in the past or present that is causing you pain, distress, guilt or frustration. If you are in any way to blame for this thing, express your regret and sorrow to the Lord. Now explicitly thank God for this, praise the Lord for it ... Tell God that you believe that even this fits into the divine plan for you and so God will draw great good from this for you and for others, even though you may not see the good. Leave this thing and all the other events of your life, past, present and to come, in the hands of God and rest in the peace and relief that this will bring.[8] As two Greek Orthodox writers observe: 'Lips forever giving thanks receive God's blessing, and a heart filled with gratitude unexpectedly receives grace.'[9]

Appreciation as praise

In Eph 1:12 we read: 'We who have first hoped in Christ, have been destined and appointed for the praise of his glory.' Heb 13:15 adds: 'Through Jesus, therefore, let us continually offer to God a sacrifice of praise – the fruit of lips that confess his name.' Again in 1 Pet 2:9 we are told that: 'You are a chosen people, a royal priesthood, a holy nation, a people belonging to God, that you may declare the praises of him who called you out of darkness into his wonderful light.' The prayer of praise helps us to escape the gravitational pull of self-absorption to become engrossed in the awareness of God. Having appreciated the gifts of the Giver, we go on to appreciate the Giver of the gifts. Praise, therefore, focuses on the person and attributes of God.

For example, on one occasion St Vincent de Paul said: 'Make every effort to conceive a great, a very great, idea of the majesty and sanctity of God. If we could penetrate even a little into the immensity of God's sovereign excellence, we could say with St Paul, that eyes have not seen, nor ears heard, nor the mind conceived anything like it. God is the unlimited perfection, the eternal being, most holy, most pure, most perfect, and infinitely glorious. God is the infinite good, encompassing all that is good, and the divine is wholly incomprehensible.'[10] This knowledge which we have, that God is infinitely above all human understanding, ought to be enough to make us esteem God infinitely, to humble ourselves in the divine presence, and make us speak of the Lord's majesty with great reverence. Our appreciation of God ought to be in proportion to our love. This love should make us have a strong desire to acknowledge God's blessings, and to be counted among those who praise the divine majesty. In chapter four we noted how God is manifested to those who pay self-forgetful attention to divine revelation. In the chapter on seeking God's will in prayer, we mentioned a four-step examen of consciousness which enables people to reflect on their religious experience, especially on their awareness of what the God of their experience is like. While there will be similarities between experiences of the Lord, like snowflakes they will all be different in subtle ways. It is this form of contemplative awareness that is the real source of genuine praise.

It is good to praise God in private prayer. I know that many people spontaneously articulate their praise in their own language. They might read a psalm of praise, or sing a hymn. As Col 3:16 urges: 'Sing psalms, hymns and spiritual songs with gratitude in your hearts to God.' Those who have the gift of praying and singing in tongues can use this resource to praise God in a sustained way. This gift of prayer was mentioned by St Paul. Having stated that he prayed in tongues more than anyone (1 Cor 14:18) and that he would like everyone to have this, the least of the gifts (1 Cor 14:5), St Paul said in 1 Cor 14:2; 14 that those who pray in a tongue 'do not speak to other people but to God; for nobody understands them, since they are speaking mysteries in the Spirit ... If I pray in a tongue my spirit prays but my mind is unproductive.' In Rom 8:27 he added: 'and God who searches the heart, knows what is the mind of the Spirit, because the Spirit prays ... according to the will of God.'

Praise in tongues
The charism of tongues is a form of pre-rational, non-conceptual prayer of the contemplative kind in so far as the human spirit prayerfully focuses its attention on God without the aid of thought or image. Commenting on the non-conceptual forms of *glossolalia*, Cardinal Suenens wrote: 'Praying in tongues is in relation to discursive prayer as is abstract art to figurative art.'[11] Eddie Ensley has indicated that throughout the ages non-conceptual prayer has been an aspect of Catholic piety in the form of

jubilation. The English word is derived from the Latin *jubilatio*, meaning 'loud shouting, whooping'. He says that there were different types. Firstly, there was musical jubilation in the form of wordless singing. St Augustine described it as follows. 'What is jubilation? It means to realise that words are not enough to express what we are singing in our hearts ... Joy brims over and ... people give themselves up to the sheer sound of singing.'[12] Secondly, there was mystical jubilation which was a flow of wordless musical sounds, often accompanied by the laughter and gestures that accompany intense spiritual experience. Richard Rolle (1300-1349), an English mystic, described how he experienced this kind of prayer: 'Whilst I sat in the chapel at night, before supper, I sang psalms, as I might, and I heard above me the noise as it were of singers. Whilst I took heed, praying to heaven with all desire, in what manner I know not, suddenly I received a most pleasant heavenly melody dwelling within my mind. Indeed my thought was continuously changed into mirth of song.'[13]

Sometimes the prayer of praise, whether in one's own language or in tongues, will be characterised by ecstatic joy. St Teresea of Avila wrote: 'The joy of the soul in this jubilation is so exceedingly great that it would prefer not to praise God in solitude, but to tell its joy to all, so that they might help it to praise our Lord, to which end it directs its whole activity.' Speaking within a Carmelite context, she described how private prayer can spill over into community life in a contagious way. 'How fortunate,' she observed, 'to be in a convent, where people won't speak against you if you praise God in this way, but will encourage you to praise God the more ... Sometimes it makes me especially glad when we are together and I see my sisters so full of inward joy that each vies with the rest in praising the Lord ... I should like you to often praise God, for when one of you begins to do so, she arouses the rest. How can your tongues be better employed when you are together than in the praises of God, which we have so many reasons for rendering?'[14]

St Teresa is correct when she says that personal praise reaches its fullest most satisfying expression in public praise. The bible says that this form of public prayer should be loud and long. For example, Ps 33:3 says: 'Sing to him a new song; play skillfully, and *shout* for joy.' Ps 47:1 adds: 'Clap your hands, all you nations; *shout* to God with cries of joy.' The Psalter ends with these words, which emphasise the role of loud musical instruments in the praise of God: 'Praise him with the sounding of the trumpet, praise him with the harp and lyre, praise him with tambourine and dancing, praise him with the strings and flute, praise him with the clash of cymbals, praise him with resounding cymbals. Let everything that has breath praise the Lord.' (Ps 150:3-6). The author of Sir 43:29-33 says: 'Where shall we find the strength to praise him? For he is greater than all his works. Terrible is the Lord and very great, and marvellous is his power. When you praise the Lord, exalt him as much as you can, for he will surpass even that. When you exalt him, put forth all your strength, and do not grow weary, for you cannot praise him enough. Who has seen him and can describe him? Or who can praise him as he is?'

Many contemporary pentecostal, evangelical and charismatic congregations have developed the skill of praising God in an enthusiastic, spontaneous and sustained way. Normally it consists of a mixture of vocal praise in their own language, hymns of praise, singing in tongues, clapping, and even dancing. Some people may read scripture texts that encourage praise, or exercise a gift of the Spirit such as prophecy or visions which would give people even more reason to praise God. For example, a number of years ago I attended a prayer meeting in Belfast. The praise was fairly pathetic. Then a woman saw an image of birds sitting on a wall. Although they had wings they never seemed to fly. The Lord gave her to understand: 'Unless the birds use the wings of praise, I will not be able to bear them up on the wind of my Spirit.' As soon as the people made the *decision* to praise, the Lord did the rest, until they were lifting the roof with enthusiastic appreciation. Those who are praising the Lord are aware that they are threatened by all kinds of problems, personal and public. But in their praises they express confidence in the victory of God, sometimes in shouts of praise. In the scriptures this form of prayerful appreciation was known as the *teruwah* Yahweh.

The festal shout of praise
In the Old Testament there are frequent references to battles. Over and over again, the people of God had to contend with

armies that were larger and better equipped. But the Israelites had one great advantage. They had confidence that if they were following the Lord's will, God would be fighting with them. No matter what odds were stacked against them, they would be victorious. As they marched into battle they would utter the *teruwah*. It was a piercing, blood curdling war cry that was intended to strike terror into the hearts of their enemies. It was also a liturgical chant that was meant to express their unshakable confidence in the One who would give them the victory.[15] There are many examples of this form of anticipatory praise in the Old Testament. We will focus on one. It is to be found in 2 Chr 20.

King Jehosophat received news that his kingdom was about to be attacked by formidable armies. From a military point of view, the position looked hopeless. Not surprisingly the king was filled with fear and anxiety. But instead of wrestling with the problem, he nestled by faith in the Lord by means of prayer and fasting. Having poured out his heart to the Lord, Jehosophat waited for a divine response. It came through one of his priests who spoke a word of prophecy. 'Your majesty,' he said, 'and all you people of Judah and Jerusalem, the Lord says you must not be discouraged or afraid to face this large army. The battle depends on God and not on you.' (2 Chr 20:15).

We are told that: 'early in the morning .... as the army set out, Jehoshaphat stood and said, "Listen to me, Judah and people of Jerusalem! Have faith in the Lord your God and you will be upheld; have faith in his prophets and you will be successful." After consulting the people, Jehoshaphat appointed men to sing to the Lord and to praise him for the splendour of his holiness as they went out at the head of the army, saying: "Give thanks to the Lord, for his love endures forever".' In other words, the priests and musicians led the soldiers in shouting the *teruwah* Yahweh as they marched into battle. The scriptures tell us what happened next: 'As they began to sing and praise, the Lord set ambushes against the men of Ammon and Moab and Mount Seir who were invading Judah, and they were defeated.' (2 Chr 20:20-22). As the Lord says in Ps 46:10: 'Be still, and know that I am God; I will be exalted among the nations, I will be exalted in the earth.'

Later in the Old Testament we find that when the chosen
people had settled down in Palestine there were fewer wars. But
they remembered the battle cry of victory. They modified it for
use in their temple worship. It became the 'festal shout' that is
sometimes mentioned in the psalms. For example, in Ps 47:1-8
we read: 'Clap your hands, all you nations; *shout to God* with
cries of joy … God has ascended amid shouts of joy, the Lord
amid the sounding of trumpets. Sing praises to God, sing praises;
sing praises to our King, sing praises. For God is the King of all
the earth; sing to him a psalm of praise.' However, Ps 89:15 sums
up the biblical attitude when it declares: 'Blessed are the people
who know the *festal shout*.' There are a number of examples of
the festal shout of victory in the Old and New Testaments. The
three young men praised God in the fiery furnace. Instead of
being burnt they were set free (cf. Dan 3:24). Jonah praised God
in the belly of the whale. Instead of being lost at sea he was
coughed up on the shore (cf. Jonah 2:9-10). On Palm Sunday, the
praises of the people constituted a festal shout that anticipated
the victory of Jesus over Satan, sin and death. As Jesus said on
that occasion, if the people didn't utter the festal shout 'the
stones will cry out' (Lk 19:40). We saw in chapter two how Jesus
praised God on the cross. The Father vindicated the Son when
he raised him from the dead. In the Acts of the Apostles we are
told how, having being unjustly scourged, Paul and Silas praised
God in the prison of Phillipi. Instead of remaining prisoners they
were liberated by an apparent earthquake (cf. Acts 16:25-26).

My personal conviction about the importance of the festal
shout of praise was nurtured during the troubles in Northern
Ireland. Ecumenically minded Christians seemed to face impossible odds and so we had to rely on God. For example, an inter-
faith conference was held in Belfast during a time of civil unrest
in the mid nineteen seventies. There was the threat of violence in
the streets. Nevertheless, over a thousand Protestants and
Catholics gathered in Church House in the centre of the city for a
'Festival of Praise.' It was a remarkable experience. There was an
outburst of strong, sustained praise such as I had never heard
before. God's anointing fell upon us and we were graced with
the festal shout, the kind that anticipates in praise the liberating
action of God. In a prophecy the Lord called upon us to be united

as God's army. 'The work and the weapons are one,' God said, 'they are praise.'

At a time when we face so many problems both inside and outside the church, those words are as relevant now as they were in the nineteen seventies. The words of Hab 3:17-18, which were written around 620 BC, express a biblical hope that is rooted in unshakable trust in God: 'Though the fig tree does not bud and there are no grapes on the vines, though the olive crop fails and the fields produce no food, though there are no sheep in the pen and no cattle in the stalls, yet I will rejoice in the Lord, I will be joyful in God my Saviour.'

Appreciation as worship

In the psalms there are many calls to worship the Lord. In Ps 29:2 we read: 'Ascribe to the Lord the glory due his name; worship the Lord in the splendour of his holiness,' and in Ps 132:7: 'Let us go to his dwelling place; let us worship at his footstool.' Finally, in Ps 86:9 the psalmist says: 'All the nations you have made will come and worship before you, O Lord; they will bring glory to your name.' Over the years I have discovered that in the prayer of thanksgiving and praise we have to cooperate with the grace of God by endeavouring to praise God in a sincere, enthusiastic way. But where worship is concerned, the emphasis shifts from what we do for God, to what God does for us by means of a special anointing. It says in Ps 22:1 that 'The Lord lives in the praises of his people.' If people lift the chalice of their personal or collective thanksgiving and praise to God, the Lord can fill it with the sweet wine of worship. It is a state of mind and heart that is the outcome of a special blessing of the Spirit which reveals the Lord's palpable presence and glory to those who are absorbed in prayer. This contemplative awareness evokes a deeper form of praise until it rests in a quiet sense of awe-filled worship. This kind of adoration is best expressed in the form of reverential silence. As St John of the Cross wrote: 'The Father uttered one word; that Word is his Son, and utters him for ever in everlasting silence; and in silence the soul has to hear it.'[16] Rev 8:1 informs us that at a particularly intense moment of worship 'there was silence in heaven for about half an hour'.

The fathers of the church have suggested that there are three interrelated liturgies, those of the heart, the altar and heaven. They intersect in the Eucharist which is the supreme Christian prayer of appreciation which gathers our prayers of thanksgiving and praise in heartfelt worship of God.[17] The artist Raphael (1483-1520) painted a fresco in the Stanza della Segnatura, entitled *Disputa*. It tried to depict these theological truths in a pictorial way. It shows the church triumphant in heaven and the church militant on earth centred around an altar on which the Eucharist is exposed. The word 'Eucharist' is derived from Greek words which mean 'to give thanks for freely given grace'. The English word 'liturgy' is also derived from Greek, and could be loosely translated as 'the people's work'. Eucharistic liturgy, then, is the people's conscious task of showing public appreciation to God for gifts and graces received, in the form of thanksgiving, praise and worship.

We can talk about the liturgy of the heart because the Holy Trinity dwells within us in virtue of our baptism. As a result the Spirit prays: 'Abba Father' (Rom 8:15; Gal 4:6) whether we are consciously aware of that prayer or not. We awaken our hearts in so far as we become consciously aware of the Spirit within praying to the God beyond. In *Teach Us to Pray*, Andre Louf says: 'Our heart, our true heart, is asleep; and it has to be woken up gradually – through the course of a whole lifetime ... Each and every method of prayer has but one objective: to find the heart and alert it.'[18] The extent to which a person is absent from the inner sanctum of his or her own heart, is the extent to which s/he will fail to have an experiential appreciation of either the liturgies of the altar or of heaven.

The liturgy of heaven is that which is conducted by the angels and saints as they praise and worship the Lord of Glory whom they see face to face. The books of Hebrews and Revelation give us some small insight into this heavenly adoration. There is a marvellous depiction of this celestial liturgy in Rev 7:9-12. It is read in the Mass of the feast of All Saints: 'After this I looked and there before me was a great multitude that no one could count, from every nation, tribe, people and language, standing before the throne and in front of the Lamb. They were wearing white robes and were holding palm branches in their hands. And they cried out in a loud voice: "Salvation belongs to our God, who sits on the throne, and to the Lamb." All the angels were standing around the throne and around the elders and the four living creatures. They fell down on their faces before the throne and worshipped God, saying: "Amen! Praise and glory and wisdom and thanks and honour and power and strength be to our God for ever and ever. Amen!" Speaking of the heavenly host, Rev 5:8-14 says: 'Then I looked and heard the voice of many angels, numbering thousands upon thousands, and ten thousand times ten thousand. They encircled the throne and the living creatures and the elders. In a loud voice they sang: "Worthy is the Lamb, who was slain, to receive power and wealth and wisdom and strength and honour and glory and praise!" Then I heard every creature in heaven and on earth and under the earth and on the sea, and all that is in them, singing: "To him who sits on the throne and to the Lamb be praise and honour and glory and power, for ever and ever!" The four living creatures said, '"Amen," and the elders fell down and worshiped.' In Col 3:1-2 the author says: 'Since, then, you have been raised with Christ, set your hearts on things above, where Christ is seated at the right hand of God. Set your minds on things above, not on earthly things.'

The liturgies of the heart and of heaven converge in the liturgy of the altar. In Rev 19:5-7 we are told that: 'a voice came from the throne, saying: "Praise our God, all you his servants, you who fear him, both small and great!"' It would seem that we are being summoned to show appreciation to God in our earthly adoration. We do this in a special way in the Eucharist when we thank, praise and worship the Father, through the Son, by the power of the Spirit who is at work within each heart, and also in the community. In this great prayer we gather together our sense of appreciation for who God is, and for all that God has done for us. Each time I celebrate the Eucharist I'm particularly struck by the words that precede the consecration of the bread and wine: 'The day before he suffered he took bread in his sacred hands and looking up to heaven, to you, his almighty Father, *he gave you thanks and praise.*' We know that as he hung upon the cross, Jesus quoted a line of Ps 22. But as we noted in chapter two, it is highly likely that Jesus went on to offer its subsequent words of praise to God. His final cry, 'Father, into your hands I commit my spirit' Lk 23:46 was his definitive festal shout of victory. It anticipated the vindication of God when he would be raised from the dead into glorious new life. We ought to do the same. When the outlook is bleak, we can look upwards, and praise God because: 'we know (like Jesus) that *in all things* God works for the good of those who love him, who have been called according to his purpose' (Rom 8:28).

Conclusion

The prayer of appreciation is an important one. As the *Shorter Westminster Catechism* says: 'Men's chief end is to glorify God, and to enjoy God forever.' Besides stressing the need for sincerity in the prayers of thanksgiving, praise and worship, the scriptures make it clear that we need to express our sense of appreciation for God and the gifts of God, by the way we live. For example, in Rom 12:1 Paul sums up this point when he says: 'I urge you, brothers and sisters, in view of God's mercy, to offer your bodies as living sacrifices, holy and pleasing to God – this is your spiritual act of worship.' When he spoke in the Phoenix Park in Dublin in 1979, Pope John Paul II mentioned the same point. Among other things he said: 'There must always be consistency between what we say and what we do … Our union with Christ in the Eucharist must be expressed in the truth of our lives today – in our actions, in our behaviour, in our lifestyle, and in our relationship with others … The truth of our union with Jesus Christ in the Eucharist is tested by whether or not we really love our fellow men and women; it is tested by how we treat others, especially our husbands and wives, children and parents, brothers and sisters.'[19] This topic will be explored in the last chapter.

Finally, I am convinced that as we express our prayerful appreciation in words and deeds it does a number of things. Firstly, it acts as a spiritual shield that puts 'out all the fiery darts of the Evil One' (Eph 6:16). In this way we are protected from evil. Secondly, if instead of magnifying our problems by concentrating on them, we magnify God by concentrating on the Lord, we not only express our confidence in the Lord we also anticipate the help that God is going to give us. Lastly, when we engage in the prayer of appreciation we not only echo the praises of heaven, and anticipate our personal hope of resurrection, we serve an apprenticeship for what we will be doing eternally in Paradise.

CHAPTER ELEVEN

Growth in prayer

Classical Western culture, from the Greeks up to the Enlightenment, stressed the importance of being, and had a cyclical, recurrent view of history. Since then, however, Western culture has stressed the importance of becoming and has an evolutionary, linear view of history. Nowadays we emphasise change rather than stability. From sub-atomic particles to the greatest galaxies, all things are in a state of flux. Civilisations rise and fall, but overall societies seem to become more knowledgeable and complex. The human body keeps on changing too. Every cell within us is replaced every seven years or so. Our personalities also develop through a succession of stages, each of which presents us with a specific developmental challenge. Relationships don't stand still either. They either grow or decline. As Cardinal Newman wrote: 'In a higher world it is otherwise; but here below to live is to change; and to be perfect is to have changed often.'[1]

The paradigm shift we have adverted to has had a big impact upon our understanding of the Christian life. That change in perspective was acknowledged in Vatican II's *The Church in the Modern World* when it stated that humankind has substituted 'a dynamic and more evolutionary concept of nature for a static one.'[2] This shift of emphasis has had important and noticeable effects on spirituality and therefore on our understanding of prayer. Instead of focusing primarily on the experience of objective religious authority, as heretofore, it now focuses mainly on the authority of subjective, but orthodox, religious experience.

Spirituality based on objective authority tends to be essentialist and dutiful in orientation. It sees Christian perfection largely in terms of obedience. For example, it could point to the following verse which describes Jesus: 'In the scroll of the book

it is written of me, see God, I have come to do your will' (Heb
10:7). In the past, Christians tended to carry out the injunction,
'Be perfect as your Father is perfect' (Mt 5:48), primarily by
keeping the commandments. Spirituality based on the experience
of Christian truth tends to be existentialist and to be motivated
by inner convictions. Instead of aspiring to a static notion of perfection, it is energised by a heartfelt desire for on-going spiritual
transformation and wholeness. This point of view stresses the
fact that Jesus 'grew and became strong, filled with wisdom, and
the favour of God was upon him' (Lk 2:40). At present, an increasing number of Christians aim primarily at developing their
psycho-spiritual potential. Their viewpoint is encapsulated in
the texts: 'Your mind must be renewed in spirit so that you can
put on ... the new self ... in order to come ... to the maturity, the
measure of the full stature of Christ' (Eph 2:23; Col 3:10; Eph
4:13).

Crisis and growth
In the latter half of the last century a number of overlapping developmental theories attempted to describe the process of
human growth. People such as Piaget, Erickson, Kohlberg and
Fowler, mapped out the dynamics of cognitive, psychosocial,
moral, and faith development respectively. By and large, these
theorists suggested that life is made up of succession of stages
characterised by relative stability which are succeeded by periods
of crisis.[3] For example, psychiatrist Jack Dominian has described
identifiable stages in marriage relationships during the early,
middle and late years of a couple's life together.[4] The *elan* of
friendship is not much different. In marriage and friendship,
growth is often the consequence of having to cope with painful
periods of transition, conflict or separation that invite the people
involved to deepen their communication and to re-examine
their respective perceptions and priorities. All of the researchers
are agreed that growth is more likely to occur during periods of
instability than during times of stability. Consequently,
Erickson speaks for them all when he refers to 'the potency of
disorder'. He says that life crises should be evaluated in a positive way, 'not as a threat or a catastrophe, but as a turning point,
a crucial period of increased vulnerability and heightened pot-

ential.'[5] Surely this point holds true in the realm of spirituality as well. As Catholic theology asserts, grace builds upon nature.

From a Christian point of view, life crises are times when we feel challenged to let go of worldly perspectives and inadequate understandings in order to embrace more fully those of the scriptures. This notion is implicit in a number of biblical stories such as the forty year exodus of the Jews. Following the relative predictability of their lives in the land of the Pharaohs, the people endured the unpredictability of having to wander for forty years in the wilderness. We are told that the Lord had wanted to test, purify and deepen their self-awareness by means of hardship and deprivation. In Deut 8:2-3 we read: 'The Lord your God has led you these forty years in the wilderness, that he might humble you, testing you to know what was in your heart.'

Having been baptised in the Spirit, Jesus was led, like the Jews of old, into the wilderness for a symbolic forty days of testing. There he not only fasted, he had to endure a number of trials and temptations. During this time of spiritual combat, the Father allowed Satan to sift him like wheat. As a result he grew in discernment of spirits and was prepared for his role as exorcist. Passion week proved to be another, more profound exodus, when Jesus faced even more formidable difficulties, such his betrayal by Judas and Peter. He was also buffeted by Satan at the very time when he felt forsaken by his Father. It was as if the Evil One were saying to the demons: 'He boasts of having God as his Father. Let us see if what he says is true and test him to see what sort of end he will have. For if the upright man is God's son, God will help him and rescue him from the clutches of his enemies. Let us test him with cruelty and with torture and thus explore this gentleness of his and put his patience to the test. Let us condemn him to a shameful death since God will rescue him – or so he claims' (Wis 2:17-20). Throughout his ordeal, Jesus trusted in the One who could save him from death (cf. Heb 5:7).

Predictable and unpredictable crises

There are two types of psycho-spiritual crisis, predicable and unpredictable. Predictable crises are the turbulent times between developmental stages, such as those that occur during adolescence and at mid-life. They are likely to happen in every decade of our lives and usually last for up to three years. Then there are unpredictable crises, when we have to cope with the slings and arrows of outrageous fortune, such as illness, bereavement, financial problems, unemployment, etc. It is not uncommon for predictable and unpredictable crises to coincide. During these times of change, the Lord removes the things which have been sustaining the worldly self. Instead of enjoying security, success, status and control, we may have to drink the bitter vinegar of failure, loss, humiliation and vulnerability. It is then that current ways of interpreting experience prove to be inadequate in dealing with the challenges and complexities of life. As the scaffolding that supported the ego is dismantled, there is often a painful sense of hurt and anger. Some people repress the anger, in an unhealthy way, so that it turns to feelings of anxiety and depression. As a result, God seems remote and prayer unreal.

It is healthier to get in touch with the anger and to admit it to oneself and the Lord. It is said that while others may stimulate our anger, the causes lie within. As we begin to get in touch with the inner roots of our anger we may come to recognise that, although we felt that we were observing the first commandment by putting God first, things like success, status, reputation, pleasure and the like, had, unbeknown to us, become our *de facto* gods. Reality dawns when the threat of losing them stimulates our anger. At such a time of disillusionment we may get in touch with a deep-seated desire for a new sense of God, self and values. This kind of spiritual desire is inspired by the Spirit and prepares us for a new revelation of the Lord and the Lord's will. As we pour out our feelings and desires to the Lord, unredeemed worldly time can become sacred, redeemed time, when we experience a new advent and manifestation of God. This kind of conversion experience can have the effect of re-focusing the personality. It begins to move away from worldly values to become more centred on Christ and his values.

Three types of desolation in prayer
At this point I would like to describe another way in which growth in prayer occurs. St Ignatius of Loyola indicated that the Lord will sometimes withdraw his consolations from people in order to purify their wills and to invite them to move from im-

mature to mature religion by being more fully devoted to the person and will of God. Like Jesus himself, every Christian has to endure spiritual dryness, darkness and distractions at one time or another. In my experience, desolation of spirit is particularly likely during life crises. Speaking about consolation and desolation, Ignatius says: 'The term spiritual consolation describes our interior life when we find ourselves so on fire with the love of God that neither anything or anyone presents itself in competition with a total gift of self to God in love. Rather we begin to see everything and everyone in the context of God, their Creator and Lord ... The term spiritual desolation describes our interior life when we find ourselves enmeshed in a certain turmoil of spirit or feel ourselves weighed down by a heavy darkness or weight.'[6]

While one can experience periods of desolation during times of relative stability in one's life, more often than not they are associated with periods of spiritual crisis and change. St Ignatius described three forms of desolation. Although they may be similar from an experiential point of view, their purpose is different. St Ignatius begins by saying that God may withdraw consolation as a result of spiritual laziness, neglect of prayer, or lack of effort in resisting sin. God allows desolation in this case in order to purify the person and to bring him or her to a point of single minded re-dedication to the things of God. As Heb 12:6-10 attests: 'The Lord disciplines those he loves ... we have all had human fathers who disciplined us and we respected them for it. How much more should we submit to the Father of our spirits and live! Our fathers disciplined us for a little while as they thought best; but God disciplines us for our good, that we may share in his holiness.'

At the beginning stages of the spiritual journey many people fail to notice that they seek the consolations of God rather than the God of consolation. In instances like this, the Lord withdraws consolation in order to wean them off a desire for pleasant or unusual experiences so that they might become more committed to Jesus, for his own sake. In the earlier stages of their spiritual lives people commonly focus on what God can do for them. If God were to ask them the question, 'what do you want?' they would respond by asking for graces and favours, such as,

'Lord grant me your mercy ... your love ... your peace, your healing ... such and such a material gift, etc.' However, as people grow spiritually, the focus shifts from what God can do for them, to what they can do for God. When they are asked by God 'what do you want?' they respond: 'Lord, because I love you, I want what you want. Reveal your will to me, that I may carry it out to your greater glory.' As Dan 11:35 says: 'Some of the wise will stumble, so that they may be refined, purified and made spotless.'

There is a third kind of desolation that is experienced by people who are mature in the Christian life. God withdraws consolation from them in order to teach them in an experiential way that the gifts of God are entirely gratuitous and cannot be acquired or earned by human effort. As Ignatius says: 'God does not want us ... to rise up in spirit in a certain pride and vainglory and attribute to ourselves the devotion and other effects of spiritual consolation.'[7] This kind of desolation is akin to the dark night of the soul described by the mystics. When some immature Christians experience the first or second forms of desolation, they mistakenly believe that they are undergoing the kind of dark night of the soul which was experienced by saints like John of the Cross and Thérèse of Lisieux. One is reminded in this connection of Paul's thorn in the flesh. Arguably it could have been desolation of spirit. 'Three times,' he says, 'I pleaded with the Lord to take it away from me. But he said to me, "My grace is sufficient for you, for my power is made perfect in weakness." Therefore I will boast all the more gladly about my weaknesses, so that Christ's power may rest on me' (2 Cor 12:8-9).

Coping with desolation

Ignatius warns that those who pray can expect to experience shorter and longer periods of desolation. As Margaret Hebblethwaite has observed: 'A down is not necessarily a sign that something is wrong. It may on the contrary be a sign of progress, in that it means we have progressed beyond our last pleasant plateau of consolation.'[8] Nevertheless, times of desolation are unrewarding periods of dryness and distraction. As a result Ignatius says that it is good to remember a number of points.

Firstly, acknowledge that your poverty of spirit, your ac-

knowledgement of helplessness and weakness is a salutary
awareness of creature feeling. It is hard to pray during desolation. The time seems long, and boring. Distractions abound.
God seems far away. One is tempted to give up reading spiritual
books, the scriptures and praying all together. Ignatius says that
it is important to resist an inclination like this with courage and
energy. He counsels that pray-ers should remain faithful to their
normal prayer practices even if they are emotionally unrewarding.

Secondly, times of desolation are times when negative feelings are common. In my experience, there can often be a conscious or a repressed sense of anger. This presenting emotion
has its roots in unmet needs and a sense of hurt, loss and frustration. Often when we acknowledge our anger we will see that it is
due to the fact that we feel that God has betrayed and deserted
us. It is important not to suppress emotions like these because of
fear of divine retribution or resentment against God. Otherwise
they will alienate us unnecessarily from the divine presence,
thereby prolonging the desolation. We not only need to acknowledge our feelings and their causes to ourselves, but also to
confess them honestly to the Lord in prayer. In this way we escape the gravitational pull of self-absorption. Furthermore, we
can try to express our faith conviction by thanking and praising
God for everything, in the belief that, providentially, God has allowed us to experience desolation for a purpose. As we do this,
the Lord can comfort rather than console us. In other words, although the Lord does not stir up pleasant feelings within, God
gives us the strength to endure with faithfulness. Often God
grants us this fortitude by means of a verse of scripture, e.g. 'We
can confidently say, "The Lord is my helper, I will not be afraid;
what can men do to me?".' (Heb 13:6). Words like this give us
the ability to battle on in the midst of desolation. Jesus may be
asleep in the boat of our personality as it is buffeted by inner and
outer forces, but we trust that we will not be overwhelmed (cf.
Ps 107:23-30; Mk 4:37-38).

Thirdly, times of desolation are periods when we can be
tempted to avoid negative feelings of an upsetting nature by
seeking consolation in escapist pursuits, e.g. comfort eating,
drinking too much alcohol or getting involved in sinful sexual
fantasies and activities. Obviously, we should try to resist inap-

propriate behaviour firm in our faith (cf. 1 Pt 5:9) while allowing ourselves to feel and disclose our negative feelings to God. If perchance we fall during the time of temptation, not only can we confess our sorrow with confidence to God, we can grow in realism and self-awareness, knowing that we are not as committed to the Lord as we had presumed during times of consolation. Pope John Paul I wrote during his brief pontificate: 'The Lord loves humility so much that he sometimes allows serious sins. Why? In order that those who committed them may, after repenting, remain humble. One does not feel inclined to think oneself half a saint, or half an angel, when one knows that one has committed serious faults.'

Fourthly, in times of desolation, says Ignatius, do not change a life-decision, such as marriage or priestly vows, which were made with associated consolation in the past, otherwise you may have the devil as your spiritual director. Due to the absence of consolation there is no sure way of discerning whether an inspiration comes from God or not. Finally, during times of desolation, counselled St Ignatius, think positively by reminding yourself that the consolation you experienced in the past will inevitably return in the future.

Times of desolation are occasions when the Lord invites us to grow in humble self-awareness, and to commit ourselves more fully in faith to the person and will of God. In this context it is worth noting that John Paul II has written: 'Faith in its deepest essence is the openness of the human heart to the gift: to God's self communication in the Holy Spirit.'[9] So growth in prayer, whether in times of consolation or desolation, leads to growth in trusting faith. As a person becomes increasingly aware of who God is and what God is like, false images of divinity are exposed, challenged and hopefully replaced. We have already noted in chapter three how positive experiences of the Lord are often followed by a fearful type of resistance that is rooted in God images of a forbidding nature. They are usually formed in early life. However, as one grows in prayerful relationship to Jesus and the Father, as they are and not as we have imagined them to be, we become increasingly aware of our own inner glory. We acknowledge that we are made in God's image, redeemed by God's mercy and are temples of God's living presence through the in-pouring of the Spirit of love.

So spiritual relatedness to the God Beyond and the God Within are interconnected. This awareness is the true source of increasing spiritual freedom. As St Paul says: 'The Lord is the Spirit, and where the Spirit of the Lord is, there is freedom' (2 Cor 3:17). Before concluding this section it is worth noting that Ignatius says that when a person enjoys spiritual consolation, and prayer is relatively easy and rewarding, there are a number of points worth remembering. We should not allow ourselves to become complacent, because it is only a matter of time before we will have to endure desolation of spirit again. Ignatius says we need to prepare by 'storing up a supply of strength as defence against that day.'[10] Then he adds that people in consolation should 'recall how little they were able to do in times of desolation, when they were left without such grace or consolation.'[11]

The stages of prayer
The stages of prayer can be described in different ways. Firstly, there is the movement from vocal to mental prayer. Beginners tend to say either formal prayers or to pray in a more personal, spontaneous way, if and when they feel like it. As they grow spiritually, however, they tend to arrange fixed times of prayer which can vary from a few minutes to an hour or more in length. Many of them find that the morning is the best time to pray, as they are fresh and relatively free from distractions. They know that later in the day there can be so many calls on their time that they would be unlikely to have the opportunity to pray.

As people mature in prayer, they tend to become more disciplined about their methods of praying. For example, some folks find that posture is important. I know that I like to sit bolt upright, without movement, with my back straight and my hands folded or resting on my knees. On other occasions, they may kneel, or prostrate themselves on the floor as an external sign of an inner attitude of reverence. A number of pray-ers like to begin their prayer time with a brief relaxation exercise as they know from experience that it is hard to be focused when one is tense.

Following these preliminaries, pray-ers may try to fix their attention on a passage from a spiritual book or a scripture text, e.g. from the bible, the liturgy of the day, or the Divine Office.

Some people like to use a scripture commentary in order to clarify the meaning of the text. Then they might go on to use a recognised method, such as the Benedictine or Ignatian, to pray about the text. As they mature in prayer they would spend less time in meditation and more in prayer and contemplation. Many men and women reserve a period at the end of their prayer time for intercessions.

Traditional Christian spirituality has also spoken about the purgative, illuminative and unitive stages of Christian prayer. During the purgative stage people learn to acknowledge and renounce sinful habits, attachments and attitudes. During the illuminative stage, they are enlightened by the Spirit of truth and acquire an intuitive understanding of God and the things of God. When the unitive stage is reached, people experience a loving union of their wills, if not their minds and imaginations, with the person and will of God, as revealed in Christ. At this stage, the attention of pray-ers moves from the knowability to the unknowability of God.

Knowing as not-knowing
Speaking about knowledge of God, one of the documents of the Fourth Latern Council stated: 'Between the Creator and creatures no similarity can be expressed without including a greater dissimilarity.' This is a paradoxical assertion. On the one hand it affirms the fact that, as we noted in chapter four, we can only come to know God indirectly by means of created things. This sense of revelation is made possible by the mediating power of feeling laden concepts and images drawn from everyday experience. The bible is full of this kind of mediated religious experience. Throughout the book I have stressed the importance of this approach in prayer. However, as the Latern Council rightly asserts, although this kind of knowledge of God is genuine, it is inadequate in so far as God is so exceedingly great, so utterly different from anything we know, that no concept or image, no matter how worthy or profound, is capable of doing justice to the incomprehensible mystery of divinity.[12]

Although the bible doesn't stress this point, it does advert to it in a number of places. For example, in Ex 3:13-14 we read: 'Moses said to God, Suppose I go to the Israelites and say to

them, 'The God of your fathers has sent me to you,' and they ask
me, 'What is his name?' Then what shall I tell them? God said to
Moses, I Am, Who Am. This is what you are to say to the
Israelites: 'I Am has sent me to you.' Notice that God does not
reveal the divine name to Moses. In biblical theology, a name
represented the nature of the nominated person. In refusing to
reveal the divine name the Lord was saying, 'I am beyond representation, there is no name that could symbolise my infinite perfection.' On Mount Tabor Jesus met with his Father. At first the
apostles were aware of his transfigured humanity, i.e. the mediated immediacy of God. But the experience deepened when a
cloud descended. It was a cloud of unknowing in which they
could no longer see the Lord although they had intimations of
his presence (cf. Mt 17:5). Some years later, the Pauline author
spoke about the limitless love of Christ 'which *surpasses knowledge*' (Eph 3:18-19) and 'the peace of God, which *transcends all
understanding*' (Phil 4:7). In other words, no image or concept
can encapsulate its greatness.

The incomprehensibility of God

Many of the saints have stressed the fact that, while beginners in
prayer focus on what can be known about God, those who are
growing in relationship with the Lord increasingly move beyond intellectual and imaginative representations of the Lord.
They are content, like the apostles on Mount Tabor, to leave
these aids behind and to rest in a loving, but agnostic, union
with God. For example, St John Chrysostom (347-407) wrote a
treatise entitled *The Incomprehensibility of God*. In it he said: 'Let
us invoke him as the inexpressible God, incomprehensible, invisible and unknowable; let us avow that he surpasses all power
of human speech, that he eludes the grasp of every mortal intel-
ligence, that the angels cannot penetrate him, nor the seraphim
see him in full clarity, nor the cherubim fully understand him,
for he is invisible to the principalities and powers and all creatures without exception; only the Son and the Holy Spirit know
him.' Many other saints have said similar things.

This notion has important implications for those who pray.
We have to move from the known to the unknown. In prayer we
begin with creation and the scriptures, but most of all with the

sacrament of Christ's humanity, his words and actions, because they are icons of God. By seeing and hearing him, we see and hear his Father. The Spirit, who searches everything, even the hidden depths of God, can reveal to us, by means of the gifts of wisdom and knowledge, the mysteries of Christ. But the Lord, having led us in this way can lead us further, to a point where the thoughts and symbols that served us well, in getting us thus far, begin to prove inadequate and dissatisfying. The pray-er finds that they no longer hold his or her attention. In moments of contemplation like these, mind and imagination can cease their activity, while the will rests in the darkness that envelops a loving God who lives in light inaccessible. Many of the mystics, such as John Cassian, Gregory of Palamas, John of the Cross and Teresa of Avila, have described different experiences of this kind of contemplative prayer.[13] I do not intend to describe, as they do, how the mind, imagination and will are purified in order to reach this point.[14] Suffice it to say that the process often occurs as a result of life crises and desolation of spirit, especially the third kind. God can use them to wean people off dependence on inadequate thoughts and images of the Godhead.

There are a number of prayer methods, such as centring prayer and the Jesus prayer, which aim to foster this kind of contemplative prayer. While use of this or a similar mantra can be excellent in itself, it should be used with caution. I'm convinced that Christians should normally engage in the scriptural forms of prayer described in earlier chapters. Then if God leads the soul to the more agnostic kinds of prayer, so be it, it is a good thing to follow the lead of the Spirit. It is worth repeating in this context that praying in tongues is a thoroughly scriptural way of engaging in prayer of a non-conceptual, contemplative kind. However, one should always return to the scriptures and the contemplation of Christ's humanity, so that conceptual and non-conceptual prayer can inform one another in a mutually enriching way.

Three Means of Growth
a) Spiritual direction

St Gregory the Great once said that 'the supreme art is the direction of souls.' Nowadays professional directors undergo a period
of intense training.[15] As a result they develop the skills they
need to help pray-ers to notice the presence and the inspirations
of God in their lives. As Cardinal Newman once wrote: 'God's
presence is not discerned at the time when it is upon us, but afterwards when we look back upon what is gone and over.'
Directors focus on the religious experience of their directees.
This form of experience, as we have already pointed out, has
four interconnected elements. Firstly, a desire to know Jesus and
the Father and to relate to them more deeply. Secondly, attention to creation and the scriptures. Thirdly, there is the revelation of who God is and what is God like. Fourthly, this awareness needs to be expressed in prayerful and practical terms.[16] As
the need arises, directors help directees to focus on these elements. They also assist them in acknowledging negative feelings
evoked either by life experiences or by false images of God that
might be blocking a conscious desire to relate and respond more
deeply to the Lord. Directors can also help their directees to see
for themselves whether a revelation or inspiration is from God,
the self or the evil one. They do this by focusing attention on tell-
tale inward states of consolation or desolation, in the belief that
those that are associated with consolation of spirit are normally
from God, whereas those that are associated with desolation of
spirit usually are not.

Anyone who wants to mature in prayerful relationship with
God would be well advised to seek the help of a director for a
fixed period of time. While there are many good priests, most of
them have not been trained in the art of spiritual direction. By
and large, I believe that a person would be better off having no
spiritual director than an unqualified one. I am reminded in this
regard of an observation of St Teresa of Avila: 'I have always
been attracted by learning, though confessors with only a little
of it have done my soul great harm, and I have not always found
men who had as much of it as I would have liked … A truly
learned man has never led me astray.'[17] Happily, there are
many qualified directors nowadays, clerical, religious and lay,

who are not only devout Christians themselves but experienced and competent in dealing with the dynamics of prayerful religious experience.

b) Directed retreats

Many lay people find that it is not easy to get away on retreat, directed or otherwise. Some will be able to attend an occasional day of reflection or renewal. However, those who can arrange to participate in a directed retreat, lasting between five, eight, or even thirty days, usually find that it provides a unique opportunity for growth in prayerful relationship with God. Incidentally, the Jesuits have developed a form of directed retreat that they refer to as the Eighteenth Annotation Retreat, that can last for months. The participants commit themselves to follow the *Spiritual Exercises* of St Ignatius in slow-motion in their homes. They also arrange to meet regularly with their spiritual director to share about how things are going. Five, eight and thirty day directed retreats are silent. Apart from the homily at Mass there are no talks. The emphasis is on spending many hours in personal prayer. Each day the retreatant goes to see his or her director to chat about the way things are going. This intensive exposure to spiritual direction can be extremely helpful in developing a more mature way of praying, one in which self-intimacy and interpersonal intimacy merge in an intimate encounter with the God who is both with us and within us.

c) Examen of consciousness

No matter what stage they are at, those who are growing in prayer need to engage in discernment of spirits. Jesus maintained that it was the intentions of the heart that determined what was good and bad. 'Do not keep judging,' he advised, 'according to outward appearances; let your judgment be according to what is right' (Jn 7:24). At another time he said, 'words flow from what fills the heart' (Mt 15:19), and again, 'From the heart come evil intentions: murder, adultery, fornication, theft, perjury, slander' (Mt 12:24). So, rather than looking at external actions, the art of discernment looks at inner states while trying to establish their origin and orientation, Do they come from God, the self or the evil one? Do they lead the person toward greater relationship with God, or do they weaken it?

It is good at the end of a prayer time, or at the end of the day, to engage in an examen of consciousness, as opposed to an examination of conscience, in order to 'test the spirits to see whether they are from God or not' (1 Jn 4:1).[18] I would suggest that you use following simple method. Relax your body. Calm your mind and imagination and affirm that God is present. Then use one or more of the following prayers:

Father in heaven ...

• Help me to recall with gratitude those occasions when I was aware of your presence today and to savour again what you meant to me.

• Help me to become aware of the promptings and inspirations you have given me and to know whether I responded to them or not.

• Enlighten my heart to recognise any unloving feeling, mood, attitude, desire, thought, word or deed that saddened your Holy Spirit.

Then one can conclude with a prayer such as the following: 'Father in heaven, thank you for the gift of your Spirit. It has urged me to see you more clearly, to love you more dearly, and to follow you more nearly. As for my shortcomings, please forgive them. In the future help me to respond more wholeheartedly to you, through Jesus Christ our Lord. Amen.' Spiritual writers are correct when they say that the examen of consciousness is a valuable means of growing in prayer.

Conclusion

In 2 Cor 3:18 there is a magnificent passage which encapsulates the spirit of contemporary spirituality. It reads: 'All of us with unveiled faces, seeing the glory of the Lord as though reflected in a mirror, are being transformed into the same image from one degree of glory to another, for this comes from the Lord; the Spirit.'[19] This verse describes how prayer can lead to spiritual growth. Paul explains what he means by unveiled faces in 2 Cor 3:16: 'Whenever anyone turns to the Lord, the veil is taken away.' It would seem, therefore, that the veil refers to those things that might separate the heart from the Lord. As we have noted, God can help us to purify our hearts by means of enlightening desolation. As the heart is cleansed, it is better able to behold and to reflect the glory of the Lord. We can behold that glory in all things, but particularly in the scriptures. As we encounter Christ and his Father in the word, we are transformed into the divine image, so that we become God bearers, witnesses to the presence and the loving mercy of the One who lives in our hearts through faith. Instead of being a definitive event, this is a lifelong process of growth. In the next chapter we will examine how our prayerful relationship with God needs to find expression in appropriate Christian action.

CHAPTER TWELVE

Prayer and praxis

We have already adverted to the relationship of prayer and action in chapter five. While it is vitally important to establish what God wants of us, it is equally important that we carry out the divine will in our daily lives. Scripture makes this connection abundantly clear. For example, Jesus concludes the parable of the sower, which is about prayerful openness to the word of God, by saying: 'Those that were sown upon the good soil are the ones who hear the word and accept it and bear good fruit' (Mk 4:20). Again in the parable of the two sons who were asked to go to the vineyard, one said he would go, but did not, the other said he would not go. Afterwards he changed his mind and actually went. Then Jesus asked his listeners, 'Which of the two did the will of the father?' (Mt 21:3), and they replied, 'The one who actually went to the vineyard.' Jesus observed on another occasion, that one shouldn't judge people's sincerity merely by what they say: 'You will know them,' he observed, 'by their fruits' (Mt 7:16), i.e. by their actions. Some years later St James echoed this point of view when he said: 'What does it profit, my brothers and sisters, if you say that you have faith but do not have good works?' (Jas 2:14).

Extrinsic and intrinsic religion

As was mentioned earlier, there is an immature form of prayer that metaphorically prefers milk, and a mature form that prefers solid meat. We adverted to the fact that psychologist Gordon Allport echoed this distinction when he maintained that there were two forms of religion, an extrinsic, immature variety, and an intrinsic, mature kind. Those who espouse extrinsic religion 'are disposed to use religion for their own ends ... Persons with this orientation may find religion useful in a variety of ways – to provide security and solace, sociability and distraction, status and self-justification. The embraced creed is lightly held or else selectively shaped to fit more primary needs. In theological terms the extrinsic type turns to God, but without turning away from self.'[1] By and large, the prayer life of people who espouse this kind of sociological religion focuses on what God can do for them as opposed to who God is, or what they can do for God. As a result, they often split prayer from life. What they believe doesn't necessarily impinge upon the way in which they live. They tend to re-write the commandments, for example in business matters and sexuality, to suit themselves. If others object, they say, 'Everybody is doing the same.' If and when religion and God seem to fail to meet their needs, they are like the people who found it hard to accept the teaching of Jesus on the Eucharist, 'Because of this many of his disciples turned back and no longer went with him' (Jn 6:66).

Allport says that those who espouse intrinsic religion 'find their master motive in religion. Other needs, strong as they may be, are regarded as of less ultimate significance, and they are, as far as possible, brought into harmony with the religious beliefs and preoccupations. Having embraced a creed the individual endeavours to internalise it and follow it fully. It is in this sense that he lives his religion.'[2] People with mature, intrinsic religion are usually those who, as a result of a religious awakening and deep personal conviction, have committed their lives to God in a real, as opposed to a notional sort of way. The prayer life of the people who espouse this kind of religion focuses on knowing the person, word and will of God. Their growing relationship with the Lord impinges more and more on the way they live. They tend to go against cultural trends by taking conscientious stands on all kinds of ethical issues, from honesty in business to the right to life. They are like the apostles who, although they found the teaching of Jesus on the Eucharist hard to accept, responded to his query, 'Do you also wish to go away?' by saying, 'Lord to whom can we go? You have the words of eternal life' (Jn 6:67).

People with intrinsic religion of the mature kind are nourished by religious experience. As I have suggested in another chapter, such experiences have four interconnected elements.

They are rooted in a God-prompted desire, which finds expression in self-forgetful attention to creation and the scriptures and is fulfilled when the Lord is manifested in one way or another. This sense of revelation can and should have practical effects on the way in which the pray-er lives. That is the focal point of this chapter.

Effects of personal prayer
In religious experiences, feelings of consolation such as joy, peace and hope, are evoked by a spiritual awareness of who the Lord is and what the Lord is like. They give new life and meaning to beliefs already held, while at the same time activating people's inner potential for a closer relationship with God. As a result of this growing intimacy, pray-ers relate more deeply to their spiritual selves and begin to see themselves as God does, i.e. in a loving, accepting way. Jesus once said: 'As the Father loves me, so I love you' (Jn 15:9). Pope John Paul II has written: 'The man who wishes to understand himself thoroughly and not just in accordance with immediate, partial, often superficial, and even illusory standards and measures must ... draw near to Christ. He must, so to speak, enter him with all his own self ... in order to find himself. If this profound process takes place within him, he then bears fruit not only of adoration of God but also of deeper wonder at himself.'[3]

As growth in wholeness and holiness occurs, the person has an increasing sense of inner freedom. As St Paul put it in Gal 5:1: 'It is for freedom that Christ has set us free. Stand firm, then, and do not let yourselves be burdened again by a yoke of slavery.' He or she moves from living a dutiful life on the basis of cheerless, impersonal moral imperatives, to living it on the basis of inner convictions born of heartfelt relationship with God. Genuine growth in relationship with God prompts the desire and provides the power to change inner attitudes and outer actions in an appropriate way. Religious experience, therefore, is the true source of ethics. They are a response to revelation, instead of being a legalistic substitute for it, as is often the case. This distinction captures the meaning of Paul's differentiation between living by the Spirit and living by the law (cf. Gal 5:16-26).

Genuine experience of God motivates Christians to express

their appreciation in two main ways. Firstly, they can respond in a prayerful manner by means of thanks, praise and worship, and sometimes in the form of heartfelt sorrow for having failed in many ways to give due honour to God in the past. Secondly, experience of God in prayer needs to find expression in the form of practical action. St Vincent de Paul was a great advocate of this point. It would be worthwhile listening to what he had to say about it. 'Making resolutions is one of the most important parts of our prayer, and perhaps even the most important. We must give our attention to making resolutions ... The main fruit of prayer consists of personal resolutions strongly and firmly made. They should be resolutions which you are convinced of and which you are prepared to execute, while taking into account the obstacles to be overcome.'[4] Vincent thought that resolutions should be single, precise, definite and possible.

It has long seemed to me that implicit in all religious experiences is the ethical imperative, mentioned in chapter five, 'be for others what God is for you'. For example, over the years I have come to appreciate just how merciful and loving God is. I find that I identify strongly with what St Thérèse of Lisieux said about the Lord. She maintained that because our Lord doesn't judge our good actions, God will not judge our bad ones either. For those who offer themselves to love, says Thérèse, there will be no judgement at all; on the contrary, God will respond to divine love present in our hearts.[5] Near the end of her short life Thérèse wrote: 'After earth's exile, I hope to go and enjoy you, Lord, in the fatherland, but I do not want to lay up merits for heaven. I want to work for your love alone ... In the evening of this life, I shall appear before you with empty hands, for I do not ask you, Lord, to count my works. All our justice is blemished in your eyes. I wish, then, to be clothed in your own justice and to receive from your love the eternal possession of yourself.'[6] Surely Thérèse's words find an echo in the momentous Catholic-Lutheran statement on justification: 'Together we confess: By grace alone, in faith in Christ's saving work and not because of any merit on our part, we are accepted by God and receive the Holy Spirit, who renews our hearts while equipping and calling us to good works.'[7] The ethical imperative implicit in this understanding of the Lord's amazing grace is: 'Be merciful even as your Father is merciful' (Lk 6:36), and 'Love one another even as I have loved you' (Jn 13:34). I firmly believe that when we show to others the merciful and reconciling love that is constantly shown to us in prayer, we are carrying out the great commission given to us by Christ when he said: 'You shall be my witnesses … to the ends of the earth' (Acts 1:8).

Witnessing to God's mercy
We begin with the need to be merciful. In the commentary on the Lord's Prayer, we saw that 'the Lord has forgiven you, you must do the same' (Col 3:13). But there is more to mercy than forgiveness. As Jesus says in Lk 6:36-39: 'Do not judge and you will not be judged; do not condemn and you will not be con-demned … for the measure you give will be the measure you will get back.' Many years ago I had a strange prayer experience that taught me what might be implicit in those words. I was lis-tening to Dvorak's *New World Symphony* and drinking a cup of coffee at the time. As I did so I had a three part mental vision. In part one I saw gentle peasants dancing joyfully in a field. Suddenly I became apprehensive when I noticed sinister look-ing soldiers marching ominously toward them, with flags wav-ing and drums beating. 'Oh no,' I thought, 'it is always the same. Those with power always oppress the innocent and the vulnera-ble.'

Then the scene changed and part two began. I could see that a lot of the peasants had been killed, others had been wounded. To my surprise, I noticed that inexplicably some of the soldiers were dead also. Spontaneously, some words from Ps 55:6 came to mind: 'O that I had wings like a dove! I would fly away and be at rest.' Then a voice seemed to speak within me, 'If you want me to take you, I will.' I understood that God the Father was say-ing that he would take me to himself in heaven. I looked at the dead and the dying, and replied, 'No, I'd better stay for their sake, the dead need to be buried and the wounded need to be comforted.' Then I noticed the cross of Christ from behind. Again I heard the inner voice. It said, 'Now you have learned the meaning of merciful love, it is compassion. My Son also wanted to fly away and be at rest, but he remained for your sake.' I un-derstood that these words referred to the anguish of Jesus in

Gethsemane and his resignation to the will of God, so that we might be saved.

Then suddenly a third scene appeared. I could see a great orb of light coming towards the earth. I knew inwardly that it was a symbol of the glory of God. As it grew closer to the earth, the soil, rocks, and plants were bleached as they became radiant with light. My body was also transfigured. By now it was rising into the air to meet the approaching orb of light. I looked back toward the earth and I could see peasants ascending, their bodies aglow, like mine, with light. I saw that graves were opening and that the dead were arising in light, including deceased soldiers. I was indignant at this sight. I said to the Lord, 'Why should the soldiers rise, those who oppressed the innocent and the vulnerable?' The inner voice replied, 'Because you didn't presume to judge or to condemn your oppressors, they too will be saved.'

Then the vision ended as suddenly and unexpectedly as it had begun. My heart was racing, my breathing rapid, my spirit exultant. I felt that the Lord had revealed a wonderful truth to me. God will never be outdone in mercy by creatures. If believers, who have known the merciful love of God in their own lives, refuse to judge or condemn those who have injured and hurt them, God won't judge them either. They will be saved through no merit of their own. As Jesus said, 'Those whose sins you forgive, they are forgiven' (Jn 20:23). Ever since that experience I have tried to abstain – with limited success I'm afraid – from judging anyone, not even Hitler or Pol Pot. I would like to be able to identify with a profound prayer found in a Word War II concentration camp: 'O Lord, when I shall come with glory into your kingdom, do not remember only the men and women of good will; remember also the men and women of evil. May they be remembered not only for their acts of cruelty in the camp, the evil that they have done to us prisoners, but balance against their cruelty the fruits we have reaped under the stress and in the pain; the comradeship, the courage, the greatness of heart, the humility and patience which have been born in us and become part of our lives, because we have suffered at their hands. May the memory of us not be a nightmare to them when they stand in judgement. May all that we have suffered be acceptable to you as a ransom for them.'[8]

Over the years I have come to see in prayer that all the aspects of merciful love come together in the notion of compassion. St Thomas Aquinas says: 'Compassion is heartfelt identification with another's distress, driving us to do what we can to help ... As far as outward activity is concerned, compassion is the Christian's whole rule of life.'[9] Vincent de Paul is the patron of all charitable action in the Catholic Church. He was chosen as a role model because he had a profound grasp of the fact that compassion without action is sentimentality, while action without compassion is condescension, but compassion expressed in practical action is Emmanuel, God-with-us.

Vincentian compassion

Vincent de Paul was ordained in 1599, at the tender age of nineteen. For a number of years he immersed himself in the outer world at the expense of his inner life. While he fulfilled his basic religious duties he was mainly preoccupied with getting a good, well-paid job. Then over a period of years, he suffered a number of painful setbacks. They began in his mid twenties when he was a captive for a couple of years in North Africa and ended with his three year battle with temptations against faith. These crises had a transforming effect. Vincent became increasingly aware both of his inner brokenness and the cry of the poor about him. He began to have a deep desire for a new revelation of God in his life. When, after a long inner struggle, he made a decision to devote his life to the service of the poor, the inner darkness lifted and he was filled with a sense of 'the length and breadth, the height and depth of the love of Christ, which surpasses understanding' (Eph 3:18).

There is evidence to indicate that, from then on, Vincent experienced God's love as compassion. He saw it as the motivating force for the incarnation of Jesus. 'The Son of God,' he said, 'could not have experienced a sense of compassion in the glorious state in which he existed in heaven from all eternity. He became man to share our miseries.'[10] On an other occasion he added: 'Ah! But the Son of God was tender of heart. I cannot help constantly turning my eyes to this model of love. He is called to visit Lazarus. He goes. Mary rises to meet him, weeping. The Jews follow and weep as well. What does the Lord do?

He weeps with them, so loving and compassionate is he. This tender love was the cause of his coming down from heaven.'[11] Vincent was also palpably aware that although worldly people seek riches, reputation, pleasure and power, Jesus in his compassion for the poor and oppressed became poor, humble, mortified and vulnerable.

It is clear from his writings that St Vincent wanted his followers, and by extension all Christians, to be men and women of prayer, people who contemplated the compassion of Christ and showed it in affective and effective ways to others, especially the afflicted. He described his understanding of *affective compassion* when he said: 'One of the effects of love is to enable hearts to enter into each other and feel what the others feel.'[12] On another occasion he said: 'When we go to visit the afflicted we should so identify with them that we share in their sufferings ... We must open our hearts so that they become responsive to the sufferings and miseries of the neighbour. We should pray to God to give us a true spirit of mercy, which is in truth the spirit of God. The church says that it is the nature of God to be merciful and to confer this spirit on us. Ask this grace of God, that he may give us this spirit of compassion and mercy, and that he may so fill us with it that, as soon as anyone sees any of us, he or she will immediately think, there goes a person full of compassion.'[13]

Speaking about the need for *effective compassion* Vincent said: 'Sentiments of love of God, of kindness, of good will, good as these may be, are often suspect if they do not result in good deeds ... We should be on our guard, for it is possible to be well mannered and filled with noble sentiments and yet stop there. When the need for action arises such people fall short. They may be consoled by their fervent imagination or content with the sweet sentiments they experience in prayer. They may speak like angels, but when it is a matter of working for God, of suffering, mortifying themselves, of teaching the poor, of seeking out the lost sheep, of rejoicing at deprivations, of comforting the sick or some other service, here they draw the line. Their courage fails them.'[14] On another occasion he summarised his understanding of the connection between affective and effective compassion when he said: 'In so far as it is possible, the hand should be conformed to the heart.'[15]

In the France of Vincent's time poverty was primarily a material thing. In the underdeveloped world of today it is still much the same. But in Western countries, like ours, although some people are materially poor, poverty is usually a psycho-spiritual phenomenon. The needs of these 'new poor' are hard to meet. Their problems, says Mother Teresa, 'are deep down, at the bottom of their hearts ... here you have a different kind of poverty – a poverty of the spirit, of loneliness, and being unwanted. And that is the worst disease in the world today, not tuberculosis or leprosy.'[16] Many people share activities and tasks, but not their hearts. Therefore, it would probably be true to say that in individualistic cultures such as ours, compassionate love is the greatest need. As Mother Teresa puts it: 'People today are hungry for love, for understanding love which is much greater and which is the only answer to loneliness and great poverty.'[17] The most effective way of answering this need is to listen to needy people. The philosopher, Simone Weil, once wrote: 'The love of our neighbour in all its fullness means being able to say: "What are you going through?" ...Nearly all those who think they have this capacity do not possess it.'[18]

St Vincent de Paul and Mother Teresa expressed compassion in many impressive ways. Both of them were outstanding for the way in which they engaged in charitable works. However, neither of them said anything about the need for social justice. The notion was not current in Vincent's day. Although it was becoming current in Mother Teresa's lifetime she said very little about it either. However, in recent years, the church has pointed out that while it is good and a necessary thing that Christians express their compassion by means of works of mercy, they also need to do research on the causes of oppression and poverty, and to work to change the unjust structures of society that may be causing them. For example, a few years ago Pope John Paul II addressed a gathering of the followers of St Vincent de Paul in Rome. In the course of his talk he said: 'Dear Fathers and Brothers ... search out more than ever, with boldness, humility and skill, the causes of poverty and encourage short and long term solutions, adaptable and effective concrete solutions.' Those who have intrinsic religion and who engage in regular prayer of a personal kind need to express their compassion in deeds of mercy and action for justice. It is not easy, but it is possible in small incremental steps.

Witnessing to God's love
Once they are consciously aware of the love of God, believers are called to show that same love to others. As St Paul wrote in Rom 13:9-10: 'The commandments, "Do not commit adultery," "Do not murder," "Do not steal," "Do not covet," and whatever other commandment there may be, are summed up in this one rule: "Love your neighbour as yourself." Love does no harm to its neighbour. Therefore love is the fulfilment of the law.' On an other occasion he echoed the teaching of Jesus when he said in Acts 20:35: 'It is more blessed to give than to receive.' In his famous hymn to love, in 1 Cor 13:4-7, St Paul described some of the characteristics of loving generosity when he said: 'Love is patient, love is kind. It does not envy, it does not boast, it is not proud. It is not rude, it is not self-seeking.'

St Thomas Aquinas points out that this kind of Christian love shows favour to another person. Literally speaking it 'holds him or her dear' and in high regard. This is so because love has a unique ability to enable one person to become aware of the essence and potential of another. It is a perfect form of love, in so far as it wants what is best for him or her. But that is not quite enough. Over the years I have come to see that benevolence needs to be accompanied by an accurate awareness of the needs of the other person, which may be quite different from one's own. St Vincent de Paul indicated how people could acquire that insight: 'The point of our Lord's teaching,' he said, 'is to unite us in mind, in happiness and in sorrow; *he wants us to get inside the feelings of one another*.'[19]

People in today's caring professions would say that St Vincent was talking about the importance of empathy. The word literally means 'feeling into.' As we noted in the chapter on prayer as attention to the self-disclosure of God, it is the intuitive ability to enter into and understand the feelings of another person and to communicate this understanding to him or her. Love of this kind can be looked at as empathic relationship or as service of a practical kind. Ideally, service of others should be the expression of empathic relationship rather than a substitute for it. Once empathic people know the real needs of others, they have both the desire and the graced ability to respond sensitively to them in emotional and practical ways. St Vincent de Paul stated that without empathy, without the ability to get inside the feelings of another and to respond to them, a person is like 'a Christian in a painting, lacking humanity.'[20]

Christian praxis

The advocates of liberation spirituality talk about the importance of praxis. The word is Greek and literally means 'to do'. It refers to the practical as distinct from the theoretical side of a subject. An understanding of prayer that focuses on praxis maintains that there is an indispensable and reciprocal relationship between knowing and doing. In prayer we get to know the Lord as the Lord is. The resulting intimacy has a transforming effect on one's personality. It also expresses itself in an increasingly merciful and loving way of living that leads to compassionate service of others, especially the afflicted and the oppressed.

This kind of action has all kinds of emotional and cognitive effects upon the people concerned. When they pray, they not only pour out their feelings and desires to the Lord, the way in which they experience God and the revelatory meaning of the scriptures is influenced by their everyday experiences. For example, in recent years I have spent time in a number of African countries. When I visited them, I encountered levels of poverty I had never come across before. For instance, while visiting the town of Ambo in Ethiopia I met a group of lepers who seemed to have stepped from the pages of scripture into the modern world. In the mountains of Eritrea I lived for a while among peasants who were eking out a living in a dry, inhospitable landscape which was littered with rocks. In South Africa I visited the shanty towns where tens of thousands of people lived in degradation just a few miles from the affluent suburbs of Capetown. In Nigeria I visited villages where all the people were destitute and most were infected by HIV and AIDS. Although I have seen real poverty in the USA and Ireland, especially amongst the travelling people, I had never experienced anything like the poverty I saw in Africa.

These experiences not only evoked my compassion, they effected my prayer. They also led me to try to raise funds which I could send to Christians in Ambo who wanted to help the lepers to help themselves. I spoke to lay friends. One of them, in particular, was led in prayer to raise a lot of money for this good cause. As a result, new huts have been built for the lepers while others have been renovated. Many of the adults have been trained to earn a living and the children are being educated. I have noticed that these experiences have influenced the way in which I interpret the scriptures. This point is worth emphasising. I have a growing conviction that the way we live, as a result of our prayerful intimacy with God, is as important as the study of theology and scripture. It influences the manner in which we come to understand Christian revelation. Indeed some spiritual writers would go so far as to say that the gospels can only be properly understood by those who, to a greater or lesser extent, are in compassionate solidarity with the afflicted and the oppressed. That identification with the less fortunate members of society, whether they are relatives, neighbours or strangers, becomes the indispensable key that enables Christians to unlock the true meaning of Christ's life and his good news message.

As pray-ers increasingly acknowledge their poverty of spirit and thereby grow in an experiential understanding of Christ and his message, they find that it helps them to see how they might be unwitting conspirators in the oppression of others. The kind of insight that comes from such awareness of the causes of institutional and structural injustice can effect the way in which pray-ers live and act in their daily lives. For instance, it might prompt a person to critique the way in which an organisation uses its power to oppress a minority group such as the handicapped, refugees, gay people, and those with psychiatric problems; or it might inspire skilled people such as doctors, nurses or teachers, to volunteer to work in the third world for a few years. As Pope John Paul II has observed: 'By doing this you will work for the credibility of the gospel and of the church.'

Conclusion
For those who have intrinsic religion, prayer and life become inseparable, one influencing the other in a reciprocal way. It is this

interrelationship that energises their desire and ability to evan-
gelise, principally by means of the witness of their lives. As Pope
Paul VI reminded us: 'Modern man listens more willingly to
witnesses than to teachers.' It is true. Actions speak louder than
words. Jesus made it clear that, at the particular judgement at
the end of our lives, we won't be judged on the basis of the orthodoxy of our beliefs or the length and frequency of our
prayers. He said: 'Not everyone who says to me, "Lord, Lord,"
will enter the kingdom of heaven, but only he who does the will
of my Father who is in heaven. Many will say to me on that day,
"Lord, Lord, did we not prophesy in your name, and in your
name drive out demons and perform many miracles?" Then I
will tell them plainly, "I never knew you. Away from me, you
evildoers!" Therefore everyone who hears these words of mine
and puts them into practice is like a wise man who built his
house on the rock' (Mt 7:21-24). Clearly, the Lord will judge the
genuineness of our prayer on the basis of the practical fruits it
bears. As Jesus said, at the general judgement on the last day we
will be judged on the basis of the mercy and love we have shown
to others, especially the afflicted and oppressed. 'In truth I tell
you, in so far as you did this to one of the least of these brothers
and sisters of mine, you did it to me' (Mt 25:40).

Epilogue

As we reach the end of this exploration of Christian prayer, it is worth noting that on at least four separate occasions the New Testament tells us to pray continuously. Luke records that: 'Jesus told his disciples a parable to show them that they should always pray and not give up' (Lk 18:1). The author of Eph 5:20 says: 'Pray at all times in the Spirit, with all prayer and supplication.' Eph 6:18 echoes this point when it says: 'And pray in the Spirit on all occasions with all kinds of prayers and requests. With this in mind, be alert and always keep on praying for all the saints.' Finally, in 1 Thess 5:18, St Paul gives this succinct injunction 'Pray continually'. In chapter two we suggested that this command could be interpreted either as a call to regular times of prayer morning, noon and night, or as persistence in supplicatory prayer. Over the centuries, however, there have been many other ways of interpreting it.

• Unceasing prayer can be understood as the liturgy of the heart, the praying of the Spirit within who aspires to the good God beyond, 'Abba Father' (Rom 8:15; Gal 4:6), whether we are consciously aware of that prayer or not.

• Unceasing prayer can also be looked at as a form of action: handing over the fruits of contemplation to others, principally by means of preaching, teaching and good works. St Basil once said: 'This is how to pray continually – not by offering prayer in words, but by joining yourself to God through your whole way of life, so that your life becomes one continuous and interrupted prayer.'[1]

• Unceasing prayer can be understood as on-going desire to known the person, word and will of God. As St Augustine wrote: 'For desire never ceases to pray even though the tongue be silent. If ever desiring, then ever praying.'[2]

• Unceasing prayer can also be seen as the permanent state of loving. The Christian life is essentially a loving response to the love of God. So it could be said that to pray is to love God and to love God in the neighbour is to pray.

Many spiritual writers have interpreted the command to pray without ceasing in another distinctive way. In the fifth century John Cassian advocated the use of a mantra. He encouraged people to say repeatedly, in every circumstance, whether good or bad, 'O Lord come to my assistance, O Lord make haste to help me.' (Ps 70:1) 'This verse,' he said, 'has rightly been selected from the whole bible for this purpose. It fits every mood, every temptation, every circumstance. It contains a call for divine help, a humble confession of faith, a meditation upon human weakness, a confidence in God's answer, an assurance of his on-going support.'[3] In the middle ages, the anonymous author of *The Cloud of Unknowing* encouraged people to repeat a single word rather than a phrase. He wrote, 'If you want to gather all your desire into one simple word that the mind can easily retain, choose a short word rather than a long one. A one syllable word such as 'God' or 'love' is best. But choose one that is meaningful to you. Then fix it in your mind so that it will remain there come what may. This word will be your defence in conflict and in peace … If your mind begins to intellectualise over the meaning and connotations of this little word, remind yourself that its value lies in its simplicity. Do this and I assure you these thoughts will vanish. Why? Because you have refused to develop them with arguing.'[4] In the nineteenth century the unknown Russian author of *The Way of the Pilgrim* discovered that he could pray unceasingly by repeating the traditional Jesus Prayer, 'Lord Jesus Christ, have mercy on me.' He testified: 'One who accustoms himself to this appeal experiences as a result so deep a consolation and so great a need to offer prayer always, that he can no longer live without it, and it will continue to voice itself within him of its own accord.'[5] In the twentieth century, a number of spiritual guides, such as John Main and Basil Pennington, have revived the use of mantras in what is known as centring prayer.[6]

At the beginning of this book I indicated how the church of

the twenty-first century needs to be revived and renewed in the power of the Holy Spirit. We need to pray continuously and to repeatedly ask for a spiritual awakening in the church. As Pope Paul VI said in November 1972: 'The church needs her perennial Pentecost, she needs ... to feel rising from the depths of her inmost personality, almost a weeping, a poem, a prayer, a hymn – the praying voice of the Spirit who, as St Paul teaches us, takes our place praying in us with sighs too deep for words.'[7] As the Lord answers this prayer in accordance with the scriptural promises, we need to go on to pray fervently in order to maintain and deepen our new found awareness of God as revealed in Christ by the Spirit. As Isaac of Nineveh wrote in the seventh century: 'Once the Spirit comes to dwell in someone, the latter will not be able to stop praying, for the Spirit will never stop praying inside him. Thus, whether he sleeps or wakes, prayer will never be absent from the person's soul. Whether he is eating or drinking, or sleeping or working, the sweet fragrance of prayer will effortlessly breathe in his heart. Henceforth he no longer prays at fixed times, but continuously.'[8]

I have always admired St Patrick as an outstanding example of this principle. In his *Confessions* he tells us that when he was captured at the age of sixteen he was a nominal Christian with extrinsic faith.[9] He says: 'I did not believe in the living God from my childhood.' However, when he was brought to Ireland as a captive he experienced the potency of disorder. In the midst of his afflictions he began to have a heartfelt desire for a revelation of God. Speaking about his subsequent spiritual awakening, he said in words characteristic of people with intrinsic religion: 'I cannot hide the gift of God which he gave me in the land of my captivity. There I sought him and there I found him. The Lord made me aware of my unbelief that I might at last advert to my sins and turn wholeheartedly to the Lord my God.'

One of the outstanding effects of his conversion was on Patrick's prayer life. 'Many times a day I was praying. More and more the love of God and fear of him came to me and my faith was being increased and the spirit was being moved so that in one day I could say as many as a hundred prayers, and at night nearly the same, even while I was staying in woods and on the mountain; and before daybreak I was roused up to prayer, in snow, in frost, in rain; and I felt no ill effects from it, nor was there any sluggishness in me, as I see now, because the spirit was fervent in me then.' Just as Patrick's constant prayer led to a Christian springtime for ancient Ireland, so the unceasing prayers of today's committed Christians will inevitably lead to the new springtime that so many of us desire.

Notes

INTRODUCTION

1. Ian Shevill, *Going It – with God* (Sydney: A. H. & A. W. Reed, 1968), 74.
2. In Jn 1, lect. 4.
3. *ST*, 1, 43, 5, ad. 2.
4. Foreword of Leon Joseph Suenens, *Renewal And The Powers of Darkness* (London: DLT, 1983) X.
5. *Mission of the Redeemer*, par. 42.
6. A Statement of the Irish Bishops, *Life in the Spirit: Pastoral Guidance on the Charismatic Renewal* (Dublin: Veritas, 1993).
7. Richard Mc Cullen, 'St Vincent and Prayer', *Colloque: Journal of the Irish Province of the Congregation of the Mission* (Spring,1995) no. 31, 44-55; Louis Abelly, *The Life of the Venerable Servant of God Vincent de Paul* Vol 3, (New York: New City Press, 1993), 59-71; Thomas Mc Kenna, *Praying With Vincent de Paul* (Winona, Minnesota: Saint Mary's Press, Christian Brothers Publications, 1994); Robert Maloney, 'Mental Prayer, Yesterday and Today: The Vincentian Tradition', *He Hears the Cry of the Poor: On the Spirituality of Vincent de Paul* (New York: New City Press, 1995), 78-98; Joseph Leonard, *St Vincent de Paul and Mental Prayer* (London: Burns, Oates & Washbourne, 1925).
8. Margaret Hebblethwaite, *Finding God in All Things: Praying With St Ignatius* (London: Fount, 1987); Jacqueline Bergan & Marie Schwan *Praying With Ignatius of Loyola* (Winona, Minnesota: St Mary's Press, Christian Brothers Publications, 1991).
9. 'The Prayer Meeting', *Maturing in the Spirit* (Dublin: Columba, 1991), 69-82; 'Teaching Young People to Pray', *Beyond the Race for Points: Aspects of Pastoral Care in a Catholic School Today*, ed. Matthew Feheney, (Dublin: Veritas, 1999), 169-181; 'Prayer for Healing', *Spirituality for the 21st Century: Christian Living in a Secular Age* (Dublin: Columba: 1999), 150-169. 'Is Unceasing Prayer Possible?', *Spirituality* Vol. 4, (Jan/Feb 1998), 40-44.
10. Gujarat: Anand Press, 1983, 9-51.
11. cf. Friedrich Heiler, *Prayer: A Study in the History and Psychology of Religion* (Oxford: Oneworld, 1997); Ann & Barry Ulanov, *Primary Speech: A Psychology of Prayer* (London: SCM Press, 1985).
12. cf. Morton Kelsey, *Encounter with God: A Theology of Christian Experience* (London: Hodder & Stoughton, 1974).

13. cf. Michael Chester and Marie Morrisey, *Prayer and Temperment* (Charlotsville, Virginia: The Open Door Inc., 1984); Robert Repicky, 'Jungian Typology and Christian Spirituality' and Thomas Clarke 'Jungian Types and Forms of Prayer' in *The Christian Ministry of Spiritual Direction: The Best of the Review 3*, ed. David Fleming, (St Louis: Review for Religious, 1988), 165-194.

14. cf. George Montague, 'Freezing the Fire: The Death of Relational Language', *America* (13 March 1993) vol. 168, no. 9.

15. Collegeville, Mn: The Liturgical Press, 1993.

CHAPTER 1: RELIGION AND PRAYER

1. *ST* II-II, Q. 83. A. 3.

2. London: Fontana, 1971, 444.

3. *op. cit*, 444.

4. *Prayer: A Study in the History and Psychology of Religion* (Oxford: Oneworld, 1997) 358.

5. *op. cit.*, 362.

6. *op. cit.*, 362.

7. P. Collins, 'Postmodernism and Religion,' *Doctrine and Life,* vol. 49, no. 1, (Jan 1999) pp. 22-31.

8. London: Ark, 1988, 202.

9. Viktor Frankl, *Psychotherapy and Existentialism: Selected Papers on Logotherapy* (London: Pelican, 1973) 51.

10. Quoted by Edward Hoffman, *The Right to be Human: A Biography of Abraham Maslow* (Wellinborough: Crucible, 1989) 277.

11. cf. David Wulff, *Psychology of Religion: Classic and Contemporary Views* (New York: John Wiley & Sons, 1991) 169-171.

12. Maltby, Lewis & Day, 'Religious Orientation & Psychological Well-Being: The Rule and Frequency of Personal Prayer', *British Journal of Health Psychology* (1999) 4, p. 874; cf. Michael Argyle, 'Mental Health', *Psychology and Religion: An Introduction* (London: Routledge, 2000) 159.

13. *England in the Eighteenth Century* (London: Pelican, 1961) 92.

14. *op. cit.*, 92.

15. *op. cit.*, 95.

16. 'An Account of the Revival of Religion in Northampton in 1740-1742 ', *Jonathan Edwards on Revival* (Edinburgh: Banner of Truth, 1987) 149.

17. *op. cit.*, 151.

18. *op. cit.*, 46.

19. *op. cit.*, 75-147.

20. Edinburgh: Banner of Truth, 1987, 75-147.
21. cf. Harvey Cox, 'Millennium Approaches', *Fire From Heaven: The Rise of Pentecostal Spirituality and the Reshaping of Religion in the Twenty First Century* (London: Cassell, 1996) 19-43.
22. *The Glory and the Shame: Reflections on the Outpouring of the Holy Spirit* (Guildford: Eagle, 1994) 31.
23. David Barrett, 'Annual Statistical Table on Global Mission: 1995', *International Bulletin on Missionary Research* 19:1 (January 1995) 25.
24. Kevin and Dorothy Ranaghan, *Catholic Pentecostals* (New Jersey: Paramus, 1969) 7.
25. cf. Ralph Martin 'New Springtime or Chastisement?', *Goodnews*, no. 141 (May/June 1999) 2.
26. Quoted in *Irish Times*, 10 Jan 2000, p. 15.
27. *Christian Initiation and Baptism in the Holy Spirit: Evidence from the First Eight Centuries* (Collegeville: The Liturgical Press, 1991) 333.
28. Ann Arbor: Servant Books, 1978.
29. London: Victory Press, 1975.
30. London: SCM Press, 1995.
31. *Gaudium et Spes*, par. 44.
32. par. 11.
33. par. 16
34. London: Fount, 1996.
35. *op. cit.*, 136.
36. New York: Dutton, 1943, 3.
37. *Dictionary of the Bible* (New York: Simon and Schuster, 1990) 697.
38. 'Models of Spirituality', *Spirituality for the Twenty-First Century* (Dublin: Columba, 1999), 13-36.

CHAPTER 2: THE PRAYER OF JESUS

1. cf. Albert Gelin, *The Psalms Are Our Prayers*, (Collegeville: The Liturgical Press, 1964) 53.
2. cf. F. X. Durwell, *In The Redeeming Christ* (London: Sheed & Ward Stagbooks, 1963) 6.
3. Section XLV, *Tennyson Poems*, vol 1, Everyman's Library 44 (London: Dent, 1962) 291.
4. cf. William Barclay, *The Plain Man Looks at the Lord's Prayer* (London: Fontana, 1967) 25.
5. *New Testament Theology* (London: SCM, 1981) 189.
6. 'Abba' in *The Central Message of the New Testament* (London: SCM Press, 1981) 30.

7. Pat Collins 'Was Jesus an Examplar of Unhesitating Faith?', *Expectant Faith: And the Power of God* (Dublin: Columba, 1998) 54-67.
8. Albert Gelin, *The Psalms Are Our Prayers* (Collegeville: The Liturgical Press, 1964) 56.
9. *New Testament Theology*, 191.
10. cf. Jonathan Edwards, *The Religious Affections* (Edinburgh: Banner of Truth, 1986) 40-41.
11. cf. Robert Solomon, *The Passions: The Myth and Nature of Human Emotion* (Notre Dame: University of Notre Dame, 1976) 129ff.
12. cf. Rom 12:12; Eph 5:20; 6:18; Phil 4:5-7; Col 4:2; 1 Tim 2:8; 5:5.
13. cf. Fabio Giardini, 'Unceasing Prayer,' *Pray Without Ceasing* (Leominster: Gracewing, 1998) 331-359.
14. Unger & White, 'Continuity', *Nelson's Expository Dictionary of the Old Testament* (Nashville: Nelson, 1980) 78.
15. See Ernst Lohmeyer, *The Lord's Prayer* (London: Collins, 1965); William Barclay, *The Plain Man Looks at the Lord's Prayer* (London: Fontana, 1967).
16. Part 4, section 2, article 2 (Dublin: Veritas, 1994) 590-609.
17. John Meier, New Testament 3, *Matthew* (Dublin: Veritas, 1984) 61.
18. par. 2817.
19. cf. Pat Collins, 'Forgiveness and Healing', *Growing in Health and Grace* (Galway: Campus, 1992) 7-26.
20. Pat Collins, 'Spiritual Warfare', *Spirituality for the Twenty-First Century* (Dublin: Columba, 1999) 170-179.
21. *Summa Theologica*, I, II, Q. 28, A. 2.
22. *Poems of the Dispossessed 1600-1900* (Portlaoise: Dolmen, 1981) 191.
23. 'Poems for all seasons of the year', *Daily Prayer from the Divine Office* (Dublin: Talbot, 1974) 585.
24. cf. George Martin, *To Pray as Jesus* (Ann Arbor: Michigan, 1978).

CHAPTER 3: PRAYER AS SELF-DISCLOSURE TO GOD

1. *Devotion to the Blessed Virgin Mary* (1974) par. 47.
2. *Way of Perfection*, ch. XXV.
3. *Story of a Soul*, ch. 10 (New York: Image, 1957) 136.
4. par. 2559
5. *The Life of Teresa of Jesus: The Autobiography of St Teresa of Avila* (New York: Image, 1960) 110.
6. cf. Edward O Connor, *Pope Paul and the Spirit* (Notre Dame: Ave Maria Press, 1978) 183.
7. c.f. *Pope Paul and the Spirit*, 69.
8. c.f. *Pope Paul and the Spirit*, 69.

9. See Pat Collins 'The Pain of Self-Discovery', *Intimacy and the Hungers of the Heart* (Dublin: Columba, 1991) 58-73.

10. *Autograph Directory 1540-1599*, no. 12 (Rome: Historical Institute of the Society of Jesus, 1955) 72.

11. *The Psychology of Love*, eds. Sternberg & Barnes (New Haven: Yale University Press, 1988) 120-122.

12. *The McGill Report on Male Intimacy* (New York: Holt, Rinehart & Winston, 1986) 157.

13. *Intimate Strangers* (London: Fontana, 1985) 129, 130.

14. *Spiritual Friendship* (Kalamazoo, Michigan: Cistercian Publications, 1974) 66.

15. Quoted by William Simpson, *Light and Rejoicing* (Belfast: Christian Journals, 1976) 87.

16. *Paying Attention to God: Discernment in Prayer* (Notre Dame: Ave Maria Press, 1990) 18.

17. See Preface VII of the Sundays in Ordinary Time.

CHAPTER 4: PRAYER AS SELF-FORGETFUL ATTENTION TO GOD

1. *ST*, I-I, Q. 12, art. 12

2. *ST*, I-I, Q. 43, art. 7.

3. 'Reflections on the unity of love: The love of God and love of the neighbour', *Theological Investigations*, vol 6. (London: DLT, 1969) 241.

4. *ST*, II-II, Q. 28, A. 3, ad. 9.

5. *The Life of St Teresa* (London: Penguin,1958) 156.

6. For more on the distinction between willfulness and willingness in contemplative knowing, see Gerald May, *Will and Spirit: A Contemplative Psychology* (San Francisco: Harper and Row, 1987) 5-7.

7. cf. Ana-Maria Rizzuto, *The Birth of the Living God: A Psychoanalytic Study* (Chicago: University of Chicago, 1979); William Meissner, *Psychoanalysis and Religious Experience* (New Haven: Yale University Press, 1984).

8. *Waiting on God* (London: Fontana, 1966) 66.

9. *Some Aspects of Christian Meditation* (1989) par. 6.

10. Section 2, *Interpretation of the Bible in the Church* (Pauline Books and Media, 1993).

11. par 2723 (Dublin: Veritas, 1994) 579.

12. *The Companion to the Catechism of the Catholic Church* (San Francisco: Ignatius, 1994) 921-928.

13. par. 2724 (Dublin: Veritas, 1994) 579.

14. Coste, *Collected Works*, XI, 420.

15. cf. *Sadhana: A Way to God* (Gujarat: Anand Press, 1983) 115.

16. 'Concerning the use of Biblical Quotations in Matters of Science', quoted by Mazlish and Bronowski, *The Western Intellectual Tradition* (London: Pelican, 1963) 153.

17. Quoted by Fabio Giardini, *Pray Without Ceasing* (Leominster: Gracewing, 1998) 192.

18. cf. Barry & Connolly, *The Practice of Spiritual Direction* (San Francisco: Harper and Row, 1982) 52-53.

19. *Religious Consciousness: A Psychological Study* (New York: Macmillan, 1920) 339.

20. Kansas City: Sheed and Ward, 1994, 135.

21. *Knowing Woman: A Feminine Psychology* (New York: Harper & Row, 1973) 12.

22. William Barry & William Connolly, *The Practice of Spiritual Direction* (San Francisco: Harper & Row, 1982) 8.

23. *Man's Search for Meaning* (New York: Washington Square Press, 1985) 57-58.

24. *Splendour of the Truth,* par. 8.

CHAPTER 5: SEEKING GOD'S WILL IN PRAYER

1. Jules Toner's *Discerning God's Will: Ignatius of Loyola's Teaching on Christian Decision Making* (St Louis: The Institute of Jesuit Sources, 1991).

2. *The Holy Spirit: Growth of a Biblical Tradition* (New York: Paulist Press) 200.

3. *God's Empowering Presence: The Holy Spirit in the Letters of Paul,* (Peabody, Mass: Hendrickson Publications Inc., 1994) 429.

4. Quoted by Fee, 429.

5. *ST*, 1, Q. 43, A. 5, reply obj. 2.

6. cf. William Johnston, 'Knowledge through Connaturality', *Mystical Theology: The Science of Love* (London: Fount, 1996) 50-57.

7. par. 64.

8. Quoted by Andre Dodin, *Vincent de Paul and Charity* (New York: New City Press, 1993) 82.

9. cf. Jn 6:44.

10. 'Treatise on the First Letter of St John', *Divine Office*, vol. 1 (Dublin: Talbot, 1974) 537-538.

11. *The Autobiography of St Ignatius of Loyola* (New York: Harper, 1974) 24.

12. Pat Collins 'Loving Empathy', *Spirituality* vol. 4, no. 19, (July-August 1998) 235-240.

13. Quoted by John Paul II, par. 58 of *Veritatis Splendor* (London: Catholic Truth Society, 1993) 89-90.

14. *In Solitary Witness: The Life and Death of Franz Jagerstatter* (London: Chapman, 1966).

15. Quoted by Basil Hume, *The Mystery of the Incarnation* (London: DLT, 1999) 57.

16. Quoted by Johannes Jorgensen, *St Francis of Assisi* (New York: Image, 1955) 57.

17. Maire de Paor, *Patrick the Pilgrim Apostle of Ireland: An Analysis of St Patrick's Confession and Epistola* (Dublin: Veritas, 1998) 253.

18. *Conferences of Saint Vincent de Paul* (Philadelphia: Vincentians, Eastern Province, 1963) 472.

19. cf. Thomas Hart, 'Christian Choices: A Method', *The Art of Christian Listening* (New York: Paulist Press, 1980) 75-85.

20. cf. Pat Collins 'A Time of Adversity', *Unveiling the Heart: How to Overcome Evil in the Christian Life* (Dublin: Veritas, 1995) 7-14.

21. cf. Pat Collins 'Praying for Healing', *Spirituality for the Twenty-First Century* (Dublin: Columba, 1999) 159-166.

CHAPTER 6: PRAYER AS PETITION

1. *Constitutions and Statutes of the Congregation of the Mission*, ch. 2, par. 2. (Philadelphia: General Curia C.M., 1989) 108.

2. cf. Aldous Huxley, *The Perennial Philosophy* (London: Fontana, 1966) 231.

3. *God's Empowering Presence: The Holy Spirit in the Letters of Paul* (Mass.: Hendrickson, 1994), 352.

4. *Life In the Spirit* (Dublin: Veritas, 1993) 7.

5. cf. Rom 8:15; Gal 4:6

6. To Antoine Portail, May 1st 1635, Quoted by Andre Dodin, *Vincent de Paul and Charity* (New York: New City Press, 1993) 88.

7. *Dominus et Vivificantem*, par. 54 (London: CTS, 1986) 103

8. Quoted by Mary Ann Fatula, *Thomas Aquinas Preacher and Friend* (Collegeville: The Liturgical Press, 1993) 138.

9. Quoted by St Thomas Aquinas in his 'Catena Aurea', *St Thomas Aquinas and the Summa Theologica on CD-ROM*, (Gervais, Ro: Harmony Media Inc, 1998).

10. *Ut Unum Sint*, ch. 1.

11. *The Problem of Pain* (New York: Macmillan, 1962) 61.

12. cf. Sharon Dowd, *Prayer, Power and the Problem of Suffering: Mark 11:22-25 in the Context of Markan Theology*, SBL Dissertation Series 105 (Atlanta, Georgia: Scholars Press, 1988) 155-158.

13. 'Petitionary Prayer', *The Practice of Faith: A Handbook of Contemporary Spirituality* (London: SCM Press, 1985) 74-75.

14. *op. cit.*, 65.
15. *Faith as a Theme in Mark's Narrative* (Cambridge: Cambridge University Press, 1994) 171.
16. *op. cit.*, 168.
17. 'Faith', *A Glimpse into Glory* (New York: Logos, 1979) 45.
18. Pat Collins, *Expectant Faith* (Dublin: Columba, 1998) 73-76.
19. *Expectant Faith, op. cit.*, 77-83.

CHAPTER 7: PRAYER AS INTERCESSION

1. cf. Ezech 13:5; 22; 30; Ps 106:23.
2. par. 2576.
3. cf. Jer 15:10ff.; 17:16; 18:20.
4. Pat Collins, 'The Compassion of God', *Spirituality for the Twenty First Century* (Dublin: Columba, 1999) 134-149.
5. *Spirituality for the Twenty-First Century, op. cit.*, 102-105.
6. *The Pope in Ireland: Addresses and Homilies* (Dublin: Veritas, 1989) 78.
7. Jn 12:31; 14:30; 16:11.
8. 'Faith and Deliverance from Evil', *Finding Faith in Troubled Times* (Dublin: Columba, 1993); *Unveiling the Heart: How to Overcome Evil in the Christian Life* (Dublin: Veritas, 1995); 'Spiritual Warfare,' *Spirituality for the Twenty-First Century*, 170-179.
9. 15 Nov 1972, quoted in *Deliverance Prayer*, eds. Linn & Linn (New York: Paulist Press, 1981) 10.
10. Pat Collins 'Atheism and the Father of Lies', *Doctrine and Life* (2000).
11. George Maloney, *A Return to Fasting* (Pecos, New Mexico: Dove Publications, 1974); Derek Prince, *Shaping History Through Prayer and Fasting* (New Jersey: Fleming H. Revell Company, 1973).
12. London: Sheldon Press, 1994.
13. Kent: Kingsway, 1985.
14. 'Revival and Renewal', *New Creation* (Jan 2000) 10-13.

CHAPTER 8: THE PRAYER OF COMMAND

1. cf. Pat Collins, *Expectant Faith* (Dublin: Columba, 1998) 90-91.
2. cf. Sharyn Dowd, *Prayer, Power, and the Problem of Suffering: Mark 11:22-25, In the Context of Markan Theology* (Atlanta, Scholars Press, 1988) 55.
3. *Prayer, Power and the Problem of Suffering, op. cit.*, 66.
4. *Faith as a Theme in Mark's Narrative* (Cambridge: Cambridge University Press, 1994) 164.
5. *op, cit.*, 121.

6. Ed. William Jurgens, 'Catechetical Lectures', *The Faith of the Early Fathers*, vol. 1 (Collegeville: Liturgical Press, 1970) 352.

7. *Jesus and the Spirit* (London: SCM, 1975) 426.

8. 'Gethsemane and the Problem of Theodicy', Sharyn Dowd, *op cit.*, 151-162.

9. This a modified version of a passage in *Expectant Faith, op. cit.*, 125-126.

10. 'Faith', *A Glimpse into Glory* (Plainfield, New Jersey: Logos International, 1979) 44.

11. *op cit.*, 45.

12. Pat Collins, 'The Devil in AD 1999', *The Irish Catholic* (4 Feb 1999) 11.

13. Francis McNutt, *Deliverence From Evil Spirits* (London: Hodder & Stoughton, 1996) 302.

14. Pat Collins, 'Exorcism and the Falling Phenomenon', *Maturing in the Spirit: Guidelines for Prayer Groups* (Dublin: Columba, 1991) 141-149; 'Faith and Deliverance from Evil', *Finding Faith in Troubled Times* (Dublin: Columba, 1993) 102-147; *Unveiling the Heart: How to Overcome Evil in the Christian Life* (Dublin: Veritas, 1995); Matthew and Denis Linn *Deliverance Prayer* (New York: Paulist Press, 1981); McNutt, *Deliverance from Evil Spirits*, (London: Hodder & Stoughton, 1996).

15. *The Holy Spirit: Unbounded Gift of Joy* (Collegeville: The Liturgical Press, 1998) 113.

16. cf. Pat Collins, 'Faith and the Anointing of the Sick', *Expectant Faith, op. cit.*, 141-150.

17. *James* (Philadelphia: Fortress Press, 1976) 254.

18. *Summa Contra Gentiles*, Book 3, Ch. 154, [4].

19. Jamie Buckingham, *Daughter of Destiny: Kathryn Kuhlman, Her Story* (New Jersey: Logos, 1978) 196.

20. *I Believe in Miracles* (London: Lakeland, 1974) 199.

21. John Wimber, *Power Healing* (London: Hodder & Stoughton) 252-273.

22. 'The Compassion of God', *Spirituality for the Twenty-First Century* (Dublin: Columba, 1999) 139-141.

CHAPTER 9: PRAYING TO MARY AND THE SAINTS

1. par. 2683.

2. 'Petitionary Prayer', *A Companion to the Philosophy of Religion*, eds. P. Quinn, C. Taliaferro (Oxford: Blackwell, 1999) 578.

3. *Mariology*, vol. 2, 262.

4. Joseph Dirvin, *The Lady of the Miraculous Medal* (Dublin: Virgo Potens) 15.

5. *Lumen Gentium*, n. 62.

6. *Papal Allocution at the Canonisation of Blessed Louis Marie Grignion de Monfort* (21 July 1947) *AAS* 39, 408.
7. *L'Osservatore Romano* (16 May, 1983) p. 1.
8. *Redemptoris Mater*, n. 41.

CHAPTER 10: THE PRAYER OF APPRECIATION

1. Quoted by Colin Wilson, *The Outsider* (London: Pan, 1967), 222.
2. Vol 1, *The Shorter Oxford English Dictionary* (Oxford: Clarendon Press, 1987) 1242.
3. Timothy Mc Dermott, ed., *Summa Theologiae: A Concise Translation* (London: Methuen, 1991) 402.
4. cf. Vatican Council I, *De Fide Catholica*, cites Rom 1:20 in support of its teaching that God can be known with certainty by the natural light of reason [DS 3004].
5. cf. C. K. Barrett, *Paul: An Introduction to his Thought* (London: Geoffrey Chapman, 1996) 62.
6. *Sadhana: A Way to God* (Gujarat: Anand Press, 1983) 131.
7. *From Prison to Praise* (Barbour Publishing, 1998). *Power in Praise* (Carothers, 1972).
8. *op. cit.*, 132-133.
9. Callistus and Ignatius of Xanthopoulus, 'Directions to Hesychasts', *Writings from the Philokalia on the Prayer of the Heart*, trans. E. Kadloubovsky & G. Palmer (London: Faber & Faber, 1992) 187.
10. Louis Abelly, *The Life of the Venerable Servant of God Vincent de Paul*, vol 3 (New York: New City Press, 1993) 72-73.
11. *A New Pentecost* (London: DLT, 1975) 101.
12. *Sounds of Wonder: A Popular History of Speaking in Tongues in the Catholic Tradition* (New York: Paulist Press, 1977) 60.
13. *Sounds of Wonder*, 86.
14. *The Interior Castle* (New York: Sheed & Ward, 1946) 301-302.
15. cf. Paul Hinnebusch, 'The Festal Shout', pt. 1, *Praise: A Way of Life* (Ann Arbor: Word of Life, 1976), 11-52; Pat Collins, 'Courageous Faith Expressed in Praise', *Finding Faith in Troubled Times* (Dublin: Columba, 1993) 95-101.
16. cf. Aldous Huxley, *The Perennial Philosophy* (London: Fontana, 1966) 223.
17. cf. Anon, *The Book of Degrees* quoted by Andre Louf in *Teach Us to Pray* (London: DLT, 1974) 94.
18. *op. cit.*, 19, 20.
19. *The Pope in Ireland: Addresses and Homilies* (Dublin: Veritas, 1979) 11-12.

CHAPTER 11: GROWTH IN PRAYER

1. Quoted from 'Development of Christian Doctrine', *The Book of Catholic Quotations*, ed. John Chapin, (London: John Calder, 1957) 153.

2. par. 5.

3. cf. Pat Collins, 'The Pain of Self-Discovery', *Intimacy and the Hungers of the Heart* (Dublin: Columba, 1992) 58-73.

4. *Marriage Faith and Love* (London: Fount, 1984) 119-147.

5. 'Reflections on Dr Borg's Life Cycle', *Daedalus*, 105 (Spring, 1976) 1-28.

6. David Fleming, *A Contemporary Reading of the Spiritual Exercises: A Companion to St Ignatius' Text* [216] (St Louis: The Institute of Jesuit Sources, 1980) 76-77.

7. *Spiritual Exercises* [322].

8. *Finding God in All Things* (London: Fount, 1987) 184.

9. *Lord and Giver of Life* [51].

10. *Spiritual Exercises* [323].

11. *Spiritual Exercises* [324].

12. cf. Kenneth Leech , 'God of Cloud and Darkness', *True God: An Exploration in Spiritual Theology* (London: Sheldon Press, 1985) 162-198; Elizabeth Johnson, 'The Incomprehensibility of God and the Image of God as Male and Female', *Women's Spirituality: Resources for Christian Development*, ed. J. W. Conn (New York: Paulist Press, 1986) 243-260.

13. cf. Pat Collins 'An Introduction to Mysticism', *Spirituality in the Twenty-First Century* (Dublin: Columba, 1999) 65-85.

14. cf. Jordan Aumann, 'Progressive Purgation,' *Spiritual Theology* (London: Sheed & Ward, 1982) 177-207.

15. Connolly & Birmingham, *Witnessing to the Fire: Spiritual Direction and the Development of Directors* (Kansas City: Sheed & Ward, 1994).

16. Pat Collins, 'Towards a Typology of Religious Experience', *Spirituality for the Twenty-First Century*, 46-56.

17. *The Life of Teresa of Jesus: The Autobiography of St Teresa of Avila* (New York: Image, 1960) 84-85.

18. cf. George Aschenbrenner, 'Consciousness Examen,' *The Best of the Review: Notes on the Spiritual Exercises of St. Ignatius of Loyola*, ed. D. Fleming, (St Louis: Review for Religious, 1981), 175-185.

19. cf. Pat Collins, 'Transformation in Christ', *Unveiling the Heart: How to Overcome Evil in the Christian Life* (Dublin: Veritas, 1995) 106-116.

CHAPTER 12: PRAYER AND PRAXIS

1. Allport and Ross 'Personal Religious Orientation and Prejudice', *Journal of Personality and Social Psychology*, no 5, p. 432-443.
2. *op. cit.*, 432-443.
3. *Splendour of the Truth*, par. 8.
4. Louis Abelly, vol 3, *The Life of the Venerable Servant of God Vincent de Paul* (New York: New City Press, 1993) 68.
5. cf. Bernard Bro, *The Little Way: The Spirituality of Thérèse of Lisieux* (London: DLT, 1974) 66.
6. *The Catechism of the Catholic Church*, par. 2011.
7. *Joint Declaration on the Doctrine of Justification by the Lutheran World Federation and the Catholic Church*, par. 15; Matthias Gierth, 'A Time to Embrace', *The Tablet* (20 Nov 1999) 1570.
8. cf. James Fowler, *Becoming Adult Becoming Christian* (San Francisco: Harper & Row, 1984) 121-122.
9. McDermott, Ed., *Summa Theologiae: A Concise Translation* (London: Methuen, 1989) 360.
10. Louis Abelly, *op. cit.*, 119.
11. 'Charity', trans. T. Davitt, *Colloque: Journal of the Irish Province of the Congregation of the Mission* (Autumn 1993) no. 28, p. 232.
12. 'Charity', *op. cit.*, 232.
13. Abelly, *op. cit.*, 118.
14. Andre Dodin, *Vincent de Paul and Charity* (New York: New City Press, 1993) 104.
15. Abelly, *op. cit.*, 119.
16. Mother Teresa of Calcutta, *A Gift for God* (London: Fount, 1981) 76.
17. Desmond Doig, *Mother Teresa: Her People and her Work* (London: Fount, 1978) 139.
18. cf. Pat Collins C.M., 'Loving Empathy', *Spirituality*, vol. 4, (July-August 1998) 235-240.
19. 'Charity', *op. cit.*, 232.
20. 'Charity', *op. cit.*, 232.

EPILOGUE

1. Quoted by Kenneth Leech, *True Prayer: An Introduction to Christian Spirituality* (London: Sheldon Press, 1980) 191.
2. Sermon 80, 7.
3. Cassian, *in The Fire and the Cloud*, ed. Fleming, (London: Chapman, 1978) 32.

4. *The Cloud of Unknowing and Other Works* (London: Penguin Classics, 1978) 69.
5. 'The Way of the Pilgrim', *The Fire and the Cloud: An Anthology of Catholic Spirituality*, ed., David Flemming (London: Geoffrey Chapman, 1978) 323.
6. M. Basil Pennington, *Centering Prayer: Renewing an Ancient Christian Prayer Form* (New York: Image, 1980).
7. Edward O Connor, ed., *Pope Paul and the Spirit* (Notre Dame: Ave Maria Press, 1978) 183.
8. Quoted by Raniero Cantalamessa, *The Holy Spirit in the Life of Jesus* (Collegeville: Liturgical Press, 1994) 59-60.
9. Quotations from Maire de Paor's translations in *Patrick the Pilgrim and Apostle of Ireland* (Dublin: Veritas, 1998) 220-265.

Index